The Charge of
the Light Brigade

Also by John Grehan
The Lines of Torres Vedras
Churchill's Secret Invasion
Voices from the Past, Waterloo 1815
The First VCs: The Stories Behind the First Victoria Crosses in the Crimean
War and the Definition of Courage

With Martin Mace
Images at War, The Crimean War
Despatches from the Front, British Battles of the Crimean War
The Battle of Hastings, The Uncomfortable Truth
Unearthing Churchill's Secret Army
Battleground Sussex
Slaughter on the Some, 1 July 1916
The Battle of Barossa, 1811
Bomber Harris, Sir Arthur Harris' Despatch on War Operations
The Western Front 1914-1916
The Western Front 1917-1918
The Royal Navy and the War at Sea 1914-1919
The War in East Africa 1939-43
Operations in North Africa and the Middle East 1939-1942
Operations in North Africa and the Middle East 1942-44
Battles of the Zulu War
British Battles of the Napoleonic Wars 1793-1806
British Battles of the Napoleonic Wars 1807-1815
The War at Sea in the Mediterranean 1940-1944
The Battle for Norway 1940-1942
The BEF in France 1939-1940
Gallipoli and the Dardanelles
The Boer War
Capital Ships at War 1939-1945
Defending Britain's Skies 1940-45
Liberating Europe: D-Day to Victory in Europe 1944-1945
Disaster in the Far East 1940-42
The Fall of Burma 1941-1943
The Battle for Burma 1943-1945
Far East Air Operations 1942-45

The Charge of
the Light Brigade

John Grehan

Frontline Books

THE CHARGE OF THE LIGHT BRIGADE
History's Most Famous Cavalry Charge Told Through Eye Witness Accounts, Newspaper Reports, Memoirs and Diaries

This edition published in 2017 by Frontline Books,
an imprint of Pen & Sword Books Ltd,
47 Church Street, Barnsley, S. Yorkshire, S70 2AS

ISBN: 978-1-84832-942-3

CIP data records for this title are available from the British Library

For more information on our books, please visit
www.frontline-books.com
email info@frontline-books.com
or write to us at the above address.

Printed and bound by TJ International Ltd. Padstow PL28 8RW
Typeset in 10.5/12.5 point Palatino

Contents

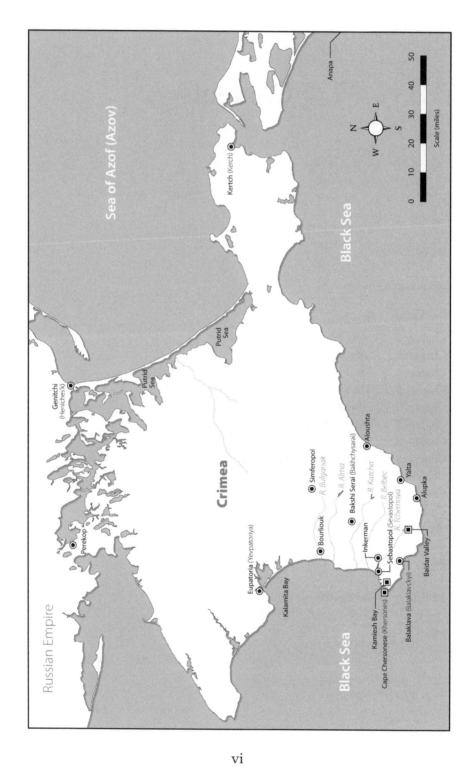

Introduction
Ours to Reason Why

I was stood on the Sapoune Heights in the public viewing area, a little to the left of the place where Lord Raglan sat on his horse during the Battle of Balaklava. I was not in the Crimea to investigate the Charge of the Light Brigade, but the opportunity to visit the famous battlefield was not one to be passed over.

I had therefore read a little about the battle before my visit and I had a fairly fixed idea in my mind of what I would see; but the panorama before me was nothing like the maps and diagrams I had seen in the few books I had consulted. I looked towards the North Valley, the 'Valley of Death'. I expected to see a narrow valley confined by dominating heights. What I actually saw was a wide plain in the centre of which was a low hill with gentle slopes. That hill was the Fedoukine Heights. To my right-centre were the Causeway Heights, the lower slopes of which were even less pronounced. In the middle-distance was a patch of white ground. It was here, our guide told us, that the Light Brigade formed up to charge the Russian guns at the head of the North Valley.

There is an anecdotal tale of three military men travelling in 1855 to see the site of the famous charge, and being as surprised as I later was with what they saw: 'Well, look yonder at that rising ground; it was there the Russians were posted,' said one of the men. 'I thought it had been on a hill or mountainside,' said another. 'Just what you see,' said the third member of the party, 'little better than an inclined plain of easy ascent.'

It is usually said that Lord Lucan, who commanded the Cavalry Division on the valley floor, was unable to see what was happening on the Causeway Heights. In fact, having later moved down from the Sapoune Heights to stand in the exact, or at least in the region of, the position occupied by Lord Lucan, it was as difficult to see down the North Valley as it was to look up the Causeway Heights, both of which were occupied by guns and enemy troops. Of all the reputed and disputed accounts of the Charge of the Light Brigade, the one I can believe wholeheartedly is Lucan's question to Captain Nolan, 'where and which guns?'

Having trodden the ground, as it was, and carrying the image of the battlefield in my mind, as well as my camera, I left the Crimea determined to investigate further. I found that the eternal question of 'who was to blame' for the most famous cavalry charge of all time, is still debated. The numerous, well-written and extensively researched books about the charge, all claim to understand, 'The Reason Why', or purport to reveal the 'Truth' about the loss of the Light Brigade. Many of these can produce no definitive answer, and leave the reader still unsure how it was that Lord Cardigan charged into the muzzels of the Don Cossack battery. A few are bold enough to state their case, deciding that it was Raglan for his wholly inadequate orders, Nolan for his impetuosity, Cardigan for completely misunderstanding his instructions, and Lucan for being, well, Lucan.

It was in fact Lord Lucan who took the fall, having to surrender his command for daring to blame his Commander-in-Chief for the whole debacle. The Earl was adamant that he was only following orders and he made his case before his peers in the House of Lords. With this he seemed to have vindicated himself, and he resumed his military career, reaching the British Army's senior rank of Field Marshal.

The general consensus at the time, and to a great extent since, was that it was Captain Nolan who let everyone down. He was, of course, an easy target, having been the first man to die as the Light Brigade trotted down the North Valley. Lord Cardigan has largely escaped censure, partly because he questioned the orders he had received (unlike Lucan), but also because he actually charged, unflinchingly, at the head of his brigade, into the Valley of Death.

So, with competing theories, the question remains unanswered. Why on earth did the Light Brigade commit to a frontal charge against a formed battery of artillery against all the accepted principles of war? There is, of course, only one way to find out – by examining the words and the deeds of those involved.

This is why I have chosen to write this 'Introduction' before starting on the quest to lay bare the details of the charge. I do not know where this investigation will take me. At this stage I do not know who was to blame, if indeed any one individual was to blame, or whether it was a combination of errors, as would at first consideration seem most likely.

Join me then on this journey, first to the Crimea, then down to Balaklava. Together we will ride with the Light Brigade into the Valley of Death, and maybe, just maybe, we really will discover the reason why that fatal charge was delivered.

*

Readers will see that in the accounts of the individuals used in this work some words were spelt differently than today, and some words were pure invention. Thus we see Colin Campbell 'manoeuver' the 93rd Highlanders when attacked by Russian cavalry and Captain Shakespeare being 'intrusted' with Major Maud's troop of the Royal Horse Artillery. Favour and favor, honour and honor were interchangeable; capital letters for common and proper nouns were used indiscriminately by some authors even in the same document. But if we are to hear the voices of the people that were living and fighting in the middle of the nineteenth century we must let them speak in their own vernacular, so spelling or grammatical errors or conflicts have been, in the main, left unaltered.

What will not be found in this book, however, are maps or diagrams portraying the charge. For when Lord Raglan ordered the fatal charge from the Sapoune Heights he did not consult such cartography, and when Lord Lucan passed on those orders the Earl of Cardigan he could see little beyond the rising ground in front of him. The problems associated with attempting to produce diagrams or plans of the Balaklava battlefield and the charge of the Light Brigade were encountered as early as 1855, when the artist William Simpson tried to create a sketch for the *Illustrated London News*: 'The Battle of Balaklava … had taken place before I arrived in the Crimea, but it was necessary for me to give pictures. I could easily make sketches on the ground, but I had to trust to those on the spot for a description of the events. Here I may mention, I had my first experience as to how men who have been actors in an event will differ in their descriptions … I then did a sketch and took it to Lord Cardigan. He gazed at it with a vacant stare, and pointing to something, asked, "What is that?" On being told, he said, "It is all wrong" and gave expression to one or two remarks of a critical kind, objecting to the picture.'

Simpson, consequently, made a second sketch, taking into account all the points that Cardigan had objected to, and presented this to Cardigan: 'On my taking this to the yacht [the Earl of Cardigan slept on his luxury yacht in Balaklava harbour throughout the war] sketch and artist were treated in much the same way as he first occasion.'

Simpson really wanted his illustration to be endorsed by the man he called 'the principle hero' of the famous charge, so he persisted, and produced a third sketch: 'I went on board a third time, and …was rewarded with the warmest praise, and was able to send it home with the expression of Lord Cardigan's highest admiration.' Simpson had realised what the honourable earl wanted to see and he had responded accordingly. 'The real truth was that in the last sketch I had taken greater care than in the first two to make sure his Lordship [was] conspicuous in the front of the brigade.'

Regimental Sergeant Major George Loy Smith of the 11th Hussars, when writing his memoirs, sought to include a diagram of the charge: 'As a proof of how little could have been known about our movements, I have at this moment before me a plan drawn by Captain Ennis ... in which the 4th [Light Dragoons] are represented inclining to the left across in rear of the 11th before arriving at the guns, and then actually on our left at the bottom of the valley close to the Aqueduct. Lord Paget [in command of the 4th] does not even say he was there, but met us [11th Hussars], returning, yet in the plate in his Journal he represents the 4th on our right pursuing the Russian Hussar Brigade, when it was known the 4th were in the battery at the time.'

Smith then goes on to write that a diagram produced for the original historian of the campaign in the Crimea, A.W. Kinglake, 'is a misrepresentation of the affair altogether'.

Instead of drawings and elaborate diagrams, therefore, are photographs of the ground, which, fortunately, has largely escaped urban development. It is from these perspectives, and the recollections of the participants and onlookers, that we must view the drama that unfolded on 25 October 1854.

John Grehan,
Shoreham-by-Sea,
January 2017.

Acknowledgements

I am extremely grateful to Mark Conrad who gave his permission for me to quote extensively from his remarkable collection of Russian documents that he has translated and are available online at his website: www.marksrussianmilitaryhistory.info.

The most extensive investigation into the Light Brigade is to be found in the late E.J. Boys website *Lives of the Light Brigade*. On this website Roy Mills and Philip Boys, who have continued Edward James Boys' work, not only lists every member of the Light Brigade who served with the Light Brigade during the Crimean campaign (almost 3,000 men), but also has, with the help of many people from across the world, investigated the careers and subsequent lives, loves and inevitable loss of many of those that charged into the Valley of Death. This is a constantly evolving source of information with new material being compiled and added as it is uncovered, or discovered.

Without question the most detailed published work on the Light Brigade is Roy Dutton's *Forgotten Heroes, The Charge of the Light Brigade*. Once again this is an investigation into the individuals of Cardigan's five regiments and their respective staffs. The accompanying volume, *Forgotten Heroes, The Charge of the Heavy Brigade*, is of equal value, and indeed essential, to anyone attempting to write about the Battle of Balaklava. Without all these above works this current book would be a poor effort indeed.

My gratitude also goes to the staff at the London Metropolitan Archives for handling the material from the National Army Museum during the latter's long period of closure.

James Bancroft kindly checked through the manuscript.

I must also thank the military artist David Rowlands for his photographs of the Balaklava battlefield. He had the foresight to take many shots and caption them when we visited the Crimea, when writing a book on the Charge of the Light Brigade had not even crossed my mind. I am equally grateful to my son Marcus for remaining unruffled when I was arrested by the military authorities in the Crimea for inadvertently trespassing where none are supposed to tread.

It was my colleague, Martin Mace, who suggested I should stop talking about the Charge and write a book about it instead – promising, therefore, that he would publish it.

Finally, I must thank Hannah. I had the joy of investigating one of the most intriguing episodes in British military history. She made the sacrifices and, like the Six Hundred, did so without questioning why.

Chapter 1

The Price of Glory

'The enemy, strongly posted on the highest point of the ridges, and with a gun to indicate the whereabouts of their artillery, kept up a steady fire upon the division as it approached,' ran the words of a report in *The Times*:

> While with his heavy cavalry the Duke [of Cambridge] occupied their attention on his left, his right was quickly thrown forward, so as to turn their position. First came England's Brigade, and then, taking ground still further on, the brigade of Guards, each throwing out skirmishers and keeping up a steady fire supported by the batteries. At charging pace, and with fixed bayonets, a battalion of Sir Richard England's Brigade, carried the heights. The other battalions, following quickly and deploying, extended their line to the right. Then came the Guards still farther on, and the batteries between the intervals. Lockyer's Brigade, in the attempt to get forward to the extreme right behind the Guards, was so impeded by the ground that it could not execute the movement in time, but its place was supplied by the light cavalry regiments and the guns of the Horse Artillery.

The report was not, as might be thought, a description of an early engagement in the Crimea. This action, in fact, took place a little more than twelve months earlier than the opening shots of the Russian war and the difficult ground described by the journalist was the rolling heath land around Chobham in Surrey. What *The Times* was reporting on was the first large-scale manoeuvres undertaken by the British Army since the Napoleonic Wars.

In the intervening decades the nature of the operations undertaken by the Army had changed significantly. The large field force assembled by

1

the Duke of Wellington, complete with its highly-sophisticated logistics and command structure, which had campaigned for six years in the Iberian Peninsula and then Belgium, had long been dissolved. Britain's enemies were no longer to be found in Europe and its army fought its battles against African chieftains or the Indian princes. Once a territory had been conquered and added to the ever-expanding Empire, the troops settled down to garrison and police the new colony.

Few troops remained in the United Kingdom but with no threat to the nation's stability other than internal ones, this was of no great concern. As it transpired, it was internal conflict that raised public awareness of the weakened state of Britain's home defence. In 1843 anti-taxation riots in Wales put such a severe strain upon the army that Lieutenant General Sir Henry Hardinge, the Secretary at State for War, was obliged to introduce a bill which allowed the Government to call the 'out-pensioners' from Chelsea Hospital to act in aid of the civil powers if required. If the Army could not put down a riot without the help of pensioners then the country was clearly in a highly vulnerable state.

This was highlighted when relations between Britain and France deteriorated just three years later over the possible union of the French and Spanish thrones. This dispute, known as 'The Affair of the Spanish Marriages' led to calls for the embodiment of the Militia but this was rejected on the grounds of cost.

Britain remained in this potentially dangerous state until 1848 when events in France mirrored those of an earlier generation when Britain stood alone against the might of Napoleon. A revolution in France led to the declaration of a Second French Republic. Preaching yet again the ideals of the First Republic, *liberté, égalité, fraternité*, it was once more a Bonaparte that led its revolutionary government. Louis-Napoléon Bonaparte was the nephew of Napoleon I and, like his uncle, he was not satisfied with merely being President of the Republic. In 1851 in a bizarre 'self-coup' he toppled his own regime to impose, the following year, a Second French Empire with himself as Napoleon III, Emperor of the French.

This, finally, concentrated the minds of ministers in Britain. Calls were once again made for embodying the Militia and for an increase in the establishment of the Army by changing the criteria of enlistment. In the debate on this subject in the House of Commons on 29 March 1852, Mr. W. Williams, the Member for Lambeth, asked why there was a need for further spending on the armed forces when there was already some 160,000 men under arms, Spencer Walpole, the recently appointed Home Secretary, replied:

It is true you have a large Army; but that Army is not a quarter of the army of Russia; not half the army of Prussia, not a third of the army of France, and very little more than the army of Belgium: but your Empire is ruled over by a Queen who has under her dominion one-sixth of the population and one-eighth of the surface of the habitable globe. You have colonial possessions which exhaust a great part of your forces. Other Powers have more compact dominions, and can, therefore, more readily concentrate their forces. Their troops are not spread abroad in weak detachments, which cannot be withdrawn, like those belonging to this country. The very greatness of your Empire, therefore is, in one sense of the word, a source of weakness.[1]

Walpole then set out the proposed changes to the terms of enlistment:

The House is aware that a recruit enlisting in the Army must not be more than 25 years of age, and that the standard of height is 5 feet 6 inches. We propose that the ages during which persons may volunteer or be balloted for, shall extend from 18 to 35 years. The consequence is, that with regard to those men who are upwards of 25 years of age, we shall not interfere with the recruiting for the Army, and as to those under that age, we shall not prevent them from enlisting if so disposed. With reference to the question of height, I may observe that the standard required by the present militia law is 5 feet 4 inches. The standard of height of the Russian infantry of the line is 5 feet 4 inches, in France it is 5 feet 1 inch English measure. [Laughter in the House.] Hon. Gentlemen may laugh at that; but, though I am speaking in the English House of Commons, we ought never to forgot that a nobler or more gallant soldiery never existed in the world than the French soldiery—and if we find that this people, who have fought throughout the length and breadth of Europe, have taken into their armies men of 5 feet 1 inch, we ought not to assume the military capacity is not to be found in men of 5 feet 2 inches.

Size, both in that of the men and in the total numbers of the Army, was not the British military's only concern. Brigade and divisional structures, with all the support services, particularly the commissariat, had, under Wellington, evolved into remarkably efficient bodies. With so many regiments away from home for many years at a time garrisoning the Empire, those structures had long since been broken up. Britain no longer had the systems in place to enable it to campaign against a modern European army. Lord Panmure, a former Secretary-at-War, raised this point in the Commons in March 1852:

> The system by which an army should be provisioned, moved, brought to action ... is non-existent ... We have no means of making general officers or of forming an efficient staff ... For great operations we are inadequate.'[2]

It is the method, or lack of it, of 'making of general officers', which is generally considered to have been the prime reason for the mistakes that led to the charge of the Light Brigade at Balaklava. It was not that the British Army lacked senior officers, the Army had plenty of those. What Pammure meant by 'making' was making them fit in terms of practise and experience in commanding large bodies of troops on campaign and in battle.

This was because it was possible for an officer to rise to senior rank without actually having any experience of battle due to the system by which commissions could be purchased. The prices of commissions were laid down in Army Regulations and ranged from £840 for an ensign in an ordinary infantry regiment to £9,000 (little short of £750,000 in today's terms) for a lieutenant colonelcy in the Foot Guards. On promotion an officer sold his original commission, which meant that he only had to pay the additional sum for the next rank. So a captain in a cavalry regiment could sell his commission for £3,225 and would therefore only need to find £1,350 to be able to purchase a majority at the regulation price of £4.575. In peace time, when opportunities for promotion were limited, few commissions were sold for the regulation price. Often a 'regimental value' was added to each commissioned rank with the more prestigious regiments commanding up to twice the regulation price. This tended to disappear in wartime as casualties led to many more vacancies and supply and demand levelled out. Another factor that influenced the value of a commission was whether a regiment was due to go on overseas service or was returning from an overseas posting. Generally, when a regiment was ordered overseas, wealthy officers would sell their commissions and purchase another one in a regiment that was staying in the UK. Thus a rich officer could move through the ranks of the Army and never see service beyond Britain's shores. Above the rank of lieutenant colonel promotion was usually dependent upon seniority.

The effect this had upon the Army in general was exemplified by the Duke of York's Adjutant-General, writing towards the end of the eighteenth century:

> There is not a young man in the Army that cares one farthing whether his commanding officer, the brigadier or the commander-

in-chief approves his conduct or not. His promotion depends not on their smiles or frowns. His friends [or his family] can give him a thousand pounds which with to go to the auction rooms in Charles Street and in a fortnight he becomes a captain. Out of fifteen regiments of cavalry and twenty-six of infantry which we have here [in Flanders], twenty-one are commanded literally by boys or idiots.

The origins of the system of purchase date back to the days of Oliver Cromwell whose so-called 'Commonwealth of England' was nothing short of a military dictatorship enforced by his generals who were professional soldiers. After the Restoration of the monarchy it was the agreed policy of the state that the Army should never again be led by professional military men. To ensure this, not only was the pay for officers meagre but each commission and step in rank had to be purchased. This meant that only the wealthiest of individuals could afford to become senior officers and such men were the rich landowners, the very people who had the least, or nothing, to gain from a military revolution. As Lord Palmerston explained:

> It was very desirable to connect the higher classes of Society with the Army … If the connection between the Army and the higher class of society were dissolved, then the Army would present a dangerous and unconstitutional appearance. It was only when the Army was unconnected with those whose property gave them an interest in the country, and was commanded by unprincipled military adventurers, that it ever became formidable to the liberties of the nation.[3]

The purchase system certainly ensured that there would never be a revolution in Britain as the Army was led, from top to bottom, by the aristocracy, the wealthy merchants and land owners; in other words, those that did not rely upon their pay and whose fortunes were dependent upon the continuance of the status quo. This led to a stability not seen in other countries and, in turn, allowed industry and trade to flourish. The purchase system contributed in no small measure to Britain becoming the most dominant nation of the nineteenth century.

Yet wealth and breeding does not necessarily equate to ability and many of the senior regimental ranks were filled with men of limited skill and little experience. Whilst officers could reach the rank of lieutenant colonel by purchase, they had to do so step by step, with a minimum period of time having to be spent at each grade. This was supposed to ensure they gained experience at every level of command but the speed at which an individual rose through the ranks depended upon how much money that person was able or willing to spend. Once the rank of lieutenant colonel had been attained, promotion through to full general was normally a matter of seniority, though the position of colonel was often an honorary one. It was possible for a deserving officer to be promoted on merit, but this was by far the exception.

Except in wartime, demand for first commissions usually outstripped supply, which of course pushed up prices, and limited the opportunities for the less wealthy. The Duke of York put in place one significant improvement, which was that those who had graduated from the recently-formed Royal Military College should be given priority for first commissions without purchase, though there was only ever a small number of such openings. Then, in 1849, it was necessary for new candidates to pass a qualifying examination before being placed on the list of potential new officers kept at the Horse Guards. The exam, though was only a formality, for it was almost unknown for anyone to fail, and being placed on the list did not mean obtaining a commission. For those without money or influence the chance of obtaining a commission was slight, as a report on the purchase system revealed:

> [they] were told that their son's names might be put down in the list, but that there was such a number before them that it was impossible that they would get commissions, and they did not get them. At that very time, a man with good interest [i.e. influence] would have got a commission at once.[4]

Notwithstanding the supposed requirement for commissions to be purchased, there were always free commissions to be had, not least because commissions were firmly ruled not to be heritable property and therefore the death of an officer automatically offered a free promotion to the most senior man below him and so on down, until ultimately creating a non-purchase vacancy for a new entrant as an ensign or second lieutenant. Where commissions were available with or without purchase within a regiment, such promotion was decided upon entirely by seniority – providing, in the case of purchased commissions, the eligible applicant had the necessary funds. Therefore, no officer was permitted to be promoted over the heads of more senior officers unless those ahead of him could not afford the asking price. Only if no officers in the regiment could afford the price of the next step in rank could that position be offered to someone from another regiment. This merely compounded the problem of entirely unsatisfactory, but wealthy, officers reaching high rank and of more deserving, but poor men, remaining in the junior ranks for decades.

Whilst it may seem clear that such a system of obtaining commissions, whether it be by purchase or seniority, was, by the mid-eighteenth century, an anachronism which had no place in the world's leading industrial democracy, it still had many supporters. Sir Frederick Peel, the Member of Parliament for Bury, stood up in the House of Commons on 4 March 1856 to give his views on the subject:

> Assuming it to be true that all men who entered the army did so with the desire of attaining as speedily as possible to the rank of colonel or general, or to some position of higher authority and greater responsibility than they were likely to reach in private life or in a civil profession, he could not understand how a system, the effect of which was to accelerate the accomplishment of such objects, could he viewed otherwise than with favour by those who had the means of bringing themselves within its operation by the purchase of commissions.[5]

This, then, was the accepted system of promotion in the British Army at the time of the Crimean War. When it became obvious that a war with Russia was unavoidable, the men at Horse Guards had to choose general officers to lead an expeditionary force from a pool of wealthy, influential men, many of whom had little or no combat experience, and who had purchased their way to the top, as a report after the war made clear:

> Whenever the … advisors of the crown are obliged to … recommend Her Majesty to name a commander for her army in the field, they must necessarily select from among those who had obtained high rank in the army. The great majority of these officers, however, will have risen by purchase, obtaining their rank not from any acknowledged fitness, but from the current of promotion and the opportunities of buying advancement. This country will therefore commence the operations of war under a disadvantage compared with foreign states, where all the officers in the higher grades will have been subjected to general selections and may, therefore, if the power of selection has been honestly and wisely exercised, be all men of known efficiency and merit.

The first selection to be made for the expected operations against Russia was that of Commander-in-Chief. Of those officers considered most suitable, Lord Hardinge, Lord Gough, Lord Combermere and Lord

Raglan, were all at the pinnacle of their professions. All, were either full generals or field marshals who had held high positions within the Army and had an enormous wealth of experience in the field. Unfortunately, only one, Lord Raglan, was under the age of seventy.

FitzRoy James Henry Somerset, 1st Baron Raglan, had become the military secretary to Sir Arthur Wellesley, the future Duke of Wellington, at the age of just twenty-two. He had proven to be extraordinarily brave, leading one of the assaulting parties that famously stormed the fortress of Badajoz in 1812. When his right arm was shattered towards the end of the Battle of Waterloo he simply walked to the rear to find a surgeon. When Somerset reached the makeshift operating theatre the surgeon told him to lie down on a table. He then removed Somerset's arm between the shoulder and the elbow with a saw. FitzRoy Somerset did not make a sound. He continued as Wellington's secretary when the Duke became Commander-in-Chief of the Army. The only problem with appointing Raglan was that he had never actually commanded any troops in battle, not even a battalion. Nothing could highlight the drawbacks of the purchase and seniority system more starkly. When his name was put forward for command of the expeditionary force destined for the Crimea to Queen Victoria, it came with the following recommendation:

> General Lord Raglan during the Peninsular War filled a most important situation on the staff of the late Duke of Wellington, and since the close of that War, from the period of the Battle of Waterloo, where he lost an arm, he has given eminent proofs of unwearied zeal and great ability in Your Majesty's Service, particularly during the many years he has conducted the arduous duties of Military Secretary since which Your Majesty has been most graciously pleased to confer upon him the appointment of Master-General of the Ordnance.[6]

Victoria actually knew Raglan very well and she was happy to agree to his appointment. He had served at Wellington's side throughout most of his successful years so, it was assumed, he must have learnt much from Britain's greatest soldier. His most notable qualities, on the other hand, seemed to be that he was a gentleman and was well liked and respected. Being an officer and a gentleman was qualification enough to command Britain's field army.

When completed, the force that sailed to the Crimea consisted of five divisions of infantry and one cavalry division with associated artillery and engineers. Of this force, cavalry was the most expensive arm to train, equip and, most particularly transport to the theatre of operations. It was also a most useful asset for keeping the peace in the UK. As a consequence, cavalry regiments were rarely sent abroad and so its officers and men had very little, or no, experience of warfare. Command of this prestigious division was placed in the hands of fifty-four-year-old Lieutenant General George Charles Bingham, 3rd Earl of Lucan. His only field experience had been more than twenty-five years earlier as an officer, strangely, on the staff of Prince Menshikov with the Russian Army. Lucan reached the rank of Major General before retiring. The prospect of war brought him out of retirement to take charge of the cavalry, a decision which some saw as a potentially disastrous. Amongst those was Major William Charles Forrest of the 4th (Royal Irish) Regiment of Dragoon Guards:

> Lord Lucan is no doubt a clever sharp fellow, but he has been so long on the shelf that he has no idea of moving cavalry, does not even know the words of command & is very self willed about it, thinks himself right ... if he is shewn by the drill book that he is wrong, he says, 'Ah I should like to know who wrote that book, some Farrier I suppose ... if any mishap should occur to the cavalry, you may be able to form a correct idea how it happened.'[7]

The most detailed history of the war in the Crimea down to the death of Lord Raglan, is found in the eight-volume work by A.W. Kinglake. In his account of the opening stages of the Battle of Balaklava, he notes Lord Lucan had the opportunity to delay the advance of the Russians with his cavalry. The ground was relatively flat and open and ideal for cavalry action. According to Kinglake, Lucan could have repeatedly threatened to charge the enemy which would have caused them to halt to receive cavalry. This, though, was beyond Lucan's ability and exemplifies one of the major drawbacks of the purchase system:

> It may be that a cavalry officer fresh from war-service would have been able to check Liprandi [the Russian commander], and to check him, again and again, without sustaining grave loss; but if a man can so wield a body of cavalry as to make it the means of thus arresting for a time an attack of infantry and artillery without much committing his squadrons, he has attained 'to high art' in his calling; and to expect a peace-service general to achieve such a task, is much as though one should take a house-painter at hazard and bid him portray a Madonna.[8]

The Cavalry Division was to be composed of two brigades, one of heavy cavalry, the other of light cavalry. The light cavalry had, since the days of Napoleon, been seen as dashing and their dress flamboyant. Apart from the Brigade of Guards, command of the Light Cavalry Brigade was the most sought-after of the positions below that of divisional commander. This position was given to James Brudendell, the seventh Earl of Cardigan, whose rise to the rank of major general was possibly the most egregious example of the injustices and inadequacies of the purchase system, as 'an old solder' wrote to the Editor of *The Times* on 25 June 1832:

> Lord Brudenell, one of the majors adverted to by you as having been allowed, on false pretences of economy, to exchange an active majority for an unattached Lieutenant-Colonelcy, was lately appointed to the command of the 15th Hussars. Lord Brudenell has not been ten years in the service, and perhaps never spent two years with his regiment, having been engaged either in attending his duty as a Tory in the House of Commons, hunting at Melton Mowbray, or running away with other men's wives. He cannot, therefore, be qualified to command a regiment of Dragoons. Yet he has been sent to supersede half the officers of the regiment, who are his seniors in the army. As if this were not sufficient to disgust and ruin one of the finest regiments in the service, he carries with him his wife, a divorcee. Are Tory lords thus to trample for ever on their brothers?

This swipe at Cardigan having a divorcee wife was the subject of much scandal when, in 1823, Cardigan, or Brudenell as he still was at that time, met Elizabeth, the wife of a Captain (later Lieutenant Colonel) Christian Johnstone in Paris. The two eloped. After the divorce trial, as it was then, Cardigan, as the guilty party, offered to 'give satisfaction' to Johnstone, i.e. fight a duel. Johnstone replied that 'he has already given me satisfaction: the satisfaction of having removed the most damned bad-tempered and extravagant bitch in the United Kingdom.'[9]

The problem with appointing Cardigan to the Light Brigade was that he detested his commanding officer, who happened to be his brother-in-law. He believed that Lucan treated his sister badly, 'kept her short of money and deprived of suitable enjoyments.'[10] Their antipathy was public knowledge and it is said that Raglan protested at the decision to place these two men together. His disapproval was noted but dismissed by the Duke of Newcastle, the Secretary at State for War.[11]

What those men whom Lucan and Cardigan would lead in the Crimea thought of the two generals was put into words by Captain Robert Portal of the 4th Light Dragoons:

THE PRICE OF GLORY

We are commanded by one of the greatest old women in the British
Army, called the Earl of Cardigan. He has as much brains as my
boot. He is only equaled in want of intellect by his relation to the
Earl of Lucan … without mincing matters two such fools could not
be picked out of the British Army to take command. But they are
both Earls.[12]

There, of course, was the problem. Both had risen to high rank and both
had money and influence. Lucan at least had some experience of
warfare and some knowledge of the Russian Army and a number of its
commanders. This was far from being the case with Cardigan, as George
Ryan wrote:

When the Earl of Cardigan was ordered to the East in command of
a brigade of our light cavalry, from club to pot-house marveled how
he would behave. Their remembrance of him satisfied all that he had
a taste for gunpowder, but they had no experience of how he could
wield a sword.[13]

Cardigan, though, had bought the right to lead men into battle in the
time-honoured and accepted tradition of the Army. It is said that he
spent £28,000 to rise from Cornet to Lieutenant Colonel in just six years.
He was then rumored to have spent between £35,000 and £40,000 for
command of the 15th Hussars, and later paid £48,000 (a staggering
£3,500,000 or so today) for the colonelcy of the 11th Hussars.

Such was the price that the seventh Earl of Cardigan paid for the
glory of leading the Light Brigade in the Crimea.

Chapter 2

Holy War

Tension had been mounting for months following the Turkish Ottoman Empire's declaration of war against Russia in October 1853. Ostensibly the breach between St Petersburg and Constantinople had been over the rights of Christians in the Holy Land which was under Muslim Ottoman rule. More specifically it had been over the keys to the Church and Grotto of the Nativity in Bethlehem. As Czar Nicholas I saw himself as the defender of the Orthodox Church in the East, the religious dispute gave the Russian autocrat the opportunity, he believed, to interfere in Turkish affairs.

This was merely the latest manifestation of what was called the Eastern Question, and for decades no answer had been found to the puzzle. That question, so often asked, was what would happen to the disparate peoples of the Ottoman Empire when that ailing conglomerate finally fell apart. For more than 500 years the Ottoman Turks had dominated Eastern Europe and the Near East from their capital at Constantinople. At its peak their Empire had encompassed more than 5,000,000 square kilometres and by the mid-1850s embraced in excess of 350,000,000 souls in thirty provinces that stretched from Budapest to Bagdad and reached almost as far south as the Horn of Africa.

But many of the states within the Empire had sought independence from Constantinople, and some had achieved this whilst numbers of others had gained varying degrees of autonomy. Its break up seemed inevitable and if it did collapse there would be no single state strong enough to defy the territorially ambitious Russia. This was a worrying situation for the other great European Powers, in particular Great Britain, who saw Russia as a potential threat to its empire in the Indian sub-continent.

Considerable efforts were undertaken by Britain, France, Austria, and for a time Prussia, to ease the mounting tension between the Sublime Port and the Czar. The Russian autocrat, however, considered that the time was right to give the Ottoman Empire the final push that would see it topple and he believed that the other countries would not dare to stop him. As a consequence, on 26 June, the following proclamation was issued from St Petersburg:

> Having exhausted all means of conviction, and having in vain tried all the means by which our just claims could be peaceably adjusted, we have deemed it indispensable to move our armies into the provinces on the Danube, in order that the Porte may see to what her stubbornness may lead.

To all intents and purposes this was a declaration of war on Turkey. In response the French Assemblée Nationale declared that this was the start of a conflict that would draw in more countries than just Russia and Turkey, or even the world's most dominant Power, Great Britain:

> If Russia and England were alone engaged in the discussion – if the war could be confined to those two Powers – we would be easily satisfied. It would even cause us some joy to see the two nations engaged, and it would not be for England that our prayers would be offered in that contest – for her mercantile asperity is more odious than the ambition by which Russia may be animated. But, once for all, itis not a private war that is in question. It is a general and interminable war. The peace of the world is at stake.[1]

This realistic appreciation led to the most unlikely of alliances – between the perennial enemies Great Britain and France, and a combined Anglo-French fleet sailed for the Eastern Mediterranean seeking by its presence to curd Russian ambitions. The British and French warships found a spacious anchorage in Bashika Bay just outside the Dardanelles to await developments and instructions from the ambassadors of their respective governments in Constantinople.

As it transpired the Turkish force in the Danubian provinces, under Omar Pasha, had fought back, surprising everyone with a stunning victory at Oltenița in October, in present-day Romania. This gave rise to fresh hopes that the Czar would be forced to climb down and pull back his forces. But Nicholas I was not so easily deterred and the Russians persisted with their offensive operations. As a consequence, on 22

October, the Allied fleet was ordered to enter the Dardanelles. Russia declared war on Turkey the next day.

Still, though, Britain and France hesitated. The most that they would commit to was to order the combined force of ten British and nine French ships of the line under the command of Vice Admiral Sir James Deans Dundas, to sail into the Black Sea to prevent the Russian fleet from attacking Turkish coastal trade. This could still be interpreted as a defensive move, though it brought the Allies a step closer to war.

Before the Anglo-French fleet could make its presence felt, the Russian Black Sea Fleet caught a force of ten Turkish sailing ships in Sinope harbour on 30 November. Captain, later Admiral, Adolphus Slade arrived at Sinope shortly after the battle:

> The shore of the bay was lined with wrecks and strewed with corpses. Havoc had done her worst. Not a mast was standing, not a timber was left whole. We found above a hundred wounded in various cafés, in every stage of suffering; some in agony, many of them frightfully disfigured by explosions.

The significance of Slade's comment about the injuries sustained by some of the wounded is that for the first time in naval history Russian warships had used explosive shells instead of the usual solid shot. Against such weapons the wooden Turkish vessels, and their crews, had stood no chance.

The incident made headline news around the world. Even as far away as New Zealand the *Wellington Independent* described the scene at Sinope after the battle, which was,

> horrible beyond description; mangled bodies and limbs of men floating about and lying strewed upon the shore; the dying and the dead, and the wounded mixed up with the wrecks and fragments of the wrecks …The worse feature of the whole affair is, that after all the ships had been destroyed, the Russians fired grape and canister on Turks whilst endeavouring to save themselves by swimming. They killed as many as they could, after all resistance had ceased.

The Times, which throughout the Crimean War proved to be the voice of the people, urged ministers to act. 'War has begun in earnest,' the lead in the paper of 13 December announced:

> A naval action has been fought upon the coast of Asia Minor, ending in the total destruction of a portion of the Ottoman fleet; and for the

14

first time in naval history a Russian squadron has returned to Sebastopol laden with the spoils of victory. The war, hitherto confined to the occupation of the Danubian Principalities and to a few partial encounters of the hostile armies, appears to have assumed on the Black Sea the character of direct aggression, and the Emperor of Russia has thrown down the gauntlet to the maritime Powers precisely on that element on which they are best prepared to meet him ... we have repeatedly urged upon the Governments of England and France the necessity of being prepared with a plan of operations adapted to such an emergency.

With war now seemingly inevitable, preparations for the assembly of an 'auxiliary' force to help the Turks was announced on 13 February. This force was being sent, in the first instance, to the British-held island base of Malta. It was to be 10,000 strong with the proportionate numbers of artillery and cavalry:

> The extent to which this auxiliary force may hereafter be increased will, of course, depend upon circumstances. The division will consist of 3 battalions of the Guards, the 4th, 28th, 33d, 50th, 77th and 93d Regiments of the line, and the 2d battalion of the Rifle Brigade. The Artillery force will include five field batteries and one brigade for small-arm ball cartridge. It is not expected that the brigade of Cavalry will leave until early in March. Its destination will be Constantinople, and it will comprise the Scots Greys, the Carbineers [6th Dragoon Guards], the 17th Lancers, the 11th Hussars, the 8th Hussars, and the Enniskellens [6th Dragons]. The Duke of Cambridge will take the command, assisted by General Brotherton and the Earl of Cardigan. Lord Raglan, we understand, has been appointed to the chief command of the expedition.

Just one day later, there was an amendment to this statement: 'The announcement of the intention to send out a cavalry force turns out for the present at least, to be premature, no decision having as yet been come to upon that point. There will, however, be five squadrons of picked men, in all 500 sabres, included in the division, probably for staff and escort service.' More information was revealed through the pages of *The Times* exactly one week later:

> When the announcement was first made that an auxiliary array was about to be despatched to Malta, which was intended, in case of need, to proceed thence to Turkey, it was understood, that the body

of troops actually under orders for that service constituted but the first divison of the British contingent destined to co-operate with our French allies in the East.

No steps had, however, been taken which could warrant the positive statement that the immediate despatch of a second force had been finally determined.

It was known that 1,200 men were about to embark for the Mediterranean, but the extent to which that demonstration was to be followed up had not been settled. We are now able to announce that another force, of equal strength, will at once be organized and despatched with the least possible delay. The regiments which are to make up this force have not yet been named, but it may be considered as quite arranged that we are to have from 24,000 to 25,000 of our best soldiers engaged in repelling the aggressions of Russia upon Turkey.

An army in all respects so perfectly equipped has never left our shores, and should unfortunately its services be required in the field, the country may look forward with confidence to the result.

With the country now expecting war to be declared other preparations were put in hand and the Foreign Office issued a statement to both British and French consular and diplomatic agents around the world on 23 February:

The time has now arrived when it is incumbent on the two Governments to prepare for all the contingencies of war; and among those contingencies it has been impossible for them to overlook the danger to which their subjects and their commerce on the high seas may be exposed by the machinations of their enemy, who, though unable from his own resources materially to injure either, may seek to derive means of offence from countries whose Governments take no part in the contest which he has provoked.

But it is a necessary consequence of the strict union and alliance which exists between Great Britain and France, that, in the event of war, their conjoint action should be felt by Russia in all parts of the world; that, not only in the Baltic, and in the waters and territory of Turkey, their counsels, their armies, and their fleets should be united either for offensive or defensive purposes against Russia, but that the same spirit of union should prevail in all quarters of the world … You will consider it your duty to protect, as far as possible, against she consequence of the hostilities in which England and France may shortly be engaged with Russia, the subjects and interests of France equally with those of England.[2]

The great alliance between Britain and France, something utterly beyond anyone's imagination just a couple of years before, had now been officially declared.

The same day that this was announced in the press, Londoners were treated to the sight of the Grenadier Guards starting their journey to join the Auxiliary Force destined for the East.

Many thousands of people crowded round the southern entrance of St George's Barracks throughout the afternoon in great, but patient expectation:

> Soon after 5, with a clash of music, the band emerged, to the immense delight of the multitude, and marched straight towards the Strand, where it took up its station. After the pause of a minute came the famous Grenadiers. …
>
> When formed, the regiment, about a thousand strong, and just showing their bayonets and black fur caps above the heads of a vast multitude which filled the Strand, marched over Waterloo Bridge to the station.
>
> The incessant cheering, the music, and occasionally the wild but hearty chorus of the mob, soon brought the sleepers to their windows, and many a strange figure was seen waving and shouting a farewell through the dusk …
>
> The Grenadiers marched, thus escorted, to the Waterloo station, and were there welcomed by fresh thousands, as they were again at Southampton, where they went on board the steamers waiting for them.

On the evening of the next day, Lord Clarendon in the House of Lords stated that he 'held out no hopes of peace; the Emperor of Russia, by the successive rejection of fair and honourable terms repeatedly offered to him, had hurled defiance at Europe, and that the challenge so offered would not be allowed to drop.'

Queen Victoria watched the last contingent of the Guards leaving for the East on 28 February:

> I shall never forget the touching, beautiful sight I witnessed this morning. By my particular desire, the last Battn of Guard (Scots Fusiliers) were to march past the Palace on the way to entraining for

Portsmouth, where they were to embark today. Got up at ½ p. 6 &
hurriedly dressed, going to the corner room of the new port to watch
what was going on in the Barrack Yard. Albert with the 4 eldest
Children joined me there, the others watching from above. We then
went into the middle room.

A large crowd was assembled outside the railings & 7 o'clock
having struck, great cheering being heard, as well as the distant
sounds of music, we stepped out on to the balcony & were loudly
cheered.

The morning was fine & calm, the sun rising red, over the time-
honoured Towers of Westminster, producing a solemn effect which
was heightened by the gradual, steady, but slow approach of the
Band almost drowned by the tremendous cheering of the dense
crowd following. At length the gates opened & the Sappers &
Miners began slowly to enter the yard, all in marching order with
their kit slung over their shoulders, followed by the Band (which
does not go) playing the 'Highland Laddie'. The crowd was so dense
that they could hardly get along or in, & had to run for it. They had
difficulty, owing to the small space, in forming line but succeeded,
& presented arms, after which they gave 3 hearty cheers, which went
to my heart.

At the beginning of March, Prussia, which had been trying to broker a
peace deal along with Austria, declared its neutrality, not wishing to be
drawn into conflict with its large northern neighbour. Austria followed
suit shortly afterwards. The French and British embassies were
withdrawn from St Petersburg as the opposing sides took the final steps
towards war.

Finally, on 27 March, France declared war on Russia. The next day
Britain made the following announcement in a Supplement to *The
London Gazette*:

It is with deep regret that Her Majesty announces the failure of her
anxious and protracted endeavours to preserve for her people and
for Europe the blessings of peace.

The unprovoked aggression of the Emperor of Russia against the
Sublime Porte has been persisted in with such disregard of
consequences, that after the rejection by the Emperor of Russia of
terms which the Emperor of Austria, the Emperor of the French, and
the King of Prussia, as well as Her Majesty, considered just and
equitable, Her Majesty is compelled by a sense of what is due to the

honour of her Crown, to the interests of her people, and to the independence of the States of Europe, to come forward in defence of an ally whose territory is invaded, and whose dignity and independence are assailed …

But, while the Russian Government repeatedly assured the Government of Her Majesty that the mission of Prince Menschikoff to Constantinople was exclusively directed to the settlement of the question of the Holy Places at Jerusalem, Prince Menschikoff himself pressed upon the Porte other demands of a far more serious and important character, the nature of which he in the first instance endeavoured, as far as possible, to conceal from Her Majesty's Ambassador. And these demands, thus studiously concealed, affected, not the privileges of the Greek Church at Jerusalem, but the position of many millions of Turkish subjects in their relations to their Sovereign the Sultan. These demands were rejected by the spontaneous decision of the Sublime Porte …

But when, in addition to the assemblage of large military forces on the frontier of Turkey, the Ambassador of Russia intimated that serious consequences would ensue from the refusal of the Sultan to comply with unwarrantable demands, Her Majesty deemed it right, in conjunction with the Emperor of the French, to give an unquestionable proof of her determination to support the sovereign rights of the Sultan … to take up arms, in conjunction with the Emperor of the French, for the defence of the Sultan.

A large proportion of the troops comprising what would become the Expeditionary Force had by this date already reached Malta, as had William Russell of *The Times*:

When the declaration of war reached Malta, the excitement was indescribable. Crowds assembled on the shores of the harbours and lined the quays and landing-places, the crash of music drowned in the enthusiastic cheers of the soldiers cheering their comrades as the vessels glided along, the cheers from one fort being taken up by the troops in the others, and as joyously responded to from those on board.[3]

Excited or not at the prospect of action, Raglan's small force amounted to only around 21,000 men and it was in no shape to conduct operations against a powerful enemy such as the Russians, as Lieutenant Frederick Stephenson of the Scots Fusilier Guards described:

Between you and me, I do not think matters have been well arranged at the Horse Guards. Excepting the Guards, no brigade has been put together yet. Hardly any of the Staff have come out, although the whole of the infantry of the Expeditionary Force has not only been at Malta for some considerable time, but has actually gone off to the seat of war, leaving the Brigadier-Generals and Staff to follow them at some later time, instead of those officers being the first to land to superintend the disembarking and first settling down in a foreign land of their respective brigades. Some 15,000 troops are now at Gallipoli, not brigaded, and with the exception of Sir George Brown and a staff of five officers, there is only one Brigadier-General (besides the Colonel of Engineers) to look after them all.[4]

The initial British force had consisted primarily of infantry but finally the composition of the cavalry arm was declared and it was to be of divisional strength, as *The Times* reported on 30 March:

It is rumoured that, in addition to the late augmentation of the army, there is to be a further increase of 30,000 men, and that the first division of the expeditionary force at Malta is now being rapidly moved on to Constantinople.

The Cavalry regiments proceeding to the East through France are each expected to occupy about nine days after crossing the Channel in proceeding to Marseilles. As the railway communication between Chalons and Avignon is incomplete, about seven days will be spent on the march, and it is believed that this will be found a useful preparatory training both for men and horses before they enter upon active service. The large number of transports that would be required in conveying the force entirely by sea is, we understand, the chief reason for the selection of this route. Those who are anticipating a military display on the occasion of the English cavalry passing through Paris will probably be disappointed, as according to present arrangements the troops will proceed on their journey by squadrons.

The infantry might have been short of officers and staff, but it was quite the opposite with the cavalry, as this letter from a cavalry officer reveals:

Hearing that two more cavalry regiments are about to be sent to Turkey, I think it right to state to you, and consequently to the public, the strength of the staff already there, and the numbers that staff have at this moment under their command. At present in

Turkey there are eight cavalry regiments, comprising 8 lieutenant-colonels, 8 majors, 32 captains, and 64 subalterns—in all 112 officers, to say nothing of two brigadiers and a general of division, to command what? Why, Sir, a handful of 2,000 men. If, instead of sending out more regiments, the Horse Guards would make the cavalry officers at home give all their time and attention to sending out effective men and horses continually to increase the strength of the regiments already gone out, I think we should have in course of time, in the East, cavalry regiments of such strength, as regards men and horses, at they would be a source of pride, instead of, as now, the laughing stock of the whole cavalry service. You don't want more officers, but you do want in your cavalry regiments more men and more horses.[5]

The French force, *l'armee d'Orient*, under the command of Marshal Saint-Arnaud, stronger than the British and much better prepared for war, had arrived in Turkey first. Enemies for so long, now Britain and France were to be allies. Surprisingly, the two armies very quickly developed a very close relationship:

> The joint occupation by French and English and French troops of the ground on the shores of the Dardanelles had yielded the first experience of the relations likely to subsist between the armies of the two nations when quartered near to each other.
> It quickly appeared that the troops of each force could be cordially good-humoured in their intercourse with those of the other. Canrobert, Bosquet, and Sir George Brown, all destined to take prominent share in the coming events, made a kindly beginning of acquaintanceship amid the between the early difficulties and discomforts of Gallipoli.[6]

Queen Victoria's cousin George, Duke of Cambridge, was a Major General in the British Army and was given command of the prestigious 1st Division, which included the Brigade of Guards. He arrived in Constantinople in May 1854, and was accommodated in one of the Sultan's palaces and was treated very well. This did not stop him writing to Victoria about the Sultan in frank terms and about the state of the Expeditionary Force:

> He [the Sultan] is, to say the truth, a wretched creature, prematurely aged, and having nothing whatever to say for himself... As to his Ministers, and in fact the whole population and country ... they are

all a most wretched and miserable set of people, and far, far worse than anything I could possibly have imagined or supposed …

As to our movements, I know nothing of them as yet, nor do I think that much has as yet been settled, but I fear we shall not be fit to move for some time; the difficulty of transport is very great, our Artillery only partly arrived, and no Cavalry. We require more troops, more particularly of the latter arm, in which the Russians are very strong. We ought to have at least 10,000 men more, and the sooner they are sent out the better. Even that number is not enough, for the French talk of 100,000 men, and we should be in a most dreadful minority unless we had 40,000 to 50,000.[7]

The cavalry were soon on their way to join the Expeditionary Force, as Troop Sergeant-Major Mathew Brown of the 2nd Royal North British Dragoons (Scots Greys) detailed in a letter to the Editor of the *Nottinghamshire Gazette*:

On the 24th July, at 7 a.m., we marched from Manchester amidst the cheers of the populace, and halted for the night at Prescott. We were next morning again on the road for Liverpool at 4 a.m., and arrived there about 6 a.m., where, notwithstanding the early hour, thousands followed us, some of them only half-clothed, to witness our embarkation at the Docks. By 10 a.m. [we] were all on board, the horses in their stalls, and them as comfortably put up as circumstances would permit.

The ship then slipped her moorings and steamed out to the middle of the river where we cast anchor. During the whole day steamers, crowded with dense masses of people, were continually putting off from the shore, and steaming round the Himalaya; bands playing lively and appropriate airs, and the people saluting us with cries of 'God speed the Greys'.

A Private of the 13th Hussars watched the horses being loaded onto the transport ships at Portsmouth:

In a few minutes every man was dismounted, and his saddle and accoutrements neatly stowed in his corn-sack, and then I saw a sight I had never seen before. Each horse was led up to the ship's side (which lay alongside the quay); a sling was placed beneath the horse's belly, and fastened to the tackling on the main-yard.

The word was then given to 'hoist away', when about a hundred convicts manned a large rope, and running away with it, the poor trooper was soon high in the air, quite helpless. He was then gradually lowered down the main hatchway (which was well padded to prevent accidents) until he arrived at the hold which was fitted up as a stable, each horse being provided with a separate stall. They were placed with their heels towards the ship's side, and heads towards each other, with a passage between them. There were strong mangers fixed beneath their heads, to which they were fastened by double halters, so that when once they were fastened there was no chance of lying down while they were on board.[8]

Now that the combined French and British forces were in theatre and the latter starting to sort out its command and divisional structures, the question to be answered was what was the best course of action to take in support of the Turks? The greatest threat to Constantinople was seen as being most likely to be delivered through the Black Sea. The Russian Fleet was the most dominant naval force in the Black Sea and its main base was Sevastopol. From a very early stage in the war an attack upon Sevastopol was contemplated and this was relayed to Lord Raglan by the Duke of Newcastle, the Secretary of State for War, on 29 June 1854:

> I have to instruct your Lordship to concert measures for the siege of Sevastopol, unless, with the information in your possession, but at present unknown in this country, you should be decidedly of opinion that it could not be undertaken with a reasonable prospect of success ... if, upon mature reflection, you should consider that the united strength of the two armies is insufficient for this undertaking, you are not to be precluded from the exercise of the discretion originally vested in you, though Her Majesty's Government will learn with regret that an attack from which such important consequences are anticipated must be any longer delayed.[9]

From this it would appear that Raglan was free to decide on whether or not an operation against Sevastopol should be undertaken. In reality he had little choice, as the rest of Newcastle's letter revealed:

> The difficulties of the siege of Sevastopol appear to Her Majesty's Government to be more likely to increase than diminish by delay; and as there is no prospect of a safe and honourable peace until the fortress is reduced, and the [Russian] fleet taken or destroyed, it is, on all accounts, most important that nothing but insuperable impediments, such as the want of ample preparations by either army, or the possession by Russia of a force in the Crimea greatly

outnumbering that which can be brought against it, should be
allowed to prevent the early decision to take these operations.

As we have seen, there was undoubtedly a decided 'want of ample
preparations', and Raglan would have been more than justified in
stating that the forces which had been assembled at Gallipoli were
wholly insufficient for the task he had been set. Yet Raglan had held
high positions in the British Army for the previous four decades. He
could hardly say that the army was ill-prepared and ill-equipped – an
army that he was such an influential member of.

The other factor which Newcastle alluded to was the size of the
opposing Russian army. Not only could Raglan have no idea how
practical the siege of Sevastopol might be – a place he had never visited
– but also he had no knowledge whatsoever of the size or composition
of the enemy forces he might have to face. The next part of Newcastle's
letter can only have added to Raglan's worries:

> It is probable that a large part of the Russian army now retiring from
> the Turkish territory may be poured into the Crimea to reinforce
> Sevastopol. If orders to this effect have not already been given, it is
> further probable that such a measure would be adopted as soon as
> it is known that the Allied armies are in motion to commence active
> hostilities.

Just to make matters even worse for Raglan, Newcastle included a
private letter along with the official one:

> The Cabinet is unanimously of opinion that, unless you and Marshal
> St Arnaud feel that you are not sufficiently prepared, you should lay
> siege to Sevastopol, as we are more than ever convinced that,
> without the reduction of this fortress, and the capture of the Russian
> fleet, it will be impossible to conclude an honourable and safe peace.
> The Emperor of the French has expressed his entire concurrence in
> this opinion, and, I believe, has written privately to the Marshal to
> that effect.

After reading these letters Raglan showed them to his friend, and
commander of the Light Division General Sir George Brown. He asked
Brown for his opinion. He replied:

> You and I are accustomed, when in any great difficulty, or when any
> important question is proposed to us, to ask ourselves how the Great

Duke [of Wellington] would have acted and decided under similar circumstances. Now, I tell your Lordship that, without more certain information than you appear to have obtained in regard to this matter, that great man would not have accepted the responsibility of undertaking such an enterprise as that which is now proposed to you.

Brown was right, of course, but he knew, as did Raglan, that he had been pushed into a corner:

> I am of the opinion that you had better accede to the proposal, and come into the views of the Government, for this reason, that it is clear to me, from the Duke of Newcastle's letter, that they have made up their minds to it at home; and that, if you decline to accept the responsibility, they will send someone else out to command the army who will be less scrupulous and more ready to come into their plans.[10]

Raglan, therefore, ordered the army to prepare for a move to the Crimea. Everything now depended on what Saint-Arnaud thought of the proposed assault upon Sevastopol. If he was opposed to it, the operation might have to be cancelled, or at least postponed. Raglan discussed the scheme with the French commander who, though excited at the idea, had reservations:

> To land in the Crimea, and besiege Sevastopol is in itself a whole campaign. It is not a *coup de main*; it requires enormous resources and a certainty of success … Supposing us landed, we should require, perhaps, more than a month's siege to capture Sevastopol, if well defended. During that time, succours arrive, and I have two or even three battles to fight … Nevertheless, despite all difficulties, all obstacles, and the lack of means and of time, Sevastopol tempts me to such a degree, that I should not hesitate, should there be even an appearance of success; and I should prepare myself accordingly.[11]

As it transpired, the first move into the Black Sea was not to Sevastopol but to Varna, in present-day Bulgaria. This was because of a Russian force threatening to cross the Danube and move down through the fortified town of Silistria. The British and French forces arrived at Varna in the early summer:

> The British camp is pitched on a plain, covered with scrub and clumps of sweet briar, about a mile from the town, and half a mile

from the fresh waterlake. The water of the lake, however, is not good for drinking – it abounds in animalcule, not to mention enormous leeches – and the men have to go to the fountains and wells near the town to fill their canteens and cooking tins …The French force [presently here] is very small, but they have got hold of some of the, best quarters, and the tricolor floats over the town from a very high flag-staff. Varna is something like Sandgate, with a white wall round it. Great efforts are being made to strengthen it, and along the sea face are mounted new guns, with earthwork and fascine parapets and embrasures. The beach is covered with heaps of rusty old shot and shell. The hills at the back completely command the place, and make it a poor military position.[12]

Henry Clifford, aide-de-camp to Brigadier George Buller who commanded the 2nd Brigade of the Light Division, was not impressed with Varna:

Houses are made of wood, two stories in height, some few with glass windows, but most without, red tiles to the houses, the streets paved with stone and slanting to the centre, which forms a sort of large drain, into which is emptied all sorts of filth … In trying to get out of the way of a dead dog the other day, I found my foot on a dead rat. The streets are never cleaned in any way, so the stench beats anything I have ever smelt.[13]

Whilst Raglan and Saint-Arnaud wrestled with the problem of how to best utilise their combined forces in support of the Turks, they had another problem to contend with – cholera. In the confined conditions of the camps the disease was spreading rapidly amongst the troops, as Margaret Kirwin, wife of Private John Kirwin of the 19th Regiment wrote:

The men were dying fast of the cholera and black fever and were buried in their blankets. No sooner had we moved up country than the Turks opened the graves and took the blankets. After this we buried them without covering, save for branches and brambles.[14]

As no particular course of action had yet been decided upon, there was nothing to occupy the troops, which can only have added to their susceptibility to illness. Captain Townsend Wilson of the Coldstream Guards painted a picture of life at Varna each morning. After reveille and breakfast, the troops, lapse into a state of semi-coma; would for the most part, compose itself to the enjoyment of a *siesta* in tents as hot as ovens; the thin canvas of course offering but feeble resistance to the blaze overhead. Take a stroll through the camp and you will find the majority ... overcome with heat and idleness, stretched flat or snoring on the ground.[15]

The cavalry division had by this time joined the rest of the force and Major General James Thomas Brudenell, 7th Earl of Cardigan, in command of the Light Brigade, did at least keep his men busy, as Trooper Mitchell wrote:

> We had plenty of drill here, generally early in the morning, Lord Cardigan seemed determined that it should not be for want of practice if we were not perfect. One of his favourite manoeuvres was to advance a squadron to the front, and at a given signal for every man to disperse and go where they pleased. He would then order the 'Rally' to be sounded to see how quick we could get into our places again. This with skirmishing drill, charging in line and by squadrons, outpost drill etc. was principally our work while here.[16]

To everyone's surprise, the Russians, who appeared to be on the verge of victory, suddenly abandoned the siege and withdrew from Silistria. The Austrians had demanded the withdrawal of all Russian forces from the Danubian provinces and Czar Nicholas, already at war with Britain, France and Turkey, could not risk making any more enemies.

When news of the Russian withdrawal reached Varna, Raglan, unaware of the reason for the sudden departure of the enemy, needed to learn what was happening and ordered Lord Cardigan to take a strong body of cavalry and investigate. With a squadron each of the 8th Hussars and 13th Light Dragoons, with some Turkish cavalry making a total of around 200 men, Lord Cardigan set off on 25 June. Already Cardigan, whose brigade was stationed at Devna, ten miles from Varna, had told Lord Lucan, his divisional commander, that he considered he had 'a separate and detached command', and that he would take orders from no-one but 'the general officer in command of the forces in the country.' Lucan, understandably, reacted angry at this 'misapprehension' of the brigadiers' position, To make things worse, Raglan then, seemingly, favoured Cardigan by asking him to undertake an independent reconnaissance, 'to try and discover the movements of the enemy' leaving Lucan behind. Lucan was, not for the last time, furious with Raglan. But the Commander-in-Chief reminded Lucan that there were still more detachments of cavalry to arrive and he needed him 'to inspect each troop carefully as it disembarks.'[17]

Cardigan, was delighted with this opportunity to show how great a cavalry commander he was. As a result, instead of simply riding up to Silistria, he continued his reconnaissance along the banks of the Danube, the whole escapade taking seventeen days instead of the expected eight days. He drove his men on at a punishing pace, and when the patrol returned the men and mounts were in terrible condition. Fanny Duberly saw them as the straggled back to camp on 11 July:

> The reconnaissance under Lord Cardigan came in this morning, at eight, having marched all night. They have … lived for five days on water and salt pork; have shot five horses, which dropped from exhaustion on the road, brought back a cart full of disabled men, and seventy-five horses which will be unfit for work for many months, and some of them will never work again. I was ou riding in the evening when the stragglers came in; and a piteous sight it was, men on foot driving and goading the wretched, wretched horses, three or four of which could hardly stir. There seems to have been much unnecessary suffering, a cruel parade of death.[18]

With the Russian threat in the Danube removed the Allied troops could serve no useful purpose at Varna and Raglan and Saint-Arnaud accepted that they would have to make the move against Sevastopol that their respective governments desired. On 24 August, the combined forces began assembling for the journey that would take them across the Black Sea to the Crimea.

Raglan decided to embark the Light Brigade only with the rest of the Expeditionary Force, with the Heavy Brigade to follow once a secure landing had been achieved. Lucan was not told when he would sail. He was not impressed:

> My Lord – Last evening [the 29th] I received a memorandum, instructing me to direct 'that the regiments of the Light Cavalry Brigade be held in readiness to embark at shortest notice under the Earl of Cardigan' and another memorandum stating that 'the internal distribution is left to the direction of the general officer commanding'. Brigadier-General Scarlett had already informed me that your Lordship had stated to him that the Heavy Brigade would be embarked at a later period under his command. I find myself left, as on former occasions, without instructions regarding myself, the

commander of the division, except, as I read them, not to accompany the Light Cavalry Brigade and not to interfere with their embarkation … I cannot conceal from myself, what has not been concealed from the Army – that during the four months I have been under your Lordship's command, I have been separated, as much as it possible to do so … and I have been left to discharge duties more properly befitting an inferior officer; whilst to Lord Cardigan has been intrusted, from the day of his arrival, the command of nearly the whole of the cavalry, having under his charge the Light Brigade, half the Heavy Brigade and any horse artillery attached to the cavalry.[19]

He told Raglan that he assumed he and Cardigan were being kept apart to prevent a 'collision' between the brothers-in-law. This was probably exactly what Raglan was trying to do, but Lucan had been appointed cavalry commander and he could not be bypassed. From that point onwards Raglan channelled his instructions, quite properly, through Lucan. The damage, though, had been done.

Chapter 3

Inaction at the Alma

A private in the 8th Hussars, who signed himself as 'G.C.' wrote a number of letters to the MP for Bristol, the Right Honourable Francis Berkeley, which were reproduced in the *Bristol Mercury*. His letter of 3 September 1854 was written from on board the transport steamer *Himalaya*:

> It was a great surprise to a good many who had fancied all along that there would be no war, to find themselves near to it. The 11th Hussars marched first; the next day the 8th Hussars, the 13th and 17th followed them. We had three days' march, and then halted near Varna, and on the next day marched down to the Quay, and there embarked on board the 'Himalaya'. I have often read of this vessel, but had no idea of her immense size and splendid accommodation. When I went on board, after my horse had been taken from the slings, I went down a staircase, and the polished railing, gilded mouldings, and splendidly-lit Saloon put me more in mind of a palace than a troop-ship. It made me wonder where they could put 400 horses, for in the transport ship I came out in, which was 1020 tons, we could only find accommodation for 54 horses.
>
> This vessel ('Himalaya') is able to carry two regiments of horse … We now have 300 horses on board, and 32 more are to be shipped this afternoon; the whole of the regiment (8th Hussars) is on board and one squadron of the 17th Lancers. Lord Cardigan and the whole of the staff are coming on board to go up to Sebastopol. We expect to leave Varna on Monday, one day's steaming will bring us in sight of the enemy.[1]

It was not until 5 September that the first Allied ships departed from Varna. Strong winds had made embarkation slow and difficult, especially for the horses of the artillery and the cavalry, and the weather in the Black Sea continued unsettled. The water was so choppy that Raglan, who had lost an arm at Waterloo, was unable to board the flagship of Vice Admiral Hamelin, the 114-gun screw battleship *Ville de Paris* for a conference of Allied commanders.

What the Allied commanders had to resolve was where on the Crimean Peninsula the Expeditionary Force and *l'armee d'Orient* was to land. It was known that Sevastopol harbour and its approaches were defended by coastal batteries and that a portion of the Black Sea Fleet lay there at anchor. A direct amphibious assault was certain to be a costly affair and was discounted. The other options available were considered by Lieutenant General Sir Edward Hamley, who at the time was a captain and aide-de-camp to Sir Richard Dacres, who commanded the artillery contingent:

> The considerations which had been the main elements in the question of the selection of a point of disembarkation were, first, a space sufficient for the armies to land together, and in full communication with each other; and secondly, that the ground should be such as the fire of the ships could protect from the possible enterprises of the enemy. Ship's guns are so formidable in size and, range that no batteries capable of rapid motion can hope to contend with them. No ground fulfilling these conditions was found on the southern coast, where the cliffs stand up steep and high out of the water, nor did the mouths of the rivers afford the necessary advantages.
>
> On the other hand, the western coast north of Sebastopol offered no harbour of which the armies could make a secure base, or even a temporary depot; while, south of Sebastopol, the inlet of Balaklava, though small, was deep and well-sheltered, where large steamers could unload close to the shore, and the small bay of Kamiesch was capable of being made a base.[2]

It was eventually decided that the wide, open coastline of Kalamita Bay, some thirty miles to the north of Sevastopol, and two to three miles south of the port of Eupatoria, offered the easiest and safest landing beaches. There were no natural defences along the beach that could be occupied by the Russians to oppose a landing and any approach by the enemy would be detected early.

Back in Russia, feelings about the Allied invasion, were probably best regarded as being mixed, as can be gauged by the views of writer Sergey Aksakov:

Without doubt the enemy's troops are better organised than ours, his weapons and shells are superior and he has the support of a huge fleet with guns which can cover the beaches at a range of two versts [2,300 yards]. But we are on our home ground and we have fresh troops ... It is not known how many troops we have in the Crimea; if we have a large force, say 100,00, then the enemy may be annihilated.[3]

The reality was that the Russian commander in the Crimea, Prince Alexander Sergeyevich Menschikoff, had less than half that number of troops and he had no intention of disputing the Allied landings.

The Allied warships and transports congregated off Kalamita Bay on the evening of 13 September, and the following morning the landing began, as an officer on Raglan's staff recorded:

On the morning of the 14th, at 3 o'clock, we weighed anchor, and from then till 8 a.m. the transports, &c., were getting into their proper places. There was some confusion in consequence of the French taking up one of our buoys as their left, so in that manner they threw us out by half a mile, which caused much crowding. The French were the first to land.

Soon after 7 a.m. they sent a boat on shore with half a dozen men, who erected a flag-staff and hoisted the French colours. Their first flat of troops landed at a quarter to 9 a.m. about 2 miles south of us.[4]

The only Russians that were seen were five horsemen, two of whom appeared to be officers. One of the officers began taking notes in a 'memorandum' book. As more troops landed, led by Sir George Brown's Light Division, the Russians made off, no doubt to report their observations, and the disembarkation continued unopposed, as described by William Russell:

By twelve o'clock, that barren and desolate beach, inhabited but a short time before only by the seagull and wild-fowl, was swarming with life. From one extremity to the other, bayonets glistened and red coats and brass-mounted shakoes gleamed in solid masses. The air was filled with our English speech and the hum of voices mingled with loud notes of command.[5]

The disembarkation continued throughout the day, but the wind grew in intensity towards evening and the landing of the horses and artillery was postponed. By that time the French had landed three divisions complete with their equipment, provisions and staff, and all four British infantry divisions were ashore, but without their equipment, particularly the tents. All that the troops could do was wrap themselves in their blankets and greatcoats as they were lashed by a torrential storm. 'The first night in the Crimea was a night long to be remembered by those who were there,' wrote Sergeant Major Timothy Gowing of the 7th Royal Fusiliers:

> It came on to rain in torrents, while the wind blew a perfect hurricane; and all, from the Commanders down to the Drummer Boys, had to stand and take it as it came. And the rain did fall, only as it does in the tropics. We looked next morning like a lot of drowned rats ... had the enemy come on in strength nothing could have saved us.[6]

On the 15th the landing of the cavalry and artillery began, the entire disembarkation lasting for a further three days. Lord George Paget of the 4th Light Dragoons wrote of this in his journal:

> We are at last landing our horses. Lucan and staff just landed. Surge rather increasing ... it is distressing to see the poor horses, as they are upset out of the boats, swimming about in all directions among the ships. They swim so peacefully, but look rather unhappy with their heads in the air and the surf driving into their poor mouths. Only one has been drowned as yet, to our knowledge. We get on but slowly with our disembarkation.[7]

Fanny Duberly had accompanied her husband, Henry Duberly, the paymaster of the 8th Hussars, to the Crimea. She wrote the following in her diary of Saturday the 15th:

> English troops disembarking in a heavy surf. The landing of the horses is difficult and dangerous. Such men as were disembarked yesterday were all lying exposed to the torrents of rain which fell during the night ... In consequence an order has been issued to disembark *the tents*. The beach is a vast and crowded camp, covered with men, horses, fires, tents, general officers, staff officers, boats landing men and horses, which latter are flung overboard and swim ashore. Eleven drowned today.[8]

Fanny then made an interesting observation. 'Lord Cardigan begins to be eager for the fray, and will be doing something or other directly he has landed, I fancy.' Cardigan's desire for action would be satisfied in little more than a month's time, in a manner he could hardly have imagined.

Albert Mitchell, of the 13th Light Dragoons, had landed from the transport ship, *Jason*:

> The sand was not above a hundred yards wide, and beyond that there was a good sized salt lake. Into the sand we drove our picket pegs, and picketed our horses for the night. It was very difficult to get the pegs to hold in the sand. As I was not on duty that night, and I found a capital bed among some hay nets which had been sent on shore all filled with hay, and laid in a heap. I slept very soundly until morning.[9]

After helping to escort a number of horses loaded with sacks of flour, Mitchell and his detachment were told off to have breakfast. This, Mitchell remarked, was easier said than done as there was no fresh water on the beach or wood with which to light a fire:

> However, we took a camp kettle and went along the shore watching the waves as they rolled in, hoping to get a fragment of wood that washed in. This was our only chance of firewood. By dint of much patience we managed to get enough to make a fire, and after we had gone about a mile we saw a crowd of soldiers, both English and French, gathered together at one spot. On arrival there we found a small well about a dozen feet deep. The only way to get the water was for one to descend into the well and dip the water up in a tin pannikin, and so fill the kettle. In this way we managed to get a little drinkable water and, having brought a little tea ashore, we soon had quite a nice breakfast.

Rather than hanging around the beach, the Light Dragoons should have been out foraging and watching out for the approach of the enemy. This was highlighted by the historian Alexander Kinglake who accompanied the Expeditionary Force to the Crimea and who compiled the most detailed account of its operations up to the summer of 1855. This, as will later be seen, may, to some degree, have contributed to the loss of the Light Brigade little more than a month later:

> In general, it would fall within the duty of light horse to sweep the face of the invaded territory and bring in supplies; but the French were without cavalry; and although the body of horse which we had landed was called 'the Light Brigade,' the Lancers, the Hussars, and

the Light Dragoons of which it consisted, were not troops of such nimble kind, and not so practised as to be all at once apt at foraging. Besides it was plain that in advancing through the enemy's country, the power of the invaders would have to be measured by the arm in which they were weakest, and a material loss in our small, brilliant force of cavalry might bring ruin upon the whole expedition.[10]

Raglan was acutely conscious of how small the cavalry force was, although Kingslake was wrong in stating that the French had no cavalry, as they had one squadron of *Spahis* and one squadron of *Chasseurs d'Afrique*, around 300 sabres in total.

The prime function of cavalry, particularly the light cavalry, was to act as the 'eyes and ears' of the army. In an alien and hostile environment, with little knowledge of the terrain or of the strength or intentions of the enemy, intelligence derived from the cavalry, scouting far in advance of the main body, is utterly essential. Raglan, therefore, could not risk losing his cavalry and he would not permit it to undertake any dangerous endeavours. This had nearly been the case when Cardigan took his men off on patrol and had got lost, as described in a letter from a trooper of the 11th Hussars published in the *Bristol Mercury* of 11 November 1854:

Immediately after landing we saddled, and Lord Cardigan took us and the 17th Lancers about 15 miles up the country. Such a mad-brained trick I should was never played before. We started at ten o'clock in the morning, at length we stopped at a Russian village about 15 miles from the place we started from; here we fed our horses and remained an hour – in fact, it was getting quite dark before we thought of going back.

We came over gigantic mountains, and as we were to go back the same way it struck us all how easily we could be attacked and the whole of us cut to pieces by men who knew the country; and, to mend the matter, his Lordship forgot the road. When we came up in the afternoon we had an immense sheet of salt water to ford, but it was only a foot and a half deep; on returning, when we came to the water, we found that instead of a foot and a half deep it was about five feet deep. We made a detour to the right, and found that the tide had, in our absence, come in, and the place we had forded in the morning was four feet deep. We were obliged then to make another detour to our extreme left, and at length got to a place where the water was only three feet deep, but it was nearly a quarter of a mile across. I thought how easily we could have been cut off when we were wandering about in search of a ford. When we got back to the beach it was twelve o'clock and the night very dark.

Nevertheless, the cavalry was there to be used, and it took up a position some three miles in front of the infantry, where the men bivouacked. They laid down, fully clothed, swords by their sides, close to their horses, so that they could be armed and mounted within moments if the enemy approached.

With all the men, stores, horses and artillery landed, the combined armies began their march on Sebastopol on 19 September. The Allied force was composed of 30,204 French, 7,000 Turks and 27,000 British. This was a formidable body of around 63,000 men with 128 artillery pieces.

The French took the right wing next to the sea, where the Allied fleet followed the land forces to provide artillery support if necessary and to transport the provisions the soldiers could not carry with them. The advance guard consisted of the 11th Hussars and the 13th Light Dragoons under Lord Cardigan, behind which was the rest of the cavalry and a detachment of the Rifle Brigade in extended order following which was the rest of the British army.

In words that the men of the light cavalry would no doubt recall when ordered to charge into the North Valley at Balaklava, Cardigan issued his instructions for engaging the enemy:

> In case we fall in with them and charge them, ride close, and let the centre be a little in advance of the flanks, and when you get within a hundred yards of them ride with the utmost impetuosity. But mind whatever you do after you have passed through their ranks, don't go too far, but turn about as quick as possible, and rally together and charge back again.[11]

The Allies were travelling through open country which invited attack and between Kalamita Bay and Sevastopol were four rivers, any of which might be defended by the enemy. The Allies therefore advanced with some caution. The first of the rivers was the Bulganak (or Bulganek) which some five or six miles to the south and it was here where the Russians were waiting. Two reports under the headline, 'The Skirmish on the 19th', appeared in the *Sheffield & Rotherham Independent* of 14 October describing the first encounter with the Russians as the Allies approached the Bulganak:

> At three we came to a little brook or stream, about 20 yards broad, which we all expected the Russians would defend at all hazards. Not

a soul was there. The river ran between steep sloping banks. We crossed, and the troops believed that we were going to stop on the opposite bank of the river for the night, and the men, in spite of their fatigue, were chasing the hares in the long grass, amid shouts of laughter; when suddenly the cavalry pickets came down to inform us that the enemy were in force in the vale beyond the hills. In an instant all was excitement and eagerness; the light cavalry dashed over the hill with a tremendous hurrah, and disappeared; staff officer began to gallop about madly; bugles blew all sorts of notes and the men fell into their divisions with as much alacrity as if they were going to a dinner.

A French naval officer had an excellent view of proceeding from the poop deck of his ship. He described how 'breathless with excitement and emotion' he watched as Prince Menschikoff, send a strong column of cavalry supported by a brigade of infantry into the valley to meet the Allied force:

> We had a capital view of the field; nothing escaped us; we could distinguish the uniforms of the regiments, the arms they carried, everything in fact. Oh the glorious and beautiful spectacle! Two armies were about to join battle under our eyes. Our friends, our brethren in arms, at last were on the point of finding themselves face to face of the enemy so long wished for, so long desired.[12]

The author of the piece in the *Sheffield & Rotherham Independent* rode in up to a little knoll where Raglan and his staff had halted:

> Beneath me was an immense deep valley, the south side of which was formed by the mountain ridge which encloses Sebastopol, and four squadrons of our cavalry were down in the centre of the valley, and facing them, and distant about 600 yards, were 18 or 20 squadrons of Cossacks. Our Lancers and Light Dragoons were preparing to charge, when the Cossacks, seeing they were unsupported by artillery, practised a *ruse*, of which our generals should have been aware. They very coolly opened their ranks, and disclosed a battery of ten or twelve field pieces, which immediately commenced a heavy fire on our cavalry … one of our cavalrymen lost his leg, and another his foot, one horse was killed, and another wounded.

The man who lost his leg was Private Henry of the 11th Hussars, who actually had his foot shot off. A sergeant of the 13th Light Dragoons also lost his right hand. William Russell saw the wounded men:

One of the wounded men, a sergeant in the 11th Hussars, rode coolly to the rear with his foot dangling by a piece of skin to the bone, and told the doctor he had just come to have his leg dressed. Another wounded trooper behaved with equal fortitude, and refused the use of a litter to carry him to the rear, though his leg was broken into splinters.[13]

Albert Mitchell, also with the 13th Light Dragoons, was involved in the skirmish and produced the most detailed of the various accounts:

> After trotting about two miles in column of troops up a gently rising ground, we came in sight of a line of the enemy's skirmishers in our front. Half of the right troop (to which I belonged) was sent out to oppose them. They allowed us to get within two hundred yards of them, when they retired. We followed until they arrived at the top of a steeper rising ground.
>
> Here they made a stand and we still advanced until we were within about a hundred yards of them. As before, their skirmishers were more numerous than ours, and they soon opened fire, which we promptly returned. They were better suited than we were, for as they were on top of the hill, they could easily rein back out of sight and then come forward and fire, and then back again. We only halfway up the hill, had no cover ... I expect we had been nearly half an hour skirmishing. They hit none of us; a few of their got hit, which proved that as bad as our carbines were, theirs were still worse.

The 13th Light Dragoons were ordered to 'Rally to the left' which meant Albert Mitchell's right-hand troop had a wide arc of ground to cover:

> Just at this time, the enemy brought a couple of guns about halfway down the hill, and before we reached the regiment. Let fly a couple of round shot at us. They both passed over our heads, making a most unpleasant noise. In another minute we were formed in our place in line on the right of the regiment. They kept on firing as fast as they could, each time with greater precision, for we were not moved, but had to sit, not quite as motionless as statues, but quite unable to do more ... Several shells burst close to us, and some fell in the ranks; one struck the Troop horse a few files on my left. It struck him in the side, and bursting inside the horse, clean him out as though a

butcher had done it. His rider and the next man were both wounded and taken to the rear, and afterwards sent home to England.[14]

Brigadier-General Thomas Strangeways, in command of the Royal Horse Artillery which was accompanying the cavalry, ordered his men to be ready to unlimber, whilst the Light Brigade moved to its left, leaving the front clear for the Horse Artillery:

> It appears Lord Raglan gave instructions that there was to be no general engagement brought on, but now sent orders to both troops [of Horse Artillery] to come into action, which they did, quickly silencing the Russian guns, and causing both guns and Infantry to retire with loss. Both troops then limbered up to the front, threw the right shoulder forward, but of course independently, and galloped into action against the Russian regular cavalry, and also the Cossacks, causing them loss.[15]

It is interesting to see, that Raglan was not willing to let his cavalry charge the enemy but, seemingly, did not mind the artillery doing exactly that. Cardigan was keen to see his men engage the Russians and was seen arguing with Lord Lucan, his divisional commander. Yet there was nothing to gain from such an attack at this early stage in the campaign and Cardigan was told to disengage.

Nevertheless, in his official despatch which mentioned the skirmish of the 19th, Raglan wrote, 'In the affair of the previous day, Major-General the Earl of Cardigan exhibited the utmost spirit and coolness, and kept his brigade under perfect command.' Likewise, Lieutenant Somerset Calthorpe, an aide de camp to his uncle Lord Raglan, was impressed with Cardigan's handling of the Light Brigade:

> The whole affair was the prettiest thing I ever saw, so exactly as one had seen it done dozens of times at Chobbam and elsewhere. If one had not seen the cannon-balls coming along at the rate of a thousand miles an hour, and bounding like cricket balls, one would really have thought it only a little cavalry review.[16]

One of the unlooked for consequences of the refusal to allow the Light Brigade to charge was that Lord Lucan acquired the mocking nickname amongst the troops of 'Lord Look-on'. This would be compounded at the next engagement, where once again the cavalry, and particularly the Light Brigade, were held back. Nevertheless, the withdrawal of the

Russians after such a brief encounter was a hopeful portent. But beyond the Bulganak Menschikoff had prepared a strong defensive position to the south of the River Alma and his troops withdrew to there.

Raglan could not be certain that the Russians would remain in their defensive position and might launch an attack of their own upon the Allies under the cover of darkness in a country they knew well. So rather than push on towards Sevastopol, Raglan chose to halt for the night but, as his force was on the Allied column's exposed left flank (the French having the protection of the sea on the right flank), he bivouacked for the night on the banks of the Bulganak with extreme caution, as detailed by Alexander Kinglake:

> The first brigades of the 2d and Light Divisions were drawn up in line parallel with the river, and some hundreds of yards in advance of it. The first brigades of the 1st and 3d Divisions were placed in an oblique line receding from the left of the Light Division, and going back to the river's bank. The troops thus deployed formed, with the river, a kind of three-sided enclosure, in which the principal part of the cavalry and the encumbrances of the army were enfolded.
>
> The second brigade of each of the divisions already named was formed in column in rear of the first or deployed brigade. The 4th Division and the 4th Light Dragoons were placed in observation on the northern side of the river … Our troops piled arms, and bivouacked in order of battle.[17]

There were no alarms during the night and the troops slept well considering the proximity of the enemy. The next morning the Allies moved up towards the River Alma where the Russians were waiting. Dr McDermott was a Staff surgeon with the army and had seen his first gunshot wounds the previous day. He sent a letter to Captain Latham of the 48th Foot who was stationed in Carlisle Castle, which was passed on to the editor of the *Carlisle Patriot* and published on 14 October:

> Next morning we could see the Russians, about six miles off, occupying the crest of a chain of hills, and separated from us by a level plain. We came up with them at one o'clock in the afternoon. They were strongly posted on the crest of the hills, numbering about 50,000. The ground they occupied reminded me forcibly of the towns about Winchester.

The easy victory at the Bulganak was illusory, for Menschikoff never had any intention of committing his forces to a combat in the open.

Instead the invaders would have to mount the heights beyond the Alma where his fifty-two infantry battalions, sixteen squadrons of cavalry twenty-four batteries of artillery and 1,100 or so Cossacks were waiting – a total of 33,600 men and eighty-four guns.[18] This position was described in more detail by Lord Raglan in his official despatch:

> The bold and almost precipitous range of heights, of from 350 to 400 feet, that from the sea closely border the left bank of the river here ceases and formed their [the Russian] left, and turning thence round a great amphitheatre or wide valley, terminates at a salient pinnacle where their right rested, and whence the descent to the plain was more gradual. The front was about two miles in extent.
>
> Across the mouth of this great opening is a lower ridge at different heights, varying from 60 to 150 feet, parallel to the river, and at distances from it of from 600 to 800 yards.
>
> The river itself is generally fordable for our troops, but its banks are extremely rugged, and in most parts steep; the willows along it had been cut down, in order to prevent them from affording cover to the attacking party, and in fact everything has been done to deprive an assailant of any species of shelter.
>
> In front of the position on the right bank, at about 200 yards from the Alma, is the village of Bouliouk, and near it a timber bridge, which had been partly destroyed by the enemy.
>
> The high pinnacle and ridge before alluded to was the key to the position, and consequently, there the greatest preparations had been made for defence.
>
> Halfway down the height, and across its front was a trench of the extent of some hundred yards, to afford cover against an advance up the even slope of the hill. On the right, and a little retired, was a powerful covered battery, armed with heavy guns, which flanked the whole of the right of the position.
>
> Artillery, at the same time, was posted at the points that best commanded the passage of the river and its approaches generally.
>
> On the slopes of these hills (forming a sort of table land) were placed dense masses of the enemy's infantry, whilst on the heights above was his great reserve.[19]

A reconnaissance undertaken by the French had found that the River Alma was not a serious obstacle and that the eastern part of the heights, those that Raglan described as 'bold and almost precipitous', were only lightly held by the Russians who evidently considered that they were too difficult to be climbed by heavily armed and equipped soldiers.

Saint-Arnaud therefore proposed that his force should tackle these heights covered by the guns of the fleet which could sail within cannon shot. With the Russians suitably distracted by the unexpected movement, the British would attack the main Russian positions on what Raglan called the high pinnacle, the Kourgané Hill, and try to turn the Russian right flank.

At 05.00 hours the French advance from the Bulganak began in silence. The British were due to begin their move two hours later but because they had had to face east during the night ready to counter a dawn attack by the Russians, Raglan had to re-position his entire force and the British were unable to advance southwards until 11.30 hours, the French having been ordered, meanwhile, to halt – much to their frustration.

The guns of the warships opened fire shortly after midday and the advance finally began. The French moved in columns on a series of narrow fronts, whereas the British deployed into line across a broad front to await news that the French had surmounted the heights. The French, therefore, made the first move, watched by Sir Edward Colebrook from the deck of HMS *Agamemnon*:

> A line of troops was passing along the shore, while darker masses traversed the plain at greater distance, their skirmishers thrown in advance and approaching the wood on the banks of the river occupied by the enemy. The village opposite [Burliuk] opposite the centre of the Russian position was already in flames, and a few Russian soldiers could be seen setting fire to the hay or corn in the fields, almost within gunshot of the French … presently a line of troops diverged from the main body, and advanced to the river about half a mile from the coast, and commenced ascending the cliff by a steep winding road. Still not a shot was fired by the enemy, and to our surprise we saw the leading battalion, apparently Zouaves, establish themselves without resistance, and form a line on the summit.[20]

It was now time for the British to attack, after having waited within cannon shot of the Russian so-called Great Redoubt on Kourgané Hill and suffered a number of casualties. The British right front in the attack upon the Alma position was formed by Sir George Brown's Light Division slightly behind and to the right of which was de Lacy Evan's 2nd Division. Behind the Light Division was the Duke of Cambridge with the 1st Division and, even further behind and to the west, was Sir Richard English with the 3rd Division. Lord Cathcart's 4th Division was in reserve to the east. The cavalry, in the shape of the Light Brigade guarded the extreme eastern flank.

Lieutenant General O.A. Kvetzenski, in command of the Russian 16th Infantry Division, watched the approach of the British:

> The mass of English troops, notwithstanding our devastating fire of shot and shell that made bloody furrows through their ranks, closed up once more and, with new forces, protected by swarms of skirmishing riflemen and supported by a battery firing from behind the smoking ruins of Burliuk, crossed the river and drove back the brave Kazan[sky Regiment] forcing our field battery to limber up and depart.[21]

In General William Codrington's brigade of the Light Division was the 7th Royal Fusiliers which included Timothy Gowing:

> From east to west the enemy's batteries were served with rapidity, hence we were enveloped in smoke on what may be called the glacis. We were only about 600 yards from the mouths of the guns, the thunderbolts of war were, therefore, not far apart, and death loves a crowd. The havoc among the Fusiliers, both 7th and 23rd, was awful, still nothing but death could stop that renowned Infantry. There were 14 guns of heavy calibre just in front of us, and others on our flanks, in all some 42 guns were raining death and destruction upon us.[22]

Despite the heavy fire and mounting casualties, the Fusiliers pushed on up the hill and finally reached the Great Redoubt:

> [General] Codrington waved his hat, then rode straight at one of the embrasures, and leaped his grey Arab into the breastwork; others, breathless, were soon beside him. Up we went, step by step, but with a horrid carnage … Into the battery we jumped, spiked the guns, and bayoneted or shot down the gunners; but alas, we were not strong enough, and we were in turn hurled, by an overwhelming force, out of the battery.[23]

The Light Division conquered the heights and drove the Russians from the Great Redoubt. Victory seemed within its grasp and then something quite unpredictable happened, as described in a supplement to the *Sheffield and Rotherham, Independent*:

> At this moment a compact column descended one of the hills. This was mistaken for a French division [the French wore dark blue coats

and the Russians dark green; from a distance both simply appeared dark], and the firing on the part of the British ceased. When within musket range this supposed French column deployed in line, and, before the error could be discovered, poured a fearful volley into the British ranks. Our loss here was frightful – the 23rd Regiment was nearly annihilated, and six officers fell on the spot. The 7th Fusiliers were equally unfortunate. The Light Division was forced to give way, and the redoubt fell into the hands of the Russians once more.[24]

The Russians had retaken the Great Redoubt but behind the Light Division came the second wave of British troops in the form of the Highland Brigade and the Guards Brigade of the Duke of Cambridge's elite 1st Division. Lieutenant, the Honourable Henry Neville was with the Grenadier Guards:

The firing commenced with the artillery, and was very severe, but they had 32-pounders, which were, of course, heavier than our field pieces. As we advanced, it got very exciting, getting out of the way of the round shot, which came hopping along and doing but little damage. After the artillery had pounded away, the Light Division advanced in line to the stream [the Alma], which they crossed, but were dreadfully cut up by the fire from the forts; we followed them, and it was certainly the most awful moment of my life – shot, shell, and musket-balls falling in every direction; and when one considers the shower of bullets, it seems a miracle how anyone escaped.[25]

The Scots Fusilier Guards were in the centre of the three Guards battalions as they pushed on up the heights. With the Scots Guards was Lieutenant John Astley:

We had fixed bayonets, and I verily believe we should have driven the Ruskies out of their battery; but just at the critical moment the 23rd Welsh Fusiliers – who had been terribly cut up, and had gathered round their colours at the corner of the battery – got the order to retire, and they came down the hill in a body, right through the centre of our line, and carried a lot of our men with them.[26]

This was a critical moment in the battle. The Russians withdrew their artillery from the Great Redoubt to prevent its capture. But three heavy columns of Russian infantry were about to charge down the hill into the Guards Brigade which was still wavering after its ranks had been disrupted by the retreating Light Division. Captain Alfred Tipping of the Grenadier Guards takes up the story:

> The order to fire was then given to us, and the Regiment being all in line, gave a cool, deliberate aim at the advancing column, and poured into them such a shower of Minie bullets, as rather checked their onward pace. Still on they came, our men coolly reloading, as if it were only a drill in Hyde Park, and discharging another withering volley, at about 150 yards distance, and in addition to this, Sir Colin Campbell had just brought his brigade of Highlanders over the crest of the rising ground … It was painful to be obliged continually to order the men to close up, as the gaps were made in the ranks by the falling of their comrades; however as fast as they could load, we kept up a continual fire upon the enemy, whom to our great delight, we now saw turn around and commence a retrograde movement up the hill, towards their encampment of the morning.[27]

To the left of the Guards was Highland Brigade, whose advance up the hill was recorded by Captain Hamley:

> On the extreme right of their [the Russians'] original position, at the top of the heights, was a battery behind an epaulment, with a flank for seven guns thrown back to prevent the right being turned. The Brigade of Highlanders being on the left of the British line, found themselves, when the first division crossed the river, directly in front of this battery, which, before it followed the other guns in their retreat, poured upon them, during their advance, a heavy but ill-directed fire, doing hem but little damage.[28]

The Highland Brigade's commander, Sir Colin Campbell submitted an account after the battle:

> The men were too much blown to think of charging, so they opened fire while advancing in a line, at which they had been practised and drove with cheers and a terrible loss both masses and the fugitives from the redoubt in confusion before them. Before reaching the inner crest of these heights, another heavy mass of troops came forward against the 42nd, and these were disposed of in the same way.[29]

Now came the decisive moment of the battle, watched by Lieutenant Calthorpe:

The whole division sent in a withering volley, which perfectly staggered the Russians, literally knocking over every man in their two front ranks. The enemy stopped, fired a random volley, turned, and fled, without another attempt at staying the victorious course of the British troops. The moment the Russians turned, down went the bayonets, and the whole division charged up the hill, dashing through the battery, and capturing a gun which some Russian artillerymen were in the act of carrying off. Cheering as they went, they bayoneted hundreds of the flying enemy. They were followed by the Light Division, which had been re-formed, and even assisted the 1st Division in repelling the advance of the Russian masses of infantry.[30]

The British volleys had a devastating effect on the Russians. When war broke out with Russia the British Army was in the process of replacing the vintage smooth-bore muskets with French-designed 1851-pattern Minié rifles. These had an effective range of around 800 yards compared with the muskets that the Russians were still using of little more than 100 yards. The British artillery had also, by this time, crossed the Alma, and joined in the action. The combined weight of fire, with the determined advance of the First Division, backed by the Light Division which had rallied and returned to the fight, was too much for the Russians, who were also being pressed by the French from the west. Lieutenant General Kvetzenski commanded the Russian 16th Division:

The English advanced in three columns and threatened to turn my right flank, and the French were coming up on my left wing ... I then decided that my aim must be to save the regiment and its colours and not the guns ... then my horse was struck down and I was wounded in the leg. As I was being carried off on a stretcher made of rifles I was hit yet again by a bullet which smashed my arm and rib.[31]

It was the same story throughout Menschikoff's force, as one newspaper report described:

The Russians retreated upon the hill in confusion and dismay, carrying off all the guns except one, which the Guards took. They gave the enemy no time to rally, but pursued them up the hill, where the supporting Russian regiments were trying to check the rout. The latter, animated by the example of their officers, attempted to rally, but the spirit of their men was utterly gone.[32]

With the battle won and the enemy in retreat, now was the time to mount

46

a vigorous pursuit and destroy the Russian army before it could reform. The moment had come for the cavalry to be unleashed. John Chadwick wrote on 22 September to his brother, Captain James Chadwick. The letter was published in the *Manchester Courier* of 21 October:

> I cannot attempt to describe the action at present, we were ordered up to pursue, and our leading troops went on and took several prisoners, but a strong column of Cossacks suddenly showed and deployed on our men and we were recalled ... it is said that had we been stronger in Cavalry we should have taken nearly all their guns and men.

Corporal George Senior of the 13th Light Dragoons provided a little more detail in a letter to his brother in Lockwood, near Huddersfield which appeared in the *Huddersfield Chronicle* on 28 October:

> Just as the Infantry captured the last fortification and drove the Russians back in disorder, we (the Cavalry brigade) were ordered to advance. We had to come down a very narrow lane, and could only ride in single file. We were obliged to halt, on account of some guns being in the way, something like a quarter of an hour. Had we or could we have charged up the heights when ordered to do so, we might have had an opportunity of charging the retreating Russians; but this delay gave them an opportunity of retreating.
>
> We came up to the top of the heights just in time to see them gain another of the heights, something in appearance to those we had then taken. When we came in sight they opened fire with some heavy guns, and several shells burst but a few yards away from where I was mounted. Our artillery opened fire at them. I had a slight accident, when charging up the heights, by coming in contact with a large bush of underwood. I had no other alternative but to leap my horse at it, when, I suppose, the horse was not strong enough to clear it, caught it with his fore legs, which pitched him on his head. I also came on my head or shako (head dress), and the horse rolled on top of me, but, thank God, did me no injury.

Sergeant-Major John Smith Parkinson was with the 11th Hussars:

> So far I had been a witness of the horrors and excitement of a battlefield from a distance. Now I was plunged into the thick of the conflict, and abruptly confronted by all the dangers of a stricken field ... The Horse Artillery had fired two rounds from each gun,

and were advancing across the valley, the Light Brigade following them. As we rode after the retreating masses I saw a Russian lying on the ground, apparently dead. Not knowing that the cavalry were following the guns, he turned on his side.

Then I saw he had his rifle underneath him, and that he had raised it and fired at one of the men, who was riding on the back of a gun-carriage. The man was badly wounded, and the Russian was instantly killed by one of our troopers as we rode past.

Captain Louis Nolan of the 15th Light Dragoons was another of Raglan's aides, but he was not impressed with his commanding officer's decision not to unleash the cavalry:

An enterprising leader would have crossed, gained the heights in the right rear of the enemy & when the Infty had driven them from their Redoubts the cavalry should have prevented them from carrying off their guns … but no attempt was made to cross the River … At no time should Cavalry stand fast to counter the opposing squadrons. Frederick the Great gave an order that any Cavalry Officer meeting the Enemy and not charging should be cashiered! When a routed army was in full retreat what excuse can any one find for those horsemen who did not do their duty & whose chief replied to an order to advance that the Russians were very numerous![33]

In an alarming episode that would be fatally repeated at the Battle of Balaklava little more than a month later, there was a 'misconception' of Raglan's orders, as Lieutenant Calthorpe put it:

The cavalry went in front of the infantry, and from some misconception of orders no prisoners were allowed to be taken. An officer of the 8th Hussars, who was somewhat in advance with his troop, and who had captured some 60 or 70 Russians soldiers, was ordered to let them go again, quite as much to the astonishment of the Russians who had been taken, as of the Hussars who had captured them.[34]

A note in the *Sheffield & Rotherham Independent* makes it clear that the failure to convert the victory into a rout was widely understood:

At five o'clock the Russians were flying in every direction, ploughed up by the splendid fire of our guns, leaving on the field an immense number of dead, three guns, drums, and ammunition. The want of

48

cavalry prevented our getting more prisoners, or of capturing a greater number of guns.

John Parkinson of the 11th Hussars, however, believed that Raglan had been wise in keeping his cavalry in hand:

> We kept up the pursuit until we were ordered to halt, and in spite of all that has been said about the feebleness of the harrying of the flying Russians, I think, as I have always thought, that if once they had pulled themselves together and rounded on us we should have been destroyed, and the heights would have been recaptured, because there were such hosts of them, and the advantages they possessed were so great.

Lieutenant Calthorpe, riding besides Raglan, presents a somewhat different side to this story, and that is rarely mentioned. According to this young aide de camp, Raglan met Marshal Saint Arnaud on the captured heights, where, after mutual congratulations, Raglan 'very much wished' that the Russians should then be pursued:

> He offered our cavalry, and I think two or three batteries of artillery, but said the infantry had suffered so much that they could not well advance without weakening too much the English force.
>
> Marshal St. Arnaud replied that he could send no infantry, and that his artillery had exhausted their ammunition: indeed he appeared to think that quite enough had been done. Lord Raglan saw there was no help for it, and therefore much against his will gave up the pursuit.[35]

Saint-Arnaud, however, saw only too clearly that an opportunity was being missed. 'If I had had some cavalry,' he wrote in his journal later that day, 'Prince Menschikoff would no longer have an army, — but ...'[36] In some respects, the calamitous mistakes that would lead to the Light Brigade charging into the so-called Valley of Death a month later were born on 20 September. The frustrations felt by the cavalrymen at not being able to take advantage of the disorganised retreat of the Russians, after seeing the glorious achievements the infantry, led to much grumbling in the ranks of the troopers and the bivouacs of the officers. Captain Nolan, who would play a leading role in the drama to come, was particularly incensed and when, at last, he would carry the order from Lord Raglan for the Light Brigade to charge, his judgement, many later believed, was already clouded by the inaction at the Alma.

Chapter 4

The Flank March

The Russians had been badly beaten, and such was the scale of the defeat, the British Press proudly announced not just a victory, but that the entire campaign had been won!

> The battle of the Alma may be ranked with the most brilliant achievements of the two valiant armies which met and fought for the first time side by side on that field of battle. But this exploit, gallant and momentous as it undoubtedly is, seems to be already surpassed by the magnitude of its immediate consequences. Telegraphic despatches of a less certain and official character, but nevertheless of high probability, have been received … stating that the fortress of Sevastopol itself surrendered on the 25th ult. To the allied armies, together with all the vast stores of war it contained, the fleet, and the Russian garrison.[1]

The Russians had certainly lost heavily. Casualties were reported to amount to 145 officers and 5,600 other ranks. Just as important was the depressing effect the defeat had on Russian morale and the confidence that the soldiers had in their generals. The announcement of the fall of Sevastopol was absurdly premature, but a rapid strike at the Russian port by the Allies might, at that moment, have had led to its swift capture.

It was certainly essential that the Allies follow up their victory as swiftly as possible whilst the enemy were still shaken by their demoralising defeat but British casualties numbered almost 2,000, and these had to be dealt with and on the 21st the troops had to clear the battlefield of the dead and the wounded, as Lieutenant Peard of the 20th Regiment recorded:

This day was employed in placing the dead bodies in rows, and counting them previous to their being buried in large pits. Several of them were buried in the batteries where they fell, being laid in the ditch and covered with earth. The dead and wounded Russians were lying in all directions.[2]

As soon as the battlefield was cleared and the wounded carried back to the ships helped by marines and sailors, Raglan urged Saint-Arnaud to begin the march upon Sevastopol. For his part the French commander was frustrated by the loss of two days whilst the British dealt with their casualties, as Baron Bazancourt wrote:

> The intention of the Marshal had been to advance, on the morning of the 22nd, upon the Katcha, in the hope of again encountering the enemy, and a second time giving them a speedy defeat. But on the morrow our allies were not ready, and compelled us to remain upon the field of battle. We placed at their disposition, mules and *cacolets* for the transport of their wounded. The English, intrepid and indefatigable in action, appear not to understand the vast importance of a day, or an hour of delay, in a warlike operation. They either know not how to hurry themselves, or will not do it. 'I have lost fewer men than they,' writes the Marshal, 'because I have been more rapid. My soldiers run; — theirs march.'[3]

Nevertheless, at 08.00 hours on the morning of the 23rd the Allied army began its march south along the Eupatoria to Sevastopol Post road, which was 'a mere beaten track marked with cart wheels, hoofs and the nails of gun-carriage wheels.' The cavalry took the lead, with everyone wondering, as Edward Hamley wrote, if they would meet the Russians again:

> The road between the Alma and the Katcha, traversed by the army on the 23d, lay as before over dry grassy plains. Here we expected the enemy to be waiting for us; but, ascending the ridge which overlooks the valley, we saw the heights unoccupied. The lesson on the Alma had been so sharp ... it would scarcely have been prudent for him [the enemy] to risk a battle where the pursuit might carry the victors into Sebastopol along with the vanquished.[4]

This first march took the Allied army to the next river that crossed their path on the way to Sevastopol, the Katcha. They reached the river at around 15.00 hours, finding it undefended. The armies settled down here, whilst Lucan, with the light cavalry pushed on as far as village of Duvanköi on the road to the River Belbek. They remained on the high ground above the village during the night.

It was on this day that the first of the regiments of the Heavy Brigade arrived from Varna in the form of the Scots Greys.

The original plan had been to attack Sevastopol from the north side, or Severnya, but it was learnt that a major outwork holding forty-seven guns, the Star Fort, protected the landward approaches on the northern side. Additional defences had been also hurriedly thrown up around the Severnya. Furthermore, Menshikov had ordered ships of the Black Sea Fleet to be scuttled across the harbour entrance which meant that the Allied warships would not be able to enter the harbour to lend their support to any landward attack. It was also discovered that the Russians had built redoubts to defend the passage of the third river to be crossed on the approach to the north side of Sevastopol, the River Belbec. Raglan's Chief Engineer, came up with what he thought would be a solution:

> It occurred to Sir John Burgoyne that, by a flank movement performed with energy and decision on Balaklava, we should turn and neutralise the effect of these batteries, secure a new base of operations ... and completely distract the enemy, who would find the weakest part of Sebastopol exposed to the fire of our batteries and our attacks directed against a point where they had least reason to expect it.[5]

This proposal was put to the French and Saint-Arnaud agreed with Burgoyne that an attack upon Sevastopol from the north was no longer the best proposition. On the morning of 24 September he wrote:

> The Russians have committed an act of desperation which shows how beaten and terrified they are. They have blocked the entrance to Sebastopol by sinking three of their large ships and two of their frigates ... This bothers me a lot, because it forces me to change my plans of attack, and take the attack to the south, the side of Balaklava.[6]

So the decision was made to march round Sevastopol to the south, to the narrow, and easily defendable inlet of Balaklava harbour, which was some eight miles from Sevastopol. Such a march was, however, an extremely dangerous manoeuvre and contrary to all the principles of war. The army would be strung out for miles with its flank completely exposed to the enemy. It also meant leaving the Post Road to take an ill-defined track through tangled and heavily-wooded terrain. Some indication of just how dangerous a move this was can be gleaned from Raglan's report to the Duke of Newcastle, which shows how completely helpless the men would have been if the Russians had attacked:

> The march was attended with great difficulties. On leaving the high road from the Belbec to Sevastopol, the Army had to traverse a dense wood, in which there was but one road that led in the direction it was necessary to take. That road was left in the first instance to the Cavalry and Artillery; and the divisions were ordered to march by compass and make a way for themselves as well as they could; and, indeed, the Artillery of the Light Division pursued the same course as long as it was found to be possible, but, as the wood became more impracticable, the batteries could not proceed otherwise than by getting into the road above mentioned.[7]

There had been little opportunity for the troops or horses to be watered, and by the time the army reached the Belbec the horses in particular were desperately thirsty. Yet instead of allowing both men and horses to drink, Lucan would not let them stop, as Troop Sergeant Major George Smith angrily recalled:

> Opposite the part we were fording sat Lord Lucan, storming and threatening that he would flog any man who attempted to water his horse, so that the men who passed over directly opposite him had great difficulty in forcing their horses through the water, as they plunged their heads into it eager to drink, not having been watered since we left the Alma. What could have been Lord Lucan's reason for this I could never make out, for a greater piece of cruelty I never witnessed.

Cardigan was, seemingly, equally unimpressed with this as he stayed well out of the way and did not enforce Lucan's instructions. Cardigan was angry and frustrated by Lucan's interference in his brigade, but as most of the regiments of the Heavy Brigade were still in transit it is hardly surprising that Lucan spent most of his time with the only cavalry he had under his command. He should, though, have commanded through Cardigan and not bypassed him but their relationship was so strained that normal communication between them simply did not exist.

Though the Scots Greys had only just arrived, the regiment was soon pressed into taking up a leading position ahead of the main British column. Gunner John Horne, of Captain Maude's Troop of the Royal Horse Artillery, wrote about this in a letter to his parents:

> While on the march our troop, with the Scotch [Scots] Greys and other light companies were sent forward to reconnoitre. Our road lay through a level wooded country, where we could not see five yards on either side of us for thick bushes and underwood. For miles we went along expecting every minute a volley of musketry fired into us.[8]

Private 'G.C.' of the 8th Hussars, in another letter printed in the *Bristol Mercury*, also described the march from the Alma:

> After we quitted this miserable spot, we marched through a dense wood, that is the 8th [Hussars], 17th [Lancers], and a battalion of Rifles, to see that the enemy were not in ambush; the main body took the High Road. We were divided into two parties, our regiment, and the 17th, each having half the Rifles attached to us. The Rifles were in advance, and we were dismounted, and what with being up all night the three last days, we were no sooner on the ground than we fell asleep, we were in this state when the alert Rifles heard the sound of wheels and cavalry, 'Mount and Gallop' was the word, and through the wood we went. I forget to say that Captain Maud's troop of Artillery was with us. On we came into a narrow lane, through a thick wood, and we found a quantity of baggage, with a strong cavalry escort and three guns, which proved to be a general and his staff thus accompanied, making his way to Sebastopol.

The slumbers of Albert Mitchell of the 13th Light Dragoons were also disturbed:

> I lay down, and after a little while fell asleep. Suddenly I was awakened by the orders 'Mount,' and then 'Gallop'. At the same time we heard the report of firearms in our front, apparently very close. In a few moments we came out upon an open space of perhaps two acres. On the left-hand side of the road stood a long low building, perhaps thirty yards long, with outbuildings in rear. Along the road, and out on the green were a number of wagons all loaded. Horses were loose and galloping about, and a party of Russian

infantry were just escaping into the brushwood. We went straight on past the house as fast as we could go. We had not gone far when we came across a dead Russian Hussar laying in the middle of the road, and a little further on an overturned wagon and a dead horse. There were plenty of clothing and provisions scattered along the road. Large black loaves and some died fish. One of our men picked up a new Hussar officer's superfine cloth jacket.[9]

Whilst the Allies had made the momentous decision to attack Sevastopol from the south, Menshikov had made a decision of similar importance. Rather than allow his army to become trapped inside Sevastopol, he believed it could defend the port more effectively from outside. His reasoning was that in the field he could operate against the invaders, therefore restricting their operations, whilst at the same time keeping open the road to the interior of Russia from where supplies and reinforcements were expected.

On the night of the 24th, Menshikov made his move, slipping out of Sevastopol, crossing the River Tchernaya. The Russian commander did not realise that he was marching right across the front of the Allied army, whom he assumed were heading towards Sevastopol. It was the rear of Menshikov's column that the British advanced guard had encountered. Lieutenant Calthorpe was riding with Raglan at the head of the column:

> After a careful reconnaissance of the town, Lord Raglan followed the road which the artillery had been ordered to take, and, trotting on, placed himself at the head of the column on the line of march. After proceeding for about 4 miles through the forest, the trees became thinner, and it was evident that we should soon be clear of it. Lord Raglan had been for some time wondering that we had not come upon the cavalry, who had been ordered in advance, and therefore sent two of the officers of his Staff into the wood on our right to try and find them. Two hussars of the escort and a staff officer were a hundred yards or so in advance of the Head-quarter Staff; these all at once came back, and reported that there were Russian troops on a road just in front of them. General Airey rode forward with his aide-de-camp to see what they were, and, returning in a minute, announced that it was evident we had come upon a Russian convoy or troops on the line of march, as there were numbers of waggons guarded by infantry passing northwards along a road at right angles to the one by which we were marching.[10]

Troop Sergeant-Major Robert Lawrence Sturtevant of the Scots Greys described this action in a letter to the editor of the *Nottingham Guardian*:

On the 25th we were saddled at day-break and off through brush-wood, going through at single-file and making our own track. After about four hours thus marching in a broiling sun we got the words, 'Greys to the front.' We were still in the bush, and hard to charge in single file. We soon came on the road, and after a charge of about two miles caught the enemy's rear guard, and sent them flying into the bush, and we also dismounted a troop, and sent them out skirmishing, and did great execution, while on the other hand not a man or horse was hurt. We killed a good many of the enemy and took many prisoners. By thus being surprised we captured the whole baggage of a division of the Russian army, and although we had only the 17th Lancers, two or three guns, and a few Rifles, they were too cowardly to face us, although there were thousands of them.[11]

The action was also described by an unnamed NCO of the Light Brigade published in *The Standard* of 23 October 1854:

All at once we heard the sound of our own artillery wheels, upon a hard road close by, and got the order to mount. Off we were like a shot. The artillery unlimbered and fired four or five shots, and then off they were again, and away went the Lancers in hot pursuit. The Greys dismounted, took to the woods with carbines in hand, and commenced firing away 'like one o'clock.' There is said to have been 25,000 of the enemy before us, but this quite uncertain. However, I saw dead and dying of several [Russian] regiments of infantry; three regiments of Hussars, viz., 2d, 12th, and 15th, and a lot of artillery. We captured about nine tons of powder, with lots of shot and ammunition, a carriage belonging to some person of note, with a great quantity baggage of all descriptions, stars, medals, and orders.

The march was resumed on the morning of the 26th along a road in a valley through the Fedioukine Heights that opened out into what became known as the North Valley of Balaklava. It was an easy march down to the village of Kadikoi on the final stage of the road to the port. It was discovered that the port was overlooked by an ancient fort but whether it was garrisoned or not was unknown. Lieutenant Colonel Lawrence with the 2nd Battalion Rifle Brigade was to the fore:

We were within 4 miles of the port of Balaklava where we were to re-establish our communications with the sea but to approach it we had to pass thro' a narrow gorge with high bare mountains on either side. I was ordered to send the Regt in advance. Norcott went to the right, Bradford to the left & I kept the centre with four Companies. We met with no opposition till we got some way when a fire of musketry made us cautious but the enemy appeared to be only a few men of the hills & having driven them in a Staff Officer reported to Ld Raglan that the coast was clear. He rode to the front & was entering the gorge when I took the liberty of remonstrating, telling him that I still saw some of the enemy up on the heights & begged that I might at least send one of my companies in advance. He assented to this but when he turned a corner of the road & approached the Fort we were saluted with a couple of shells which marvellously did not hurt a creature of the 200 people on the road.[12]

Raglan and his staff sensibly withdrew while the Rifle Brigade assaulted the fort, supported by the guns of HMS *Agamemnon*. The small garrison, seeing no point in further resistance, surrendered.

When William Russell arrived at Balaklava he was shocked at how small and confined the port, which was where the two armies were supposed to form their operational base:

> I never was more astonished in my life than when on the morning of Tuesday Sept. 26th, I halted on the top of one of the numerous hills of which this portion of the Crimea is composed, and looking down saw under my feet a little pond, closely compressed by the sides of high, rocky mountains; on it floated some six or seven English ships, for which exit seemed quite hopeless. The bay is like a highland tarn, and it is long ere the eye admits that it is some half mile in length from the sea, and varies from 250 to 120 yards in breadth. The shores are so steep and precipitous that they shut out as it were the expanse of the harbour, and make it appear much smaller than it really is. Towards the sea the cliffs close up and completely overlap the narrow channel which leads to the haven, so that it is quite invisible.[13]

It was immediately apparent that Balaklava was far too small to accommodate both armies and after a brief discussion it was agreed that the French would leave Balaklava in British hands whilst Saint-Arnaud's men moved to the west to the harbours of Kazach and Kamiesch.

The flank march, which so easily could have proven disastrous if Menchilov had realised that the Allies were marching across his front, had succeeded and Captain Nolan, so highly critical of Raglan, actually was full of praise for this risks that the Commander-in-Chief had taken:

> The flank march is unmatched in the annals of war for its strategic importance, bold conception and brilliant execution ... Our army drawn now to a narrow thread by the difficulties and impediments ... could have been cut through at any time by a bold and erudite enemy. Our men were exhausted, our artillery horses actually drifting down and dying on the roadside ... we had but one line of march, the road on our right lay under the guns of the enemy the country on our left was occupied in force, thus this movement hazardous at all times was 'neck or nothing' in our case, and a little dash and daring on the part of our foes have brought our expedition to a ... less glorious close than we now fervently anticipate.[14]

Nolan was mistaken, however, for there would be no glorious close to the campaign, merely months of brutal attrition leading to a far from celebratory conclusion. Nolan and Raglan would not even see that unsatisfactory end to the war; one would die broken in body, the other broken in spirit.

Chapter 5

The Siege of Sevastopol

On 27 September, the British troops had their first view of Sevastopol. The 4th Light Dragoons were called from their post as rear guard to take the lead on the approach to the city, one of its number being Private Robert Stuart Farquharson with the regiment's first squadron:

> Coming to the front, we threw out a squadron into skirmishing order, and advanced at a slow pace till we came to the top of the hill on the south-east side of Sevastopol, where we had a glorious view of the doomed city. It was a fine summer evening, the atmosphere as clear as any the poet could imagine, or painter depict. The golden-domed churches sparkled and glittered in the declining rays of the sinking sun; while long lines of well-built houses, the barracks, and the tremendous fortifications were spread out before our gaze like a panorama.[1]

'We are in sight of Sebastopol,' wrote Lord George Paget in his journal entry of that late September day, adding 'up here, indeed, there is a beautiful view of it. I rode up with Cathcart ... I walked with him and his staff a little more to the front, and as we lay on the ground with our telescopes out, he said, "I could get in there tonight with my division, if they would let me. I have tried hard, but I am not allowed to make the attempt."'[2] Lieutenant General Cathcart had indeed tried to make his point, writing to Raglan shortly after first examining Sevastopol from high ground (that would become known as Cathcart's Hill) taken up by the 4th Division that overlooked the port:

> If you and Sir John Burgoyne would pay me a visit you can see everything in the way of defences, which is not much. They are

working at two or three redoubts, but the place is only enclosed by a thing like a loose park wall not in good repair. I am sure I could walk into it with scarcely the loss of a man at night or an hour before day-break if all the rest of the force was up between the sea and the hill I am upon. We would leave our packs and run into it even in open day only risking a few shots whilst we passed the redoubts.[3]

Raglan was certainly keen to attack Sevastopol without further delay but Burgoyne advised against it:

The works of defence are not formidable in themselves, consisting of some high masonry casemated buildings, loop-holed walls, and earthen batteries, but with a great abundance of artillery, and a large garrison, probably not less than 20,000, including their sailors, who are also good soldiers.[4]

Raglan still believed that an immediate assault would succeed and bring the campaign to the speedy conclusion that had been expected from the outset, but when he approached General Canrobert who had taken over the command of the French force after Saint-Arnaud finally succumbed to his illness, said that he was fearful of 'any check or reverse … [as] the safety of the whole army would be compromised'.[5]

The French, who since the days of Vauban had considered themselves the masters of siege warfare, saw Sevastopol as a fortress that had to be taken by formal assault. This meant a regular siege, but if conducted with urgency Sevastopol could still be taken before winter. The next operation, therefore, was the unloading of the siege guns and this began almost immediately. The British siege train consisted of twenty 8-inch guns, of which four were newly-designed rifle-barrelled 'Lancaster' guns, thirty 24-pounders and ten 15-inch mortars. The French had a total of fifty-three guns.[6]

Soon after the British had occupied Balaklava it was apparent that the port was highly vulnerable to attack. Whereas the French had the sea on their left flank and the British on the right, Raglan's eastern flank was, in military terms 'in the air'. With the bulk of the army conducting siege operations in front of Sevastopol some three or four miles to the north, the port was dangerously exposed. So, shortly after arriving at Balaklava, three artillery batteries were established in redoubts on high ground to the east of the entrance to the valley leading to the port from Kadikoi. These faced north and looked out over the South Valley of Balaklava and were manned by marines from the fleet. Consequently called the Marine Heights, the force there consisted of 1,000 or so Royal

Marines with six artillery pieces. Vice Admiral Sir James Dundas also arranged for a large number guns and men from the fleet to supplement the siege guns in front of Sevastopol, as he told the Admiralty on 3 October:

> On the 1st instant I despatched from the fleet to Balaklava fifty 32-pounder guns, of 42 cwt. Each, with shot, shell, ammunition, and some platforms, together with 1,040 officers and seamen, under the command of Captain Lushington ... on the 2nd I sent a further force of 220 marines, and this morning twenty field-pieces complete with ammunition, for the same service.[7]

George Tryon was Acting Mate aboard the eighty-four gun warship HMS *Vengeance*:

> We were sent off the other day with fifty siege guns to assist the siege train and more are landing now. We have from a hundred to a hundred and fifty men from each line-of-battle ship on shore – a merry party, as long as the fine weather lasts ... We run our guns by hand, landed from the ships, much faster than the artillery. Everyone seems to be delighted with the progress we have made, but there is an immense deal to be done.[8]

During the course of 30 September and the following three days the remainder of the British cavalry arrived at Balaklava and disembarked. 'We landed the day before yesterday and had to bivouac on the shore,' wrote Lieutenant Temple Godman of the 5th Dragoon Guards on 3 October. 'I found an empty cart in which I took up my abode for the night, not a very comfortable lodging. The Cavalry are encamped about four or five miles from the town.' At last Lucan had his division with him in its entirety.

Almost from the outset Prince Menshikov aimed to disrupt the siege by threatening the British base at Balaklava. The inhabitants of Sevastopol were working feverishly on the city's defences which, with the passing of every day, became increasingly more formidable. Anything that delayed the operations of the besiegers was of help to the men and women of Sevastopol. In a bid to counter such threats to Balaklavas, Lucan issued an instruction to the Light Brigade on 4 October: 'The chief duties of the Light Cavalry are to ensure the safety of the Army from all surprises ... It is not their duty needlessly, without authority to engage the enemy ... on no account should any party attack or pursue, unless specially instructed to do so.'

As a result, pickets – both outlying and 'inlying'[9] – were posted to warn of any approach by the Russians and the cavalry was constantly on the alert, as Robert Farquharson of the 4th Light Dragoons complained:

> The nights were awfully cold, and the heavy dews would almost drench us, till the blood felt like ice, and what with 'outlying' and 'inlying' pickets, almost always in the saddle, and never undressed, sickness, want of food – and I've gone entire three days without food – we were very queer indeed. Every day now the Russians loitering or moving in great masses about the Chernaya, keep us on the alert morning, noon and night. If we came in from picket fagged, cold and hungry, we might hear the trumpet sound 'boot and saddle' at any moment.[10]

Troop Sergeant-Major Norris of the 1st Dragoons also complained of the repeated alarms:

> There are 10 cavalry regiments encamped opposite Balaklava, which is our place of unshipment, I cannot say one word about the entrenchments, as we are not allowed to move a foot from our horses, for there is a large army of Cossacks and Russians in our rear, waiting and trying to get into Sebastopol, but it is of no use. They annoy us very much by skirmishing with our pickets and outposts; but they will not stand and fight us. We made an advance on them one morning with the whole of our cavalry, ten regiments, and Captain Maude's troop of horse artillery, but they escaped and fled into the mountains. The artillery fired twelve shots at them, but they were rather out of range, but we saw many horses without riders.[11]

Similar complaints were voiced by many of the horsemen, including Lieutenant Edward Seager of the 8th Hussars:

> The cavalry have been worked very much, as we do all the outpost duty, night and day. We cover Balaklava, being encamped in the valley leading to the town and we have to find patrols, pickets, and vedettes for all the country around our position. We are protecting the rear of our position from attack, and what annoys us most is there is scarcely a day passes that it does not sound turn out the whole, and away we have to go to look at a few Cossacks, perhaps to remain there for many hours.[12]

One patrol in particular was mounted each morning along a narrow road that was cut into the side of one of the steep hills. This patrol was particularly hazardous, being considered 'a most dangerous one and not fit for cavalry at all' and caused much 'grumbling' amongst the troopers.[13]

Meanwhile on the Chersonese Plateau the siege operations began in earnest with the French being the first to break ground on 9 October. The following night Lieutenant Colonel George Bell's 1st (Royal Scots) Regiment was ordered to prepare 700 men for work under the instructions of Captain Chapman of the Royal Engineers. Bell recorded the night's endeavours:

> I advanced in the dark with caution and silence for about two miles, with the whole of my regiment. Captain Chapman laid out with his white tape for the first line of the trenches. I divided the men some six feet apart. Each man being provided with a pickaxe and shovel, laid down his firelock and went to work. Thus we broke the first ground for the 3rd Division batteries – 'Chapman's', or the 'Greenhill battery'. By four in the morning we had worked under cover, although the ground was rocky, which gave us double trouble in carrying earth from the rear to fill up the embankments. We stole away back to the camp undiscovered before dawn, being relieved by another corps. And so I had the honour of breaking the first ground before Sebastopol.[14]

The area on the Chersonese plateau where the British siege lines would be formed was split in two by the deep Woronzov Ravine. This necessitated the division of the British effort into what became known as the Left and Right attacks. The battery in the Left Attack, Chapman's Battery, was the one started by Bell's 1st Regiment on the 10/11th and was to consist of forty-one guns, whilst that of the Right Attack, was to hold thirty-six pieces. The battery in the Right Attack, like Chapman's Battery, was named after the directing Engineer, Captain Gordon.

Work on the batteries continued over the course of the following week with the various battalions taking their turns, including that of Captain George Frederick Dallas' 46th Regiment:

> These last few days [he wrote on 12 October] we have been having really desperate hard work & though one is utterly exhausted it is infinitely better than the stupid inaction we have been suffering from for nearly a fortnight. We are all hard at work preparing the Trenches & the position for our guns. The ground is as hard as iron

& full of stones so that the work is most laborious. One party works in the Trenches & another armed Party protects them. We are quite close to the Town when at work, & the enemy keeps up a constant cannonade on us, but does little harm as we all 'duck' behind the Trenches when a shot is seen coming. This goes on constantly night & day.[15]

Work on the batteries continued, though perhaps without the degree of urgency that might be expected, as Lieutenant Gerald Graham, responsible for No.2 Battery, complained:

I was in the trenches all yesterday under the heaviest fire. Two men were killed at my battery by the cross-fire from a heavy Russian battery ... My battery is manned by sailors, who work capitally, whether fighting their guns or throwing up intrenchments. I have tried both soldiers and sailors, and I consider 100 sailors as a working party worth at least 150 soldiers of the Line. The reason of this is not only the willing spirit of the men but the fact that their officers exert themselves and direct their men, which is more than I can say for the officers of the Line, who do not appear to be at all aware of the importance of speedily completing the work, and instead of energetically encouraging their men, generally (particularly if at night) retire to some sheltered place and go to sleep. As the whole of the working parties—field officers and all—are under the direction of the Engineer officer, I always make a point of turning out these sleepy gentlemen (when I can find them) with a polite request that they will make their men work a little better. They are obliged to attend to this, knowing that a report from me would bring down on them severe censure from the commander-in-chief.[16]

The tardiness of the men was not just because of an understandable dislike of work in the trenches, the men were also tired and weak due to a lack of food and widespread illness. The terrible conditions that prevailed in the British camp shocked Anthony Home, Assistant Surgeon with the 8th Hussars:

The cholera is still raging ... When taken ill we have no medicines, no place to be nursed in, no one to care a straw about us ... In fact, people taken ill may recover, but by a sort of miracle. One officer of the 77th, Crofton, a man I knew, died in a ditch by the road-side, with as little ceremony as a dog. When the officers are so badly off, I leave you to guess how the men are. I am myself so weak from diarrhoea that I can hardly sit on horse-back, indeed, I am quite prepared to see it turn to cholera as I cannot stop it … I went to the General Hospital yesterday [6 October], and the horrible sight of so many dying of cholera, and all suffering horribly, quite stunned me. The surgeons have all along done their duty well, and have died in heaps.[17]

Despite the weakened physical condition of the men and intense fire from the Russian guns, by the morning of 17 October, the Allies were finally ready to begin the bombardment of Sevastopol, in conjunction with a barrage from the guns of the French and British fleets. It had been expected that the Russian guns would be silenced after a short bombardment, and Sevastopol's defences smashed, in preparation of an infantry assault that would capture the city. But things went badly from the start. General Burgoyne wrote despairingly of this in his journal of the 18th:

> The affair of yesterday was sadly disjointed. The batteries all opened by signal at 6½ A.M., and ours continued throughout the day with energy and effect. About half-past ten a magazine in the midst of the French batteries blew up, and their batteries were in consequence paralysed for the rest of the day, *all* of their batteries.
>
> Then the fleets had an uninfluential fight all to themselves against the outer harbour batteries, at twelve or one o'clock.
>
> The French are to be re-established, and with new batteries, to-morrow morning, when we shall re-commence.[18]

Despite Burgoyne's misgivings, the Allied guns had severely damaged Sevastopol's southern fortifications, especially the Redan bastion, where a magazine had exploded and all but demolished the building. The defenders fully expected the Allies to mount an assault and they stood ready behind their crumbling defences. But no attack had been planned and the Russians took advantage of the darkness of the night to repair the damage. The days passed with despairing familiarity for the attackers, with the Russians rebuilding their defences, and even improving them, each night. Their ability to recover from each bombardment, and the apparent unwillingness of the enemy to launch an assault, engendered a growing confidence in Sevastopol. Maybe the city could hold out until reinforcements – which were known to be on their way – arrived to bolster Menshikov's field force?

With every sign that the siege was not going to be brought to a conclusion any time in the near future the security of the British base at

Balaklava was of paramount importance. The defence of Balaklava had been placed in Lucan's hands but this was not considered a wise move by many, including Major William Forrest of the 4th Dragoon Guards, as he noted in a letter written on 12 October:

> We have no faith in the generalship of my Lord Lucan, we all agree that two greater muffs than Lucan and Cardigan could not be, we call Lucan the cautious ass and Cardigan the dangerous ass, between the two they got us into two or three very awkward positions at Alma and also on the previous day and then began to dispute who commanded the brigade – Cardigan abused the officers of the 11th [Hussars] and called them a dead set of old women – the officers sent [Lieutenant Colonel John] Douglas to remonstrate with him, when Lord Cardigan asked him what he meant by speaking to a Major General in that way – In the evening he sent for Douglas and Peel to his tent and said that under the excitement he had made use of some nasty expressions. He is now on board a ship with a touch of diarrhoea and we hope he will remain there![19]

This, in part, probably explains why on 14 October Raglan put Major General Colin Campbell in charge of the defence of Balaklava. The repeated threats by the Russians could not be ignored and it made sense to have a properly coordinated defence of the port. Though Lucan still retained his 'independent' command, this appointment in effect placed Campbell over Lucan despite the fact that the cavalry commander was senior in rank. Raglan clearly had little confidence in the noble lord.

On 13-14 October, 3,000 Turkish troops landed at Balaklava from Constantinople to reinforce the garrison. They were immediately set to work building five redoubts on the Causeway Heights that flanked the landward approach to Balaklava, which were armed with twelve iron 12-pounder guns. At the same time, the French built a redoubt on what became known as Canrobert's Hill, on the most distant outcrop of the Causeway Heights. This became No.1 Redoubt. By the 25th, four of the six redoubts were complete and occupied.

The redoubts were numbered from east to west, with the most easterly being No.1 Redoubt. This was around 2,000 yards from the River Baidar and some 1,000 yards from No.2 Redoubt. Nos.2 and 3 Redoubts were only 500 yards apart, whilst No.4 Redoubt was 800 yards from No.3. Altogether six redoubts were planned but by the 25 October Nos. 5 and 6 were still under construction and were unmanned. No.1 Redoubt was armed with three British 12-pounder guns with the other three having just two 12-pounders each. Though the redoubts were each garrisoned by Turkish colonial troops, two Royal Artillery NCOs were assigned to No.1 Redoubt and one to each of the other redoubts to supervise the operation of the guns. Another Turkish battalion was stationed at Kadikoi, as was Captain G.R. Barker's 'W' Battery of field artillery. All of this was under Campbell's authority as well as a battalion of infantry from his Highland Brigade, the 93rd (Sutherland) Highlanders and, of course, the two brigades of cavalry.

Captain Nolan approved of the measures that were being taken to protect Balaklava:

> At last to my great satisfaction it has been decided to occupy and strengthen the chain of heights from which Balaklava is first seen on crossing the bridge of the Tchernaya. For this purpose two battalions of Turks have been lent to us by the French. These are now posted on the heights which are to have 5 enceinte redoubts and hold each 250 men. The works ... will be thrown up by the Turks themselves who are excellent workmen.[20]

The fear of an attack upon Balaklava was ever-present and the cavalry were permitted no relaxation, as Lieutenant Temple Godman told his brother Frederick in a letter written on 17 October:

> We have been saddled all day in expectation of a turn-out, and Lord Raglan expects an attack daily, so the sooner they come the better, and let us have it over. We are confined to camp all day and threatened with arrest for leaving it ... We have turned out two or three times since I last wrote [he wrote to his parents on 12 October] but only ending in a skirmish, though the whole army was said to be advancing, and pistols were capped and got ready etc., but they did not like to face us, or had some reason for not doing so, as about they went.[21]

The Russians certainly had some reason for not engaging the British. These manoeuvres were merely reconnaissance missions to investigate the British defences and to see how the defenders reacted when threatened. Again at dawn on 18 October a large body of Russians advanced into the Balaklava plain, and came under fire from the Turks in the new redoubts on the Causeway Heights. An officer of the Royal Marines wrote of the incident in a letter home:

> I had scarcely ... taken my *al fresco* ablution, and was preparing for breakfast ... when our drums beat to arms – the Highland pipes

brayed – and all was accoutre and arm. The Russians, in force, were on the plain below – artillery, cavalry, and infantry – in all about 10,000. Their cavalry appeared to be their largest arm. Our cavalry and horse-artillery, with some Turkish battalions … advanced … the Russians retired without coming to an action. Our field-guns opened on them; but they retired, out of range.[22]

The Russian probe was also watched by William Russell:

On the 18th, early in the morning, a vedette was seen 'circling left' most energetically – and here, in a parenthesis, I must explain that when a vedette 'circles left', the proceeding signifies that the enemy's infantry are approaching, while to 'circle right' is indicative of the approach of cavalry. On this signal was immediately heard the roll-call to 'boot and saddle'; the Scots Greys and a troop of Horse Artillery assembled with the remaining cavalry on the plain, the 93rd got under arms, and the batteries on the heights were immediately manned. The distant pickets were seen to advance, and a dragoon dashed over the plain with the intelligence that the enemy was advancing quickly. Then cavalry and infantry moved upon the plain, remaining in rear of the eminences from which the movements of the vedettes had been observed. This state of things continued for an hour, when, from the hills, about 3,000 yards in front, the Turks opened fire from their advanced entrenchments. The Moskows then halted in their onward course and in the evening lighted their watch-fires about 2,000 yards in front of our vedettes, the blaze showing bright and high in the darkness. Of course, we were on alert all night, and before day broke were particularly attentive to our front. If the Russians had intended to attack us at that time they could not have had a more favourable morning, a low dense white fog covering the whole of the plain. The sun rose, and the mist disappeared, when it was found the Russians had vanished too.[23]

The Russian incursion worried Canrobert who wrote the following to Raglan:

My Dear General,
The cavalry of the enemy, who are very numerous, and are growing in strength every day is composed of Dragoons that pass for being good troops; their infantry is also numerous: these considerations have caused me to examine this evening your defensive position and I have suggested the following disposition:

I would create at the Pass of Balaklava a barrier, which would be sufficient obstacle to the cavalry. It is the matter of a few pickaxes to make. If, at some point, the totality of the Russian infantry marched against the left and against the English right, this would certainly give serious problems… and if at the same time the enemy launched on the pass of Balaklava with six thousand cavalry that might go galloping on, three squadrons wide, it be more than a few guns or gunshots that would stop this avalanche. Your right would be turned and the besieged at your back.

Always lend the force to his enemy, and in this order of ideas, we must predict as I indicate. Make therefore tomorrow your ditch. It must be a sufficient obstacle to stop the momentum of a large body of cavalry.[24]

The Russians seemed to be getting bolder and, more significantly, stronger, as Captain Edward Hamley could not help but notice:

Hitherto the attention of the Allies had been concentrated on the fortress, but on the 20th October a new element forced itself into their calculations. Russian troops showed themselves on the cluster of low heights which, as before mentioned, divide the valley of the Tchernaya into two defiles. Some Cossack horsemen lounged about the meadows, at about 2000 yards from our position, and about fifty infantry soldiers, emerging from a ravine in the heights, crossed to the river for water, remaining for some time on the bank of the stream and returning with a deliberation which showed they felt secure of support if molested. A body of cavalry with some guns also positioned itself on the Bakshi-serai road, near the bridge which crosses the Tchernaya there, and close to the meadow where our own artillery had bivouacked on the night of the flank march. From day to day this force seemed to be augmented, and was judged to be the rearguard of an army whose numbers, being hidden in the farther defile, were unknown.[25]

Later on that day, the 20th, the Russians undertook another feint against Sevastopol, and this time in greater force than previously. This was recorded by the 'Special Correspondent' of the *Illustrated London News*:

The Russians attempted a diversion, by marching several battalions of infantry, and a quantity of cavalry and guns to the front of Balaclava. The Turks fired several rounds at them from their new redoubts [on the Causeway Heights], and Sir Colin Campbell thought it necessary to send for reinforcements. General Goldie's brigade moved out at three in the morning to the front of Balaclava. Lord Lucan's brigade of Cavalry struck tents, but the Russians retired without having molested us.

Robert Portal of the 4th Light Dragoons had just settled down for dinner,

> ... when the trumpet sounded for the whole of the cavalry to turn out at once ... We were marched to our front and came up to the Turkish fortifications that surround it. They (the Turks) were all under arms and ready to drive back the enemy when he appeared; the artillery came up and my regiment was ordered to advance if required with the guns. We had a speech made us by Lord Lucan, who commands the Cavalry, upon the desperate manner we were to charge if such was required. Altogether we expected that, at last, we were to meet the enemy, but none appeared.[26]

It was no illusion that the Russians appeared now to be operating with greater numbers, for Menshikov had received reinforcements in the form of Lieutenant General Liprandi's No.12 Infantry Division of 4 Corps (comprising the Azovsky, Dneprovsky, Ukrainsky and Odessky regiments) with one field and one light artillery batteries, as well one line infantry battalion with an accompanying battery from the 17th Division along with a rifle battalion and a Black Sea Cossack infantry battalion. Also recently arrived in the Crimea were six reserve battalions of the Minsky and Volynsky regiments. Lieutenant General Ryzhov's cavalry force had also been augmented to give him two hussar, two uhlan, and two Cossack regiments. This gave the Russian commander 65,000 men, with the prospect of another 25,000 men in the form of the Nos. 10 and 11 Infantry Divisions soon to join his field army.[27]

Confirmation that the Russians were massing in strength on the Allied flank was received from a Turkish spy employed by Brigadier Rustem Pasha of the Ottoman army on 24 October.[28] This individual made his way to Campbell's headquarters to warn the British that the Russians were planning to attack Balaklava. Campbell took the matter seriously and discussed it with Lucan. Both regarded the information as authentic and wrote a note to Raglan which was delivered to the Commander-in-Chief by Lord Bingham, the Earl of Lucan's son. Raglan had heard a number of such warnings in recent days, yet none of the enemy's probes had been conducted with any determination. Two days earlier Charles Cattley, who was the head of the mysterious Secret Intelligence Department, had given Raglan similar information after having interrogated a number of Russian deserters. As a result, Cathcart's 4th Division had marched all the way down from its encampment before Sevastopol and the cavalry had been kept under arms throughout the entire night. It was bitterly cold and the men suffered terribly with one man, Major Willet of the 17th Lancers, dying of exposure. The Russians did not make an appearance.[29]

All the warning signs indicated an imminent attack in great force but the men and horses of the cavalry were worn out from being kept in the saddle and frustrated by the cat-and-mouse tactics of the Russians and all the false information and rumours. Raglan dismissed the latest news with a 'Very well', and a polite request to be kept informed, but left it at that. Yet whilst Raglan chose to downplay these reports, others were genuinely concerned for the security of the British base, including William Russell who had been visiting the cavalry camp that same evening:

> I was told that 'the Ruskies were very strong all over the place', that reports had been sent to headquarters that an attack was imminent, and that Sir Colin Campbell was uneasy about Balaklava. As I was leaving Nolan overtook me. The evening was chilly. He remarked that I ought to have something warmer than my thin frock coat, and insisted on my taking his cloak – 'Mind you send it back to me tomorrow; I shall not want it tonight.' Nor did he next day or ever after! All the way back he 'let out' at the Cavalry Generals, and did not spares those in high places. 'We are in a very bad way I can tell you.'

In reality Menshikov had skilfully anesthetised the British who had been numbed by the repeated feints. Indeed, on the 24th, just when it was needed more than ever, the dangerous and unpopular morning cavalry patrol was discontinued. It seemed to serve no purpose. The truth was that many in the British camp believed that after the Alma the Russians were reluctant to cross swords with the Allies again and their actions since that time had done nothing to dispel such a belief. But those seemingly hesitant probes had served their purpose, and as well as exhausting the minds and the muscles of Raglan's men they had provided the Russian leadership with a good indication of the strength and state of the British defences. In just a few hours those defences would be put to the test.

Chapter 6

'The Brilliant Attack'

The first news the British public had of the Battle of Balaklava and the Charge of the Light Brigade was in *The Times* of Tuesday 14 November. Bearing the headline 'The Cavalry Action at Balaklava, October 25'. William Russell's report, his longest of the war, caused a sensation when it was published three weeks after the battle. It translated a single, comparatively small cavalry action into the most memorable event of the entire war.

Like so many since, Russell sought to explain the events of that day. He therefore opened his report by describing the exasperation felt throughout the army regarding the handling of the cavalry in the campaign so far. This frustration, which we have seen had been mounting over the preceding weeks, was widely known throughout the army:

> If the exhibition of the most brilliant valour, of the excess of courage, and of a daring which would have reflected lustre on the best days of chivalry can afford full consolation for the disaster of to-day, we can have no reason to regret the melancholy loss which we sustained in a contest with a with a savage and barbarian enemy. I shall proceed to describe, to the best of my power, what occurred under my own eyes, and to state the facts which I have heard from men whose veracity is unimpeachable, reserving to myself the exercise of the right of private judgment in making public and in suppressing the details of what occurred on this memorable day.
>
> Before I proceed to my narrative, I must premise that a certain feeling existed in some quarters that our cavalry had not been properly handled since they landed in the Crimea, and that they had lost golden opportunities from the indecision and excessive caution of their leaders. It was said that our cavalry ought to have been

manoeuvred at Boulganak in one way or in another, according to the fancy of the critic. If was affirmed, too, that the light cavalry were utterly useless in the performance of one of their most important duties–the collection of supplies for the army–that they were 'above their business, and too fine gentlemen for their work;' that our horse should have pushed on after the flying enemy after the battle of the Alma, to their utter confusion, and with the certainty of taking many guns and prisoners; and, above all, that at Mackenzie's farm first, and at the gorge near Inkermann subsequently, they had been improperly restrained from charging, and had failed in gaining great successes, which would have entitled them to a full share of the laurels of the campaign, solely owing to the timidity of the officer in command. The existence of this feeling was known to many of our cavalry, and they were indignant and exasperated that the faintest shade of suspicion should rest on any of their corps. With the justice of these aspersions they seemed to think they had nothing to do, and perhaps the prominent thought in their minds was that they would give such an example of courage to the world, if the chance offered itself, as would shame their detractors for ever.

Many have cited this as a reason for the misguided Charge of the Light Brigade. As events will show, this was not a deciding factor. No one can doubt that the cavalrymen were eager to demonstrate their prowess, having been mere spectators at the Alma. But the reality is that the men of the Light Brigade, officers and troopers alike, had no say in the matter. Nevertheless, after giving his opinion on the mental state of the cavalrymen, he set the scene, describing the Balaklava battlefield:

> Supposing the spectator, then, to take his stand on one of the heights forming the rear of our camp before Sebastopol, he would see the town of Balaklava, with its scanty shipping, its narrow strip of water, and its old forts on his right hand; immediately below he would behold the valley and a plain of coarse meadow land, occupied by our cavalry tents, and stretching from the base of the ridge on which he stood to the foot of the formidable heights at the other side; he would see the French trenches lines with Zouaves a few feet beneath and, distant from him, on the slope of the hill; a Turkish redoubt lower down, then another in the valley, then, in a line with it, some angular earthworks, then, in succession, the other two redoubts up to Canrobert's Hill … The camp of the Marines, pitched on the hill sides more than 1,000 feet above the level of the sea, is opposite to you as your back is turned to Sebastopol and your right side toward

Balaklava. On the road leading up the valley close to the entrance of the town and beneath these hills, is the encampment of the 93d Highlanders.

The cavalry lines are nearer to you below, and are some way in advance of the Highlanders but nearer to the town than the Turkish redoubts. The valley is crossed here and there by small waves of land. On your left the hills and rocky mountain ranges gradually close in toward the course of the Tchernaya, till, at three or four miles' distance from Balaklava, the valley is swallowed up in a mountain gorge and deep ravines; above which rise tiers after tiers of desolate whitish rock, garnished now and then by bits of scanty herbage, and spreading away towards the east and south ... It is very easy for an enemy ... to debouch through these gorges at any time upon this plain from the neck of the valley or to march from Sebastopol by the Tchernaya and to advance along it towards Balaklava till checked by the Turkish redoubts on the southern side or by the fire from the French works on the northern side, i.e., the side which, in relation to the valley to Balaklava, forms the rear of our position.

It was evident enough that Menschikoff and Gortschakoff had been feeling their way along this route for several days past, and very probably at night the Cossacks had crept up close to our pickets, which are not always as watchful a might be desired, and had observed the weakness of a position far too extended for our army to defend and occupied by their despised enemy, the Turks.

An officer of Engineers likewise was critical of the Balaklava defences:

> The outer line was between 2,000 and 3,000 yards in front of this inner position, and crowned the line of low eminences which extend across the plain of Balaklava from the village of Kamara to the plateau of Sebastopol. Four small redoubts, each capable of holding from 250 to 400 men, had been hastily constructed along this line by the Turks, under the direction of Lieut. Wagman, and they were armed with seven 12-pounder iron guns. These works, being of very slight profile, were little calculated to resist a powerful attack, and they were too far to the front to be properly supported.[1]

In contrast to these two men, Riding Master George Cruise of the 1st Royal Dragoons had a more positive opinion of the Balaklava position:

> The 93rd Highlanders were posted on our right front so as to protect the road leading to Balaklava, there was also a larger body of Turks

74

on the right of the Highlanders. The heights round Balaklava were well defended by Sailors and Marines so that the Russians will have a difficult job to retake place. The Russian army was posted some few miles behind the heights which were defended by the Turkish redoubts, and the whole of the heights around that spot and near the village of Kamara had picquets and videttes posted on them. We thought ourselves in a pretty decent position forgetting that our Countrymen did not defend the Redoubts.[2]

The pickets Russell had referred to were certainly not very watchful. Indeed, as Kinglake remarked, they were almost captured by the advancing Russians on the morning of the 25th:

> Far from detecting the earliest signs of an advance in force, and being at once driven in, our outlying picket enjoyed its tranquillity to the last, and was only, indeed, saved from capture, by the 'field officer of the day,' [Captain Charteris] who learnt, as he rode, what was passing, and conveyed to the men of the watch—just in time to secure their escape—that warning of the enemy's approach which they themselves should have given.[3]

Amongst those pickets was Private George Winterburn of the 5th Dragoon Guards:

> About daybreak the first shot was fired. I was on outlying picket at the time, and we were preceding to the spot on which to place our videttes to watch the surrounding country, when, having ascended a hill near the village of Camara, we suddenly came upon the vanguard of the enemy. We were only 18 men in all, therefore we retired as fast as our horses could gallop, pursued by about 200 of the Russian cavalry. We, however, proved too swift for them, gained the plain on which our brigade by this time was formed, and rejoined our regiments.[4]

As usual the Cavalry Division had turned out an hour before daybreak, as one trooper of the 8th Hussars remembered:

> We groomed and saddled our horses as well we could, wiped the dews off our swords and scabbards, which were red and rusty despite all our care, got our cloaks, equipments, and so on, in order, with thirty rounds of cartridges in our wallets and thirty more in our pouches, and moved up to the brow of the hill.[5]

According to Private James Henry Herbert of the 4th Light Dragoons this had been the case for the last few days:

> We thought we were to attack the Russians on October 22nd or 23rd, 1854, but we did not do so until the 25th, the day of the charge. Of course our staff must have observed a movement amongst the Russians, whom they could see through their glasses; but to us, with the naked eye, they were invisible. We had been continually standing to our horses, and were doing so during the greater part of the 24th, returning to our camp late at night. It was the custom on active service in those days to turn out and stand to our horses for two hours before daybreak, and on the 25th we turned out about four o'clock. The weather was cold and miserable, and we had slept on the ground under our tents, fully dressed and armed. We had nothing to eat or drink before turning out.[6]

The division was still standing to its horses when Lord Lucan and his staff appeared from the darkness on their normal early morning ride. Lord George Paget in command of the 4th Light Dragoons, trotted up to join them and fell in with Lord William Paulet, Assistant Adjutant General, and Major McMahon, Assistant Quartermaster General who were some fifty yards behind the Lieutenant General. What happened next was permanently etched in Paget's mind:

> We rode on at a walk across the plain, in the direction of the left of 'Canrobert's Hill' in happy ignorance of the day's work in store for us; and by the time we had approached to within about three hundred yards of the Turkish redoubts in our front, the first faint streaks of daylight (for the sun had not yet appeared on the horizon), showed us that from the flag-staff, which had, I believe, only the day before been erected on the redoubt, flew two flags, only just discernible in the grey twilight.
>
> 'Holloa,' said Lord William looking up to the Causeway Heights. 'there are two flags flying; what does that means?' 'Why *that* surely is the signal that the enemy is approaching,' we replied. We were not long kept in doubt! Hardly were the words out of McMahon's mouth, when *bang* went a cannon from the redoubt in question, firing on the advancing masses of the enemy.'[7]

The earlier Russian probes towards Balaklava had brought back the information that the defence of the port was principally entrusted to Turkish troops in redoubts on the Causeway Heights. The Russians had come to respect the best of the Turkish regiments in their fighting in the Danube provinces, particularly when in a strong defensive position. But the soldiers in the redoubts were second line colonial troops, mostly Tunisians who, until recently, had been used by the French as porters. It is said that they were poorly trained and poorly led. They had also 'sat there for several weeks [*sic*] and had done little to prepared the positions', indicating that the redoubts were far from formidable structues.[8]

Like the cavalry, the Royal Horse Artillery attached to the Division had also been up and ready for action an hour before daybreak. As it was clear that the Russians were mounting a serious attack, the cavalry and Captain George Maude's 'I' Troop were brought forward in readiness for action.

Maude was the first to respond. taking his guns rapidly eastwards along the South Valley and then onto the Causeway Heights between Nos. 2 and 3 Redoubts to engage the Russian artillery. In the dim morning light, 'nothing could be distinctly seen but the flashes of the Russian guns,' Maude later wrote, 'on which accordingly our guns were laid.'[9]

This early artillery duel was seen by George Paget:

> We advanced from our bivouac lines in echelon of brigades from the right (the Heavy Brigade to our right) … (our left shoulders being slightly thrown forward), Captain Maude's troop of Horse Artillery having during our advance galloped to the front, and taken up its position on the ridge in front, from whence it opened fire. The outlying picket, which had been for some days previously stationed some quarter of a mile beyond the village of Kamara, had been surprised early in the morning, and had a narrow escape of being taken prisoners … Ere this, all eyes had become riveted on the redoubts in our front, including Canrobert's Hill, and presently a sort of 'Spread Eagle' was seen against the horizon, the splinters of broken guns, horses' legs, etc., shooting up in the air, reminding one of a battle picture.
>
> Five minutes later, the mangled form of poor Maude, as he was carried past us to their rear, too truly confirmed our surmises of the total havoc caused by the bursting of a shell among the guns of his battery. He was actually covered in blood, that of the horse probably mingled with his own.

Lieutenant Calthorpe had taken up a position on the Sapoune Heights which gave him a commanding view across most, though not quite all, of the battlefield:

> Early on the morning of the 25th instant it was discovered from the most advanced of the Turkish redoubts that large bodies of troops were marching towards Balaklava. Lord Lucan was in the redoubt at the moment, and lost no time in ordering the cavalry division under arms; an affair of only a few moments, as the cavalry are always ready to turn out an hour before daylight. Information of this was sent to Sir Colin Campbell and Lord Raglan. In the mean time Barker's battery (9-pounders) and Maude's troop (6-pounders) of horse artillery were ordered up, supported by the Greys. Our guns opened a smart fire on the enemy, but, the distance being too great, they did not tell with much effect.[10]

The Russian force, under the command of Lieutenant General Liprandi, consisted of seventeen battalions of infantry and thirty squadrons of cavalry, supported by forty-eight guns of foot artillery and sixteen of horse artillery. In total Liprandi's corps numbered something in the region of 20,000 to 25,000 men. It was a force that hugely outnumbered the defenders of Balaklava – 1,000 Royal Marines, 600 men of the 93rd Highlanders and around 2,000 Turks (two and a half battalions in the redoubts and another battalion by Kadikoi), plus Captain Barker's 'W' Battery Royal Artillery. In addition, was, of course, the Cavalry Division along with its accompanying 'I' Troops RHA which, as we have read, had lost its commander, Captain Maude, in the early artillery exchanges.

In total there was little more than 5,000 men to defend Balaklava plus 100. The odds were a daunting 5 to 1.

A young Russian cavalry officer related the objectives of Liprandi's operation:

> According to the deployment orders, it was proposed to take from the Turks four redoubts built on the Balaklava heights and drive them out of the village of Komary. Then we were to send the Kiev and Ingermanland Hussar Regiments across the already-occupied Balaklava heights to the enemy artillery park located to the right of the village of Kadykioi. Once the hussars had put the park's wagons out of order, they were to retreat. After this, artillery fire was supposed to blow up the park, the enemy already having been deprived of the means to move it away.[11]

The Russian officer was misinformed as there was no such artillery park but this demonstrates the lack of clear purpose of Liprandi's attack, which ultimately contributed to its failure. Liprandi submitted his own report on the battle the following day, the 26th, to Prince Menchikov, describing the opening moves:

> According to the orders of your highness, the troops of the division intrusted to my command and those attached to it executed on the 25th of October, a general movement in advance from the village of Tchorgoum, and attacked the fortifications of the heights forming the valley of Kadikoi [the Causeway Heights].
>
> Conformably with the arrangement which I had made on the evening of that day ... all the troops of the detachment left, at five o'clock in the morning, the village of Tchorgoum by two defiles. A regiment of chasseurs of the Ukraine, under the command of Major-general Lévoutsky, marched by the principal defile leading from Tchorgoum to Kadikoi, with four guns of the battery of position No. 4, and six guns of the light battery No. 7. These troops advanced with precision, and, on approaching the heights of Kadikoi, opened their fire upon the redoubts Nos. 1 and 2. After them the Azoff infantry regiment, the 4th battalion of the regiment of the Dnieper, with four guns of the battery of position No. 4 and six guns of the light battery No. 6, moved on under the command of Major-general Semiakine.
>
> By the second defile, leading to the valley of Baidar, an advance was made under the command of Major-general Gribbe, of the first three battalions of the infantry regiment of the Dnieper, with six guns of the light battery No. 6, four pieces of the battery of position No. 4, a detachment of the regiment No. 53 of Cossacks of the Don, and a squadron of the combined regiment of the lancers. Major-general Gribbe, who had marched in advance, occupied the village of Kamary, after having dispatched the detachment of Cossacks in the direction of the valley of Baidar. Simultaneously with this movement Major-general Semiakine in taking up his position to the left of the regiment of the Ukraine, covered by the fire of the artillery and a chain of riflemen, formed by the second company of the [4th] battalion of riflemen with the carabineers of the infantry regiment of Azoff, advanced rapidly with the latter regiment in two lines by columns of companies, there not being a space of more than 100 paces between the two lines, and in a third line the first battalion of the regiment of Azoff and the 4th battalion of the regiment of the Dnieper, by columns of attack.[12]

It was soon apparent to Raglan, who had now arrived on the Sapoune Heights with his staff, that this was a far larger and more determined

Russian probe than that of the previous occasions and that Colin Campbell's small force was likely to be overwhelmed. He sent one of his aides to warn Canrobert and another to the Duke of Cambridge, commanding the 1st Division. He also despatched Captain Ewart to instruct Sir George Cathcart to bring up his 4th Division from in front of Sevastopol as quickly as possible. Captain Ewart covered the one and a half miles in ten minutes or so. He presented himself to the sixty-year-old general and the following conversation then took place:

> STAFF OFFICER. – 'Lord Raglan requests you, Sir George, to move your division immediately to the assistance of the Turks.'
> CATHCART. – 'It's quite impossible, sir,' he snapped back, 'for the 4th Division to move.'
> STAFF OFFICER. – 'My orders are very positive. And the Russians are advancing on Balaklava.'
> CATHCART. – 'I can't help that, sir. It is impossible for my division to move, as the greater portion of the men have only just come from the trenches. The best thing you can do, sir, is to sit down and have some breakfast.
> STAFF OFFICER. – 'No thank you, sir. My orders are to request that you will move your division immediately to the assistance of Sir Colin Campbell. I feel sure every moment is of consequence. Sir Colin has only the 93rd Highlanders with him. I saw the Turks in full flight.'
> CATHCART. – 'Well sir, if you will not sit down in my tent, you may as well go back to Lord Raglan and tell him I cannot move my division.'[13]

Faced with this entirely unexpected response Ewart left Sir George's tent and got back on his horse. As he rode back towards Balaklava he considered just what he was going to say to Lord Raglan and, bravely, the young captain rode back to Sir George's tent and said that he was not going to return to Balaklava without the 4th Division. Very well, said, Sir George, 'I will consult with my staff-officers, and see if anything can be done.' Three days earlier, during the Russian probe against Balaklava, Cathcart had marched his division to the port only to find that the enemy had withdrawn. His reluctance to disturb his tired men again for possibly no reason was understandable. He no doubt thought that if he delayed his response, a galloper would soon be on his way to countermand the order.

Though the 4th Division was yet to move, the 1st Division had responded quickly and was soon on the march. In stark contrast to

Cathcart's sluggish response, Captain Brandling, on his own initiative, had also set off for Balaklava with his 'C' Troop, RHA, as soon as he learnt of the Russian attack.

Canrobert galloped up to the Sapoune Heights and joined Raglan at around 08.00 hours to assess the degree of danger posed by the Russian force before calling up some of his troops to support the British. Having seen the extent of Liprandi's operation the French commander summoned the infantry brigades of generals Vinoy and Espinasse and two cavalry regiments of Chasseurs d'Afrique under General d'Allonville.

These units were ordered to take up a position at the foot of the Sapoune Heights.

Lieutenant Koribut-Kubitovich was with Colonel Yeropkin's Combined Lancer Regiment and wrote one of the more detailed Russian accounts of the battle:

> At eight o'clock General Liprandi moved his infantry to the approaches to Redoubt No.1. Under the leadership of Colonel Krüdener, the Azov men went forward in company columns in a fine, orderly fashion. Accurate enemy artillery and rifle fire did not make them waiver … with each casualty they closed up as if on training manoueuvres. And now in a well-formed mass they reached the foot of the hill … A drawn-out shout of 'Ura!' breaks forth and the steep slope is covered with a dense crowd of soldiers making their way up. With such a quick, brave attack, success cannot be long in doubt.[14]

General Todleben, the man in charge of the defensive works of Sevastopol, wrote a history of the siege which included an account of the Battle of Balaklava:

> At five o'clock on the 25th of October, in obedience to the order given the preceding day, the troops of the detachment of Tchernaya began to march towards the Redoubts. General-Major Levoutzky, having approached the heights of Kadikoi, advanced his artillery and opened fire on Redoubts No. 1 and No. 2.
>
> General-Major Gribbe, marching on Komari, drove out the enemy's advanced posts and established himself there. A sotnia [squadron] of Cossacks, which had been dispatched along the road which led to Baidon, at once occupied St. John's Chapel. After this first success he established his artillery on the heights, and opened a cannonade against Redoubt No. 1.

By the occupation of Komari our left flank was protected from the attacks of the enemy, General Semiakine [Semiakin] following Levoutzky's [Levutski] column, and, protected by the fire of the artillery and a line of skirmishers, advanced rapidly and took up his ground on the left of the column. Having arrived at 150 paces from the hillock on which Redoubt No. 1 was placed, he ordered the Regiment of Azoff to begin the attack. Notwithstanding the obstinate resistance of the Turks who held the redoubt, it was carried by assault, and at half-past 7 a. m., the Regiment of Azoff planted its standards upon it. The camp and three pieces of artillery fell into our hands.[15]

The Azov Regiment mentioned by Todleben was commanded by Colonel V.M. Krudener:

Neither the great steepness [of the ground], nor the well-aimed fire [of the Turks] could stop the brave Azovs. In any loss they closed their lines until they came to the bottom of the hill in good order. The drawling 'Hurrah!' rang out and all at once the slope was covered with the crowd. The Azovs, as only they could, charged the fortification like a swarm of bees; some ran round the rear and others went through the embrasures, and then the bayonet work of the Russian soldier began.[16]

Todleben continued with his narrative:

Struck by the brilliant attack executed by our troops against the principal hill, and by the rapid occupation which was the result, and perceiving also the battalions of the Regiment of Ukraine which advanced towards Redoubts Nos. 2 and 3, the Turks charged with the defence of the works abandoned them, leaving five guns, which fell into our hands.

Meanwhile the Light Infantry Regiment of Odessa advanced with eight guns against Redoubt No. 4. But the enemy, terrified by our success, did not want to fight at that point either. Abandoning the three pieces of artillery which defended the redoubt, the Turks retired towards Kadikoi.

Besides the eleven guns we found also in the intrenchments tents, powder, and pioneers' tools, which the enemy had left. The Redoubt No. 4, which was situated too much in front, was at once levelled, the guns which remained were spiked, the wheels of the carriages broken, and the pieces thrown down the hill. After this expedition, the Regiment of Odessa came with eight guns to join the right wing of the line of battle.

William Russell watched the Russians capture the redoubts, describing seeing the Turks 'fly' from No.2 Redoubt:

> They ran in scattered groups across towards redoubt No.3 and towards Balaklava; but the horse-hoof of the Cossack was too quick for them, and sword and lance were busily plied among the retreating herd. The yells of the pursuers and pursued were plainly audible. As the Lancers and Light Cavalry of the Russians advanced they gathered up their skirmishers with great speed and in excellent order – the shifting trails of men, which played over the valley like moonlight on the water, contracted, gathered up, and the little *peloton* in a few moments became a solid column. Then up came their guns, in rushed their gunners to the abandoned redoubt, and the guns of No.2 redoubt soon played with deadly effect upon the dispirited defenders of No.3. Two or three shots in return and all was silent. The Turks swarmed over the earthworks, and ran in confusion towards the town, firing their muskets at the enemy as they ran.

Evelyn Wood, a Midshipman at the time, who later transferred to the Army and rose to the rank of Field Marshal, also wrote about the early stages of the battle.

> While the troopers of the Cavalry Division were 'standing to their horses' before daylight on the 25th, the Turks opened fire on the advancing Russians. Liprandi brought thirty guns into action against Redoubts Nos.1 and 2, being answered by five of the 12-pounders in the earthworks and two batteries which, escorted by the Scots Greys, came into action on the Causeway Heights. The three 12-pounders in No.1 Redoubt were soon silenced, but the battalion of 500 Moslems stood fast, undauntedly awaiting the attack by five battalions, which were closely supported by six others; at 7.30 A.M., however, the Redoubt was carried, the Turks leaving 170 dead in it. When the Turks in Redoubts Nos. 2, 3, and 4 saw their comrades in No.1 overwhelmed without the British cavalry coming to their assistance, and that the nearest British battalion was 3000 yards away, they fled, carrying off most of their camp equipment, with which they streamed across the plain towards Balaklava: some were sabred in this retreat. The British Cavalry Division fell back to

the North of No.6 Redoubt, with its back to the wall-like cliff of the Upland.[17]

The Cavalry Division was indeed moved forward initially along with 'I' Troop on the right of No.3 Redoubt. The Light Brigade was instructed to remain under the southern slopes of the Sapoune Heights whilst the Heavy Brigade was pushed forwards to threaten the approaching enemy forces. It seems that Colin Campbell advised Lucan to do no more than 'demonstrate' with the heavy cavalry and not risk sending them against what was already quite obviously a very powerful enemy force. It was then at 08.00 hours, a full hour after the battle had been raging, that Raglan issued his first order of the day to Lord Lucan to fall back as Midshipman Wood had described. This order read as follows: 'Cavalry to take ground to the left of the second line of redoubts occupied by Turks.' This is a very poorly-worded instruction. Firstly, there was only one line of redoubts, and secondly the Turks had already abandoned the redoubts. Even worse, from a man who had witnessed at first hand the very precise orders given by the Duke of Wellington on a dozen or more battlefields, was his order for the cavalry to take up ground 'on the left.' Where the left was depended entirely on where one was stood. Little wonder, then, that Lucan asked the aide that had delivered the message to remain with him whilst he carried out the manoeuvre to make sure that he had interpreted it correctly.

Lucan moved his division to the south of No.6 Redoubt where it was out of range of the Russian guns but also out of sight of the main body of the Russian force. A Non-Commissioned Officer of the 1st Royal Dragoons wrote of this withdrawal in a letter written on the 26th:

> About half-past six the guns (which had been placed by us at the commanding points at the end of the plain which extends about three miles at the end from Balaklava, and near the village of Camara [Kamara]), began to open fire upon the enemy, who were advancing in great numbers. These guns were held by Turks. We advanced to the end of the plain and within range of the Russian guns, which began to play upon us in a very rapid manner. A large 32-pound shot passed through our squadrons, breaking the legs of two horses, and we soon began to think it was time to move off, as in another a minute a ball struck a man right in the head, and of course, killed him instantly. Several other casualties took place in the Right Squadron ... I am sorry to say that the Turks gave way very soon, and the Russians sent up vast columns, took the heights, drove the Turks away; and, of course, captured all the guns which

had been placed there in the earthworks. Our light field guns were no match for the immense artillery which the enemy brought against us, besides, our artillery began to suffer severely in men and horses. As we were not supported by British infantry, of course we were obliged to retire, which we did for about four miles, or about one mile in the rear of our camp, having ridden over all our tents and their contents.[18]

Sergeant Troop Sergeant-Major George Cruse, also with the 1st Royals, likewise described the withdrawal of the cavalry to a safer position:

The Russian guns began to advance and several round shot fell into [our] ranks, breaking the legs of two Horses and one large ball struck a man named Middleton right in the face, of course killing him instantly. The shot began to fall so thick around us that the Men began to bob their heads which made Lee and I pitch into them for being so foolish, just as if they could avoid a thirty-two pound shot by moving their heads one way or another. Just about this time the Turks fled in confusion down the hill towards us, abandoning the redoubts in shameful manner.

The Russians came up in dense Masses and bringing up their heavy guns with them (besides turning those which the Turks had abandoned) they opened such a fire upon us we could do nothing but retire which we did about half a mile behind our encampment. Our tents had in the meantime been struck but because of the confusion they could not be packed up and we had the pleasure of galloping over all our little property.[19]

It is hardly surprising that the Turks abandoned the Heights, having seen the Cavalry Division make no attempt to stop the Russians, leaving the men in the redoubts entirely unsupported. Nevertheless, the Turks put up a stiff fight before they fled from the redoubts, leaving, as we have seen, 170 dead behind them – not far short of one-third of their number.

Private Woodham of the 11th Hussars also wrote about the withdrawal and it is worthy of note that whilst in the original position he could not see the advance of the Russians along the valley but he was well aware of the cavalry's role:

Every morning we used to turn out a little before daybreak, and stand by our horses' heads in the expectation of an attack from the enemy. On the 25th October, 1854 ... we were in support of the

Turkish redoubts, being ranged on the plain just behind them. We could not see the Russians advancing, as we were on the brow of the hill, but we saw the Turks driven out of the redoubts, and run towards the 93rd Highlanders, who were near to the village of Balaklava [Kadikoi]. We retired from the position that we had previously held when the Russians captured the redoubts.[20]

The British cavalry, as Woodham had correctly stated, was supposed to support the Turks in the redoubts, but they received no help from the British. Troop Sergeant-Major Loy Smith watched in despair:

As they [the Turks who ran down from the redoubts] gained the plain, a number of Cossacks swept round the foot of the hill, killing and wounding many of them. Some of them unarmed raised their hands imploringly, but it was only to have them severed from their bodies ... Had a dozen or two of us been sent out numbers of these poor fellows might have been saved.[21]

Lucan believed that he was quite justified in making no attempt to help the fleeing Turks:

Lord Raglan not having acted on the communication sent him the day previous by Sir Colin Campbell and myself informing him of the approach of a considerable Russian Army, and leaving us altogether without support, we considered it our first duty to defend the approach to the town of Balaklava; and as this defence would depend chiefly upon the cavalry it was necessary to reserve them for the purpose.[22]

Fanny Duberly had not felt well and was still on board a ship in Balaklava harbour that morning and was looking through her stern cabin window when, at around 08.00 hours, she saw her horse saddled and waiting for her, being held by the Duberly's 'soldier-servant'. She was handed a note from her husband, Henry: 'The battle of Balaklava has begun, and promises to be a hot one. I send you the horse. Lose no time, but come up as quickly as you can: do not wait for breakfast.'
As she rode up from the harbour:

The road was almost blocked up with flying Turks, some running hard, vociferating, 'Ship Johnny! Ship Johnny!' while others came along laden with pots, kettles, arms, and plunder of every description, chiefly old bottles, for which the Turks appear to have a great appreciation. The Russians were by this time in possession of three batteries from which the Turks had fled … Looking on the crest of the nearest hill [the Causeway Heights], I saw it covered with running Turks, pursed by mounted Cossacks, who were making straight for where I stood, superintending the striking of our tent and the packing of our valuables.[23]

The new position taken up by the cavalry was described by an NCO of the 11th Hussars:

> Shortly after we took up a position on the left rear of our encampment with our backs to Balaklava, facing the opening of the top of the valley through which it was thought the Russian cavalry would come, so as to prevent them getting in our rear. We were out of sight of the enemy, but expected every moment to see them. Occasionally we heard a bullet from the Russian infantry that had occupied the Redoubts.[24]

Liprandi's men, with their speed and determination, had taken command of the battlefield. They had seized the first redoubt and witnessed the abandonment of the others, enabling them to take possession of the easternmost range of the Causeway Heights. The British cavalry had withdrawn to a position under the Sapoune Heights which was actually an excellent spot as it placed them on the flank of any enemy columns that might try to advance upon Balaklava. But if the Russians pressed home their attack and broke through to Balaklava, the mass of British ships, berthed side in the tiny harbour with its very narrow entrance, would never be able to escape. There is no doubt that disaster loomed. The next few moves would determine the course of the war in the East.

Chapter 7

'That Thin Red Streak'

Lieutenant General Liprandi had captured the redoubts on the Causeway Heights and, apart from the seemingly ineffectual British cavalry, all that stood between his forces and the port of Balaklava were Lieutenant Colonel Ainslie's battalion of the 93rd Highlanders which was lying down behind the crest of a small area of rising ground in front of Kadikoi, and a battery of four pieces of Barker's 'W' Field Battery on its left flank. Formed up on either side of the Highlanders were around 1,000 of the Turks that had rallied alongside the battalion stationed with the Highlanders after abandoning the redoubts. Liprandi was therefore able to mount the next stage of his operation:

> When all the redoubts had been occupied, I ordered the advance of the cavalry, with the regiment No. 1 of the Cossacks of the Ural and three sotnias of the regiment No. 53 of Cossacks of the Don, upon the enemy's camp, situated upon the other side of the mountains.[1]

The approach of the Russian cavalry prompted Raglan to issue his second order of the day to Lucan. Having watched the Turks abandon their positions on the Causeway Heights after the cavalry had left them, Raglan was worried that the Turks might also retreat from their new post. He therefore sent the following message to Lucan which he hoped would bolster the morale of his allies. This order was timed at 08.30 hours: 'Eight squadrons of heavy Dragoons to be detached towards Balaklava to support the Turks who are wavering.'

This order was delivered by another of Raglan's aides, Captain Hardinge. It was another strange instruction. There were only ten squadrons of heavy cavalry. Why leave just two squadrons behind? Lucan, nevertheless, complied. There was, in reality, little else he could do. Each order from Raglan was timed, and he knew therefore how long

88

it had taken for them to be delivered. Going back up the Sapoune Heights would take far longer than the aides had taken to ride down. This meant that it would have taken more than half an hour for Lucan to send a message to his commander and receive a reply. In the midst of battle, such a delay could prove fatal. So Lucan had either to obey or refuse to follow an order. However stupid an order might seem, Lucan was not going to place himself in a position where he could be accused of insubordination. So, he ordered Scarlett to move eight squadrons towards Balaklava, as requested.

The position taken up by the remainder of the Cavalry Division was noted by Lieutenant Calthorpe:

> In the meantime the Russians had been collecting their forces on the most commanding ground. A large mass of infantry was posted close to the village of Kamara: some were also hid from our view, between it and Canrobert's Hill; whilst opposite, extending from there to the Tcheranya river, were several battalions of infantry, three or four batteries, and another large body of Cossacks; and on some high ground close to the river, projecting into the valley, was a battery of 8 guns, supported by a regiment of infantry. On seeing these preparations on the part of the Russians, Lord Raglan ordered the brigade of light cavalry to take post on the ridge, just at the foot of the plateau where we were standing.[2]

Raglan was correct in being worried about the defence of Balaklava as the Russians continued their advance towards the port. Todleben provided an account of these next moves in a little more detail than Liprandi but, as can be seen, he understood that the objective of the attack was not to seize the port but to wreck an artillery park. This seems to be extremely short-sighted but probably represents Prince Menshikov's well-known opinion that he would never be able to defeat the Allied army. So his policy was merely to delay or hinder the siege operations. Destroying an artillery park was entirely in keeping with this (albeit that no such park existed). It was the artillery which was the embodiment of the Allied siege:

> After the capture of the redoubts, General Liprandi advanced the Brigade of Hussars, nine sotnias of Cossacks, and two horse artillery troops on the slope of hills looking towards the enemy's camp, and ordered General-Major Rijow [Ryzhov] to make an attempt to destroy the park of artillery placed near Kadikoi. The two horse batteries, and the Light Battery No. 12, and the Battery of Position

No. 3 of the division advanced rapidly, took up a position, and opened fire.[3]

Lucan was in a difficult position, with his command now split and the Russians bearing down upon his little force in huge numbers, as George Paget realised:

> Our gradual retreat across that plain by 'alternate regiments,' was one of the most painful ordeals it is possible to conceive – seeing all the defences in our front successively abandoned as they were, and straining our eyes in vain all round the hills in our rear for indications of support. We had regained the vicinity of our lines long before there was any sign of our infantry from the plateau of Sebastopol, and, even when we first saw them, they were at such a distance as to give us no hope of the *immediate* support necessary in the event of a sudden forward movement of the enemy.[4]

Indeed, this was a critical moment in the battle for which speed, the sudden movement by the Russians that Paget feared, could have had monumental consequences. The Highlanders, a few cannon and two depleted cavalry brigades could not hope to stop a full onslaught by the enemy. But Menshikov had not instructed Liprandi to seize the British port at all costs. The operation of 25th October was little more than a delaying action in the eyes of the Russian commander, who was convinced that Sevastopol was bound to fall to the invaders eventually. Consequently, the force Liprandi was now about to despatch to destroy the supposed British artillery park was cautiously small, only around 4,000 men though admittedly, it still outnumbered those that stood in its way.

Having seized the redoubts far more easily than had been anticipated, there was a brief delay whilst Lieutenant General Ivanovich Ryzhov's (or Rijow's) officers composed their respective formations for the final push towards the imagined artillery park. Lieutenant Koribut-Kubitovich, of Lieutenant Colonel Vasilii Ivanovich Yeropkin's Composite Reserve Lancer Regiment, wrote of the Russians' next move:

> In the meantime, almost at the very beginning of the battle, a Scottish regiment, the only enemy troops near the attacked point, and alarmed by our attack, deployed in front of the village of Kadykioi in the main path of our force's advance. The Turks who had run from the redoubts closed up on their flanks. A little later, the English cavalry division of Lucan deployed on the Scots' left

flank. The appearance of the English cavalry made us glad; we hoped that our wish to fight them would come true.[5]

Koribut-Kubitovich's wish was about to be granted, as the Leuchtenberg and Weimar Hussar Regiments, the Ural Cossack Regiment, and Horse Battery No. 12 moved forward towards Balaklava. Koribut-Kubitovich's regiment, initially, was held in reserve. Ryzhov explained the next moves:

> My work began once the last redoubt was taken—work that incontrovertibly was the most difficult of that whole affair. I fully understood the task laid on me: with the 6th Division's hussar regiments, in a weakened state though they were (they did not have more than ten files in each platoon, and some squadrons had even less), ascend a slope on which were all the English cavalry and even some of his infantry, in a fortified position. But it was not mine to reason why. It was enough that I received an order and I considered it a sacred duty to carry out what I had been charged with as best I understood it, placing my trust in God's help. When General Liprandi's adjutant transmitted the order to me, I moved my brigade, formed into columns of divisions into the attack in two lines, with the Leuchtenberg Regiment in front. I ordered the movement to be at a quick trot, and did not set off at full speed as had been ordered, solely due to my experience with cavalry and keeping in mind that I had about a mile to cover before meeting the enemy.[6]

After Captain Maude had been carried from the field, command of 'I' Troop fell to 2nd Captain John Shakespear, and he was amongst the first of those down in the valley to see the approach of the Russian cavalry. 'In the course of an hour or so our two brigades of cavalry and Horse Artillery formed column under the heights of the Sebastopol plateau, when suddenly about 5,000 Russian cavalry in line, with columns in support, poured down the grass slope.'[7] As the Russian cavalry moved down the valley, it divided in two, with a small force of around 400 men bearing down on Kadikoi. Ahead of them were, in addition to the approximately 550 men of the 93rd Highlanders, were some thirty or forty men of the Guards who had happened to be in Balaklava that morning. The two young officers in charge of the party, Verschoyle and Hamilton, had quickly realised the danger that the port was in and they rushed out to lend their support to Campbell. There were also around 100 invalids in Balaklava under Colonel Daveney drawn up on the left of the 93rd, as well as Captain Barker's 'W' Battery of six 9-pounders.

Kinglake was watching the drama unfold from the Sapoune Heights:

> Meanwhile the main body of the Russian cavalry continued to advance up the North Valley; but some squadrons detached themselves from the mass, and came shaping their way for the gorge of Kadikoi—the ground Campbell stood to defend.
>
> When these horsemen were within about a thousand yards of him, Campbell gave a brisk order to his little body of foot, directing them at once to advance, and again crown the top of the hillock. This was done at the instant by the Highland battalion and the few score of English soldiers who had come up to range alongside it. The troops did not throw themselves into a hollow square (as is usual in preparing for cavalry), but simply formed line two deep. On this slender array all was destined to rest.[8]

This was clearly a critical moment in the engagement, and the British Commander-in-Chief, as William Russell noted, was visibly worried:

> There was no trace of the divine calm attributed to him by his admirers as his characteristic in moments of trial. His anxious mien as he turned his glass from point to point, consulting with Generals Airey, Estcourt, and others of his staff, gave me a notion that he was in 'trouble'.[9]

Surgeon George Munro was stood with the Highlanders watching the approaching Russian cavalry and confirmed Raglan's suspicions that the Turks were wavering:

> Sir Colin ordered the 93rd and the Turks to re-form line on the crest of the [Kadikoi] hill; and as we were doing so, the two companies of the regiment, which had been detached, under the command of Major Gordon, arrived, and took up their positions in the line. Thus we stood for a few seconds, while the cavalry was rapidly nearing us; but the Turkish battalions on our flanks began to get unsteady, and at last fairly turned, broke, and bolted.
>
> A stalwart Scottish wife was employed at the time washing some articles of clothing besides a little stream that flowed through a vineyard at the base of the hill, on the crest of which the 93rd stood in line, apparently, and really, I believed, quite unconcerned about the battle, and unmoved by the sound of roundshot which passed over her head. When she saw the Turks rushing down the hill and

amongst the tents, she thought that they were bent on plunder, and watched them for a minute with suspicious eye; but when they swept past her, and trampled on things which, being washed she had spread out to dry, she broke into a towering rage, and seizing a large stick that lay on the ground near her, laid about her left and right in protection of her property.[10]

Lieutenant Colonel Anthony Sterling was with Sir Colin Campbell and he also saw the Turks making off for Balaklava:

> As soon as the [Russian] Cavalry began to charge C [Campbell] advanced his men to advance to the crest again … The Turks ran away to the rear, into the village of Balaklava, crying 'Ship, ship!' However, the Commandant, an old officer of the Royals (Lieutenant Colonel Daveney), put a sentry to stop the vagabonds. One of my native servants (all trembling) went off with two of my horses, and was not found for hours afterwards.[11]

Campbell had been shorn of two-thirds of his strength just as the Russian cavalry bore down on the 93rd. Nevertheless, the old Scot was confident his men would hold their ground. He rode down the line, and said to the Highlanders, 'Remember there is no retreat from here, men! You must die where you stand!" The men cheerily answered his appeal saying, "Ay, ay, Sir Colin; we'll do that."'

Private Charles Howell of the 1st Dragoons gave the following account of the battle, in his own particular grammatical style:

> During the time that the Russian infantry were taking those redoubts, we saw two large bodies of cavelery to our left from coming over the low hills to actak us cavelery as we supposed. Now on our right and across the road that leads to Balaklava, Sir Colin Campbell with 3 company's of the 93rd Highlanders was form [ed], and on that small body of British soldier's came at full gallop one of the large one of these bodies of cavelery, and as they passed in front of us a few hundred yards, the thought was in my mind, oh the poor 93rd they will be cut up theire is more than fifty to one against them. But the fine old Sir Colin and his men stood their ground as British soldier's. Two deep the front ranks kneeling to resist cavelery. As we sat on our horses we heard quite plain the sharp words, kneeling ranks ready present and in an instant many a Russian soldier's saddle was empty.[12]

Howard Russell's description of those Highlanders, though usually misquoted and often inappropriately applied, has become part of the English lexicon:

> The ground flies beneath their horses' feet; gathering speed at every stride, they dash towards that thin red streak topped with a line of steel. As the Russian come within six hundred yards, down goes the line of steel in front, and out rings a rolling volley of musketry. The distance is too great; the Russians are not checked, but still sweep onwards through the smoke, with the whole force of horse and man, here and there knocked over by the shot of our batteries above. With breathless suspense every one awaits the bursting of the wave upon the line of Gaelic rock; but ere they come within two hundred and fifty yards, another deadly volley flashes from the levelled rifle, and carries terror among the Russians. They wheel about, open files right and left and flee faster than they came.

Captain Christopher Edward Blackett wrote to his father:

> A dense black column of I should say twelve or fourteen very strong squadrons bore right down on us. We were in line with Turks, on either flank, who on seeing the Cavalry took to their heels, but were rallied by some of our Officers driving them back, as soon as the enemy got within about five hundred yards we opened a fire of Minié rifles on them that some began to drop their horses, the nearer they got the hotter it became for them till when they arrived to within about three hundred yards they edged off to the left and fairly cut …[13]

Hector McPherson was also with the 93rd Highlanders and his account was also published in the British press, this time the *Stirling Observer* of 28 December:

> We declared that we would die to a man rather than not maintain the position assigned to us, and, wheeling in line to our right so as to front the enemy, and with our brave general at our head determined to give them battle, numerous although they were, if they advanced upon us. By this time the Enemy had occupied a rising ground to the left of our line, and with their guns began to play fiercely upon us. Here we remained for an hour, when the Enemy's cavalry, to the number of 4,000, were discovered making their appearance on a rising ground about 1,000 yards in front of us. When they had

wheeled in column and actually fronted us, they halted, and, after viewing us for a minute or so, they began to advance at a walking pace, we still lying on the ground and in line, never moved. After they had advanced a few paces they began to trot, then at full speed came rushing down upon us, when we sprung to our feet, and waited with the utmost coolness and determination until they came within about 200 yards of us, when we opened a well-sustained and well-directed fire upon them. Still they continued to advance, until within 50 yards of our line, when, finding that instead of flinching we became more bold and determined, they wheeled to their left, evidently with the intention of attacking us on the right flank; but instantly perceiving their design, we charged first upon our right, and bounding after them with the quickness of fury, were fronting them again, before they were able, although at the gallop, to complete their movement, and at the same time we still sustained our destructive fire, which soon forced them to their heels.

Colin Campbell submitted his report on the battle to Brigadier-General Estcourt, Adjutant-General, on 27 October from his camp by Battery No.4:

Sir,- I have the honor to inform you that on the morning the 25th inst., about 7 o'clock, the Russian force which has been, as I already reported, for sometime among the hills on our right front, debouched into the open ground in front of the redoubts Nos. 1, 2, and 3, which were occupied by Turkish infantry and artillery and were armed with 7 12-pounders (iron). The enemy's forces consisted of the 18 or 19 battalions of infantry, from 30 to 40 guns, and a large body of cavalry. They attack was made against No. 1 redoubt by a cloud of skirmishers, supported by 8 battalions of infantry and 16 guns. The Turkish troops in No. 1 persisted as long as they could, and then retired, and they suffered considerable loss in their retreat. The attack was followed by the successive abandonment of Nos. 2, 3, and 4 redoubts by the Turks, as well as of the other posts held by them in our front. The guns, however, in Nos. 2, 3, and 4 were spiked. The garrisons of these redoubts retired, and some of them formed on the right, and some on the left flank of the 93d Highlanders, which was posted in front of No. 4 battery and the village of Kadikoi.

When the enemy had taken possession of these redoubts, their artillery advanced with a large mass of cavalry, and their guns ranged to the 93d Highlanders, which, with 100 invalids under

Lieutenant-Colonel Daveney in support, occupied very insufficiently, from the smallness of their numbers, the slightly-rising ground in front of No. 4 battery. As I found that round shot and shell began to cause some casualties among the 93d Highlanders and the Turkish Battalions on their right and left flank, I made them retire a few paces behind the crest of the hill. During this period our batteries on the hills, manned by the Royal Marine Artillery and the Royal Marines, made most excellent practice on the enemy's cavalry, which came over the hill ground in front. One body of them, amounting to about 400 men, turned to their left, separating themselves from those who attacked Lord Lucan's Division, and charged the 93d Highlanders, who immediately advanced to the crest of the hill and opened their fire which forced the Russian cavalry to give way and turn to their left, after which they made an attempt to turn the right flank of the 93d, having observed the flight of the Turks who were placed there, upon which the Grenadiers of the 93d, under Captain Ross, were wheeled up to the their right and fired on the enemy, which manoeuver completely discomfited them.

During the rest of the day the troops under my command received no further molestation from the Russians. I beg to call Lord Raglan's attention to the gallantry and eagerness of the 93d Highlanders under Lieutenant Colonel Ainslie, of which his Lordship was an eye-witness; as well as the admirable conduct of Captain Barker of the field-battery under his orders, who made most excellent practice against the Russian cavalry and artillery while within range.[14]

Temple Godman was with the 5th Dragoon Guards:

We retired to our camp, which had been struck, and everything was nearly packed. We had no sooner formed in rear, than the enemy who had formed all along the heights sent down their cavalry in two masses into the plain, one went at full split at some Turkish infantry, but the 93rd who were lying down, jumped up and gave them such a volley that they wheeled to the left, and rode off as hard as they could go in good order, the artillery pounding them all the way.[15]

The infantry had driven off the small body of cavalry that had broken off from the main body, some 2,000 strong (estimates vary) which was now bearing down on the Heavy Brigade. The Russians had mounted the Causeway Heights and then moved down the slope into the South Valley.

There is no doubt that Lucan and Scarlett were taken completely by surprise when the Russian cavalry appeared. This was because the ground was undulating and the view of it from the bottom of the valley was obstructed by orchards or vineyards. Neither general would have been able to see the approach of even a large body of troops until they were almost upon the British cavalry. Had either of the cavalry generals posted videttes on any of the numerous nearby knolls or ridges, they would have been able to spot the advance of any enemy force long before it was close at hand and reacted accordingly. This basic principle was forgotten in the excitement of the battle.

Equally, Ryzhov's men did not have a clear view of the British cavalry once they had left the Causeway Heights. Indeed, as the Russians bore down on Scarlett's men they actually rode unwittingly past the Light Brigade on their right flank. The Russians, though, knew they were moving down to engage their enemy and so were prepared for the ensuing clash. Scarlett with his detachment, on the other hand, was still crossing the valley to take up the position ordered by Raglan when the Russians came galloping into view. Scarlett had set off across the South Valley with the 5th Dragoon Guards, the Scots Greys and the 6th Dragoons. The 4th Dragoon Guards were following some distance behind.

The Heavies were marching in an unhurried fashion and widely spread, believing themselves safe within their own lines. It was Elliot, Scarlett's aide riding by his side, who first saw the danger and alerted his general. Much has been made of the fact that as soon as Scarlett realised what was happening he ordered his men to charge, even though they would be moving uphill and therefore would be at a considerable disadvantage. However, it is a basic principle that cavalry should never receive a charge stationary. Scarlett simply knew he had to charge. 'Scarlett's resolve was instantaneous,' wrote Kinglake, 'and his plan simple. He meant to form line to his left, and to charge with all six of his squadrons. Accordingly, he faced his horse's head towards the flank of the column, and called out, "Are you right in front?" The answer was, "Yes, sir!" Then Scarlett gave the word of command, "Left wheel into line!"'

That the Russian cavalry was also unsighted until almost the last moment can be gleaned from General Ryzhov's report:

> When I rode up onto the height, the following sight met my eyes: the entire English cavalry no more than 500 yards from me, drawn up in one line, resting its right flank on rough terrain and, in addition, protected by a rather strong battery emplaced in Kadykioi village.

On its left flank, about 200 yards away, stood infantry in echeloned columns. The Ural Cossack Regiment had edged far to the right of the enemy, along the edge of the heights, in the same formation as they had started, which is to say—in sixes. They moved with a frightful 'Ura!' and quickly shifted back and forth in a long row like some kind of flock or flight of birds, but not, however, closing with the enemy.

At this same time the hussar columns began to ascend. First was a division of the Leuchtenberg Regiment under the command of the truly brave Colonel Voinilovich, whom I ordered to bear to the left as much as required to be face to face with the red English dragoon guards. As the rest of the divisions each came up the slope, I directed them to parts of the enemy formation, since to conform to the extended English front I was forced to also stretch out both my regiments in a single line, and was left without a reserve.

Ryzhov's redeployment cost him vital moments, and impetuous. This gave Scarlett a chance to form his men into some kind of order. A trooper of the 5th Dragoon Guards, known to us only as 'W.B.', wrote to his brother on 22 November:

Our regiment formed the centre of our line – 6th Dragoons on the left; the 4th on our rear; and the Grey's upon the enemy's right flank. They kept advancing upon us until they were within a very few yards. Then came the tightening of the reins, and grasping of swords. The 4th Dragoons got the word 'Charge!', the Greys being upon the right flank. The 6th Dragoons were immediately surrounded. Then came *our* turn. Our impetuosity was very great to assist our comrades, who in a few moments would have been cut up. The next moment there was a cheer and a shout, and the 5th 'Green Horse', dashed into the enemy's ranks, who soon made their blades strike fire in the air. For fifteen minutes there was nothing to be heard but the clashing of steel. Then the next movement was the retiring of the enemy. Some you would see with heads falling off, and arms broken at the charge. I felled two at once, by leaping my mare upon two of the Russians, when they were upon the point of retiring. Both horses and men fell never to rise again. I have often read of battles being fought, but never could it compete with this![16]

A letter from an unnamed officer of the Scots Greys found its way into the *Manchester Times* of 25 November 1854:

The old Greys and Inniskillens had the honour of meeting the first charge of three times our number. They regularly surrounded us. I belonged to the left squadron (likewise the left of the line), and had two squadrons, each of double our strength, who tried to turn our flank, opposed to us. We went clean through them, and back again, and you never saw such a fight. They say you could not see a red coat, we were so surrounded, and for *ten minutes* it was dreadful suspense; but they couldn't stand it, and were soon cutting away like anything, or re-forming. The realities of war were very apparent; excited cheering and congratulations from men covered with blood and cut about dreadfully.

Another Scots Grey, Private James McPherson, was knocked from his horse and he laid stranded on the ground. He called out for help as seven enemy horsemen closed in on him, sabres bared. Death stared him in the face as the Russians close in for the kill, but in an instant twenty-seven-year-old Sergeant Henry Ramage dashed into the midst of the Russians and drove them back, his long, heavy sword carving a clear passage through which the trooper could escape. Ramage saved McPherson's life and this act, along with another incident following the charge of the Light Brigade, led to Ramage later being awarded the Victoria Cross.

The *Bath Chronicle and Weekly Gazette* of Thursday, 23 November 1854 printed a letter from another soldier of the 5th Dragoon Guards:

A lot of Russian cavalry came to attack us. I suppose they thought we would run. At first we thought they were our Light Brigade till they got about twenty yards from us; then we saw the difference. We wheeled into line. They stood still, and did not know what to do. The charge sounded, and away we went into the midst of them. Such cutting and slashing for about a minute, it was dreadful to see; the rally sounded, but it was of no use –none of us would come away until the enemy retreated; then our fellows cheered as loud as ever they could.

When we were in the midst of them, my horse was shot; he fell and got up again, and I managed to get loose. While I was in that predicament a Russian Lancer was going to run me through, and I could not help myself. Macnamara came up at the time, and nearly severed his head from his body; so, thank God, I did not get a scratch. I got up and ran to where I saw a lot of loose horses; I got one belonging to one of the Enniskillins, and soon was along with the regiment again. When I had mounted again, I saw a Russian who had strayed from the rest; he rode up to try to stop me from joining the regiment again. As it happened, I had observed a pistol in the holster pip, so I took it out, and shot him in the arm; he dropped his sword, then I immediately rode up to him and ran him through the body, and the fellow dropped to the ground.

One Dragoon was positively exhilarated by the charge. To him it was 'glorious':

> Oh, such a charge ... From the moment we dashed at the enemy I knew nothing but that I was impelled by some irresistible force onward, and by some invisible and imperceptible influence to crush every obstacle which stumbled before my good sword and brave old charger. I never in my life experienced such a sublime sensation as in the moment of the charge. Some fellows speak of it as being demonic. I know this, that it was such as made me a match for any two ordinary men and gave me such an amount of glorious indifference as to life as I thought it possible to be master of. Forward–dash–bang–clank–and there we were in the midst of such smoke, cheer and clatter as never before stunned a mortal ear. It was glorious. I could not pause. It was all push, wheel, frenzy, strike, and down, down they went.[17]

Equally, Major Robert Kingscote of the Scots Fusilier Guards was with Raglan's staff on the Sapoune Heights:

> This charge was out and out the most exciting thing I ever saw or shall see again. Being on the high ground and close by one could see the fellows coming to hand to hand blows beautifully, and our fellows did not spare them. We had to charge up hill and had not the room to get our men into a swing or we should have shaken them still more. The Greys did their work well, so they all did, but the Greys looked beautiful.[18]

It was quite the reverse for an NCO of the 1st Royals who was actually disappointed with the way the affair was handled:

> The Greys and part of the Inniskillings were the first to meet them [the Russians] and, to do the enemy justice, they advanced in much better order than we did; but they could not stand a moment the charge of the British Cavalry, for one squadron of Grays [sic] upset

a whole regiment of them. We were soon at the support, and the enemy retired, but not in confusion. I fully expected we should follow and charge them again, as I am confident we could have taken the whole of them prisoners, but, marvellous to say, the order was given to Retire, and a more confused rabble was never seen. However, the Russians retired beyond the heights which they had won, and very soon after our infantry began to arrive, as the news had reached Lord Raglan of our perilous state, and he sent the First and Fourth Divisions to our aid, and I felt quite comfortable as the Guards and Highlanders came in. I was never so vexed in my life to think that 3,000 Russian cavalry were within our grasp of our small force, and our commander allowing them to retire unmolested![19]

Major William Charles Forrest of the 4th Dragoon Guards was another who did not share such excitement:

For my part I think the Heavies might have done much better. The Greys charged at a trot and our pace was but little better, but we had very bad ground to advance over, first thro' a vineyard, and over two fences, bank and ditch, then through the Camp of the 17th [Lancers], & we were scarcely formed when we attacked, & had but very little good ground to charge over still we did not go in so good a pace as we might have done. Once in, we did better, but the confusion was more than I had expected, the men of all regiments were mixed and we were a long time reforming. If we have to do it again I hope we shall do it better.[20]

Similar sentiments were expressed by an officer of the Scots Greys: 'They say it was a magnificent charge; but it did not come up to my idea at all; it was more like a row at a fair.'[21] Another member of the 5th Dragoons was Troop Sergeant-Major William Stewart, whose actions on 25th October were remembered by another NCO, Henry Franks:

We had a Troop Sergeant-Major named William Stewart, who had no less than three horses shot that day. The first one was by a rifle bullet. Stewart caught another horse belonging to the 4th Dragoon Guards, and he had hardly got mounted when a shell burst under him and blew him up. Stewart escaped without a scratch and managed to catch another loose horse which he rode for a while, until a cannon ball broke one of the horse's legs. Stewart, who was still without a scratch, took pity on the poor dumb brute and shot him. He then

101

procured another horse, which made the fourth he had ridden that day. Very few men, I should say, have had such an experience as this and all within an hour.[22]

Temple Godman, also of the 5th Dragoon Guards, said that the Russians were very steady and well-disciplined and that their curved sabres were very sharp. The long, straight swords of the British heavy cavalry, however, made 'fearful havoc' amongst the enemy:

The Greys and Inniskillings went first, then we came in support of the Greys, their [the enemy's] front must have been composed of three regiments, and a very strong column in their rear, in all I suppose about 1,500 or 2,000, while we were not more than 800, however the charge sounded and at them went the first line; Scarlett and his A.D.C. well in front. The enemy seemed quite astonished and drew into a walk and then a halt; as soon as they met, all I saw was swords in the air in every direction, the pistols going off, and everyone hacking away right and left. In a moment the Greys were surrounded and hemmed completely in; there they were fighting back to back in the middle, the great bearskin caps high above the enemy.

This was the work of a moment; as soon as we saw it, the 5th advanced and in they charged, yelling and shouting as hard as they could split, the row was tremendous, and for about five minutes neither would give way, and their column was so deep we could not cut through it. At length they turned and well they might, and the whole ran as hard as they could pelt back up the hill, our men after them all broken up, and cutting them down right and left. We pursued about 300 yards, and then called off with much difficulty, the gunners then opened on them, and gave them a fine peppering. It took some little time to get the men to fall in again, they were all mixed up together of course, all the regiments in one mass.

The enemy being gone, and we all right, had time to look around, the ground was covered with dead and dying men and horses. I am happy to say our brigade lost but seven men dead, but had a considerable number wounded, some mortally. The ground was strewn with swords, broken and whole, trumpets, helmets, carbines, etc., while a quantity of men were scattered all along as far as we pursued. There must have been some forty or fifty of the enemy dead, besides wounded ... Lord Raglan who was looking down from a hill close by sent an A.D.C. to say 'Well done the Heavy Brigade.'[23]

Lieutenant General Ryzhov painted quite a different picture of the engagement:

> All my attention was turned to this bloody fight. I held my breath, waiting to see how this would end. As I did not have any reserve, if the hussars turned back I would not have anything with which to stop the enemy, while the descent from the heights, with its unavoidable disorder, would help the enemy cavalry deal us a great defeat. With God's help, the end was glorious for us. The hussars slashed away at a standstill for about seven minutes, and although they suffered significant losses (of the Leuchtenberg men – 18 field and company-grade officers and 122 lower ranks, while for the Weimar Regiment – 12 field and company-grade officers and 105 lower ranks) we nonetheless forced the stubborn enemy to show us his rear. The English cavalry turned back and took cover behind his infantry. I saw that it was necessary to halt the hussars chasing after them, considering that moment most suitable for returning back …
>
> I had served for 42 years, taken part in 10 campaigns, been in many great battles such as Kulm, Leipzig, Paris, and others, but never had I seen a cavalry attack in which both sides, with equal ferocity, steadfastness, and—it may be said—stubbornness, cut and slashed in place for such a long time, and even in the whole history of cavalry attacks we do not find many such instances. Senior and junior officers served as examples for the soldiers, as evidenced by such a large number of wounded, and for the most part all these wounds were in the face or head … My horse was killed under me. Even those most ill-disposed to us cannot call this fight anything but most daring, decisive, and exemplary, and in its own time it will take its place in the history of cavalry actions. [24]

Troop Sergeant Major John Linkon of the 13th Light Dragoons was a spectator to the charge of the Scots Greys, portraying the scene through a number of analogies, in a letter to his brother on 8 November 1855:

> Picture to yourself a dozen policemen going into one of our election mobs in Parker's Place or into the Senate House at the time of the students taking degrees, or into a crowded church when a popular preacher was holding forth or any other place where a small party would be swallowed up and lost to sight.[25]

Captain Robert Scott Hunter was with the Scots Greys and wrote about the battle to his sister two days later:

The scene was awful, we were so outnumbered, & there was nothing but to fight our way through them, cut & slash. I made a hack at one, & my sword bounced off his thick coat, so I gave him the point & knocked him off his horse. Another fellow just after made a slash at me, & just touched my bearskin, so I made a rush at him, & took him just on the back of his helmet. I didn't wait to see what became of him, as a lot of fellows were riding at me, but I only know that he fell forward on his horse, & if his head tingled like my wrist, he must have had it hard, & as I was riding out, another fellow came past me, whom I caught slap in the face. I'll be bound if his own mother wouldn't have known him.[26]

The Heavy Brigade had just ten men killed but ninety-eight were wounded. Temple Godman survived the charge with only superficial injuries:

I had one of two shaves for it during the day, my coat sleeve was cut through and my wrist bruised, but not cut, as I had on some very thick jersies. My coat was torn in the back, which was not done in the morning, I think it must have been a lance thrust that tore it. I was within an ace of being knocked over more than once by round shot, and once I had just galloped up from our rear squadron to the leading one, when a shell came close over my head, I looked round and saw it fall and burst exactly where I had just left, knocking over some four horses.[27]

An anonymous sergeant of the 5th Dragoon Guards also escaped serious injury, though his letter to his parents printed in the *Manchester Times* of 22 November 1854, was sent from the hospital in Scutari:

The Russian cavalry came thick upon us, eight thousand in number, which caused us to do something else than play with them. At one time I was surrounded with about ten Cossacks, and with the assistance of my long sword (which is the only thing you can depend upon with those Cossacks), I got clear of them, with two wounds in my head and one in my right hand, all sabre cuts; and what is more remarkable, I have eleven cuts in my helmet. My helmet has been shown all over the hospital and barracks. Just fancy ten fellows cutting at you on all sides! The morning after the battle wounded were removed from the Crimea to the General Hospital; and I am glad to say my wounds are doing very well.

Watching from high on the Sapoune Heights, William Russell had an excellent view of the action:

> the Grays and Enniskilleners pierced through the dark masses of Russians. The shock was but for a moment. There was a clash of steel and a light play of sword blades in the air, and then the Grays and the redcoats disappear in the midst of the shaken and quivering columns. In another moment we see them emerging and dashing on with diminished numbers, and in broken order, against the second line, which is advancing against them as fast as it can to retrieve the fortune of the charge. It was a terrible moment. 'God help them! they are lost!' was the exclamation of more than one made, and the thought of many. With unabated fire the noble hearts dashed at their enemy. It was a fight of heroes. The first line of Russians, which had been smashed utterly by our charge, and had fled off at one flank and towards the centre, were coming back to swallow up our handful of men. By sheer steel and sheer courage Enniskillener and Scot were winning their desperate way right through the enemy's squadrons, and already gray horses and red coats had appeared right at the rear of the second mass, when, with irresistible force, like one bolt from a bow, the 1st Royals, the 4th Dragoon Guards, and the 5th Dragoon Guards rushed at the remnants of the first line of the enemy, went through it as though it were made of pasteboard, and, dashing on the second body of Russians as they were still disordered by the terrible assault of the Grays and their companions, put them to utter rout.[28]

When Private James Aucinloss of the 4th Dragoon Guards read Russell's report in *The Times* he took exception to what he called the Special Correspondent's 'mis-statement' and 'want of correct information', regarding Russell's description of the Greys and Inniskillings charging 'in the first line'. The cavalry was not in two-deep line, he contended, but in a column of squadrons in successive parallel lines. He therefore put pen to paper in a letter to his cousin to put the record straight:

> I will tell you how we charged, and how we were placed when the Russians came upon us. After retiring out of range of the [guns in the] Turkish redoubts, which were in possession of the Russians, and, immediately after the Russian cavalry came over the hill to charge the Highlanders, when we came to our Front we were in

Column, or rather, moving 'en echelon' of Squadrons, left in front; and after getting through a vineyard, in which we were nearly bogged down, we Changed Front to our Left, which brought us into Column of Squadrons ... Each regiment had two squadrons up, and there being five regiments, we had ten squadrons. Well, while moving 'En Echelon', the Inniskillings and 5th took too much ground to their right, which caused then, when we changed to the left, to be some distance to the right of the parallel, and when we Wheeled into Line our regiment was next to the Greys; and the Inniskillings, finding no space to act in front attack[ed] the left flank of the Russians, whilst we, not five seconds after the Greys attacked the front, charged the Russian's right flank.[29]

Also watching the success of the Heavy Brigade was Cardigan and the entire Light Brigade, all envious of the glory the heavies had just won, and eager to show their own worth. With the Russian cavalry retiring in disorder, the Light Brigade had a wonderful opportunity to strike at the enemy. Cardigan, nevertheless, remained immobile in his saddle, cursing the 'damn' heavies. Unable to restrain himself at seeing such an opportunity go begging, Captain William Morris who had taken command of the 17th Lancers after the death of Major Willett, rode up to the General:

'What are you doing, Captain Morris? Front your regiment!'
'Look there, my lord,' said Morris, pointing with his sword at the Russian cavalry flank now exposed by the impact of the Heavy charge.
'Remain where you are, sir,' Cardigan replied, 'until you get my orders!'
With the Russians retreating in disorder, Morris tried again. 'My lord, are we not going to charge the flying enemy?'
'No,' Cardigan replied. 'We have orders to remain here.'
'Do, my lord, allow me to charge them with the Lancers. See my lord, they are in disorder!'[30]

Many saw, indeed overheard, this exchange, including Private James Wightman of the 17th, who later recorded that Cardigan said to Morris, 'We must not stir from here,' and that Morris turned to his fellow officers and angrily shouted, 'Gentlemen, you are witnesses of my request.'[31] Cardigan, astonishingly, flatly denied such a conversation ever took place:

I entirely deny that Captain Morris ever pointed out to me my opportunity of charging the enemy, or said anything to me of the kind; and it is quite untrue that I said I was placed in that particular spot, and should not move without orders, or anything to that effect. I further deny that Captain Morris ever begged me to be allowed to charge with his regiment alone, or that he ever gave me any advice, or uttered one word to me upon the subject of attacking the enemy. I remember upon one occasion during the engagement, after the Light Brigade had been ordered to join the Heavy Brigade in the valley, Captain Morris broke away from the column with his regiment without orders upon which I asked him, sharply, why he did so and desired him to fall again into column. That was all that occurred on the day in question, between myself and Captain Morris.[32]

This prompted a response from Morris:

Having read a letter from Major Calthorpe, in which he throws between Lord Cardigan and myself the settlement of the question as to whether I asked Lord Cardigan, on the 25th of October 1854, to attack the Russian cavalry in flank at the time they were engaged with the Heavy Brigade, and which Lord Cardigan most positively denies, I wish to declare most positively that I did ask Lord Cardigan to attack the enemy at the time and in the manner above mentioned.[33]

Lucan, always happy to paint his brother-in-law in the least flattering light, stated that he told Cardigan he was 'to attack anything and everything that shall come within your reach, but you will be careful of columns or squares of infantry.' Cardigan, as might be expected, claimed that he had been placed in a particular position by Lucan and told 'on no account to leave it, and to defend it against any attack by the Russians, they did not however approach the position'.[34]

What had been forgotten in all this, was that Lucan could quite easily have ordered Cardigan to attack the Russian cavalry, as one commentator pointed out: 'A swift horseman … could have reached Cardigan in ample time with instructions to take the enemy in right-rear with a part, or the whole of the Light Brigade.'[35] Lucan, it scarcely needs to be said, refuted this, claiming that 'they were altogether out of my reach, and that to me they were unavailable.'[36] He then further justified his failure to act, being obviously untroubled by the contradiction in the statements he had made:

Lord Raglan not having acted on the communication sent him the previous day by Sir Colin Campbell and myself informing him of the approach of a considerable Russian Army, and leaving us altogether without support, we considered it our first duty to defend the approach to the town of Balaklava; and as this defence would depend chiefly upon the cavalry, it was necessary to reserve them for the purpose.[37]

Regardless of who failed to do what, and whose version of events we can believe, the chance to destroy Ryzhov's cavalry had been lost and the Russians withdrew up the slope to reform in readiness to charge again. But then Captain Branding's 'C' Troop arrived on the scene 'and fired forty-nine shot and shell at them, at a range between 700 and 800 yards, with admirable results, the 24-pounder howitzers making splendid practice,' wrote Colonel Whinyates. 'This effectually prevented the Russians rallying, and they quickly retired, keeping a little inside the crest of the ridge, and thence over into the outer plain.'[38]

The Russian cavalry had been driven off and two British infantry divisions were on their way. Soon Raglan would be in a position to take the offensive. The Battle of Balaklava was far from over.

Chapter 8

'Forward the Light Brigade'

General Liprandi's initial attempt to threaten the British base at Balaklava had been repelled by Campbell's and Scarlett's men and the British artillery. The defeat of Ryzhov's cavalry had deprived Liprandi of the screen which was to have protected the flank of his advance across the South Valley, and the artillery that had entered the North Valley with the cavalry had been withdrawn and was now drawn across the far end of the valley. The Russians, though, had not lost many of their number and held a commanding position on the Causeway Heights as well as the Fedioukine Heights which they had occupied with infantry and artillery. Exactly what Liprandi considered doing next is not clear. All that can be gleaned from Liprandi's subsequent report is that the Russians were consolidating their hold of the heights before their next move:

> Our cavalry advanced rapidly, even to the [British] camp; but, attacked in flank by the fire of the enemy's riflemen, and in front by the English cavalry, it was compelled to halt, and afterwards resumed its first position at the right wing of the general order of battle, being so placed that its front did not present a right line, the direction of one of its wings forming an angle with that of the centre.
>
> At this time Major-general Jabrokritsky [Zhabokritsky], with a detachment of the infantry regiment of Vladimir (three battalions) and that of Souzdal [or Suzdal], ten guns of the battery of position No. 1, four guns of the light battery No. 2 of the 16th brigade of artillery, two companies of the battalion of riflemen No. 6, two squadrons of the regiment of hussars of the Grand Duke of Saxe-Weimar, and two detachments of the regiment No. 60 of Cossacks (of Popoff), advanced upon the heights to the left of our cavalry, and occupied them.[1]

109

Raglan was also considering his next step. Liprandi's only achievement so far that morning had been to capture the redoubts. As the Russian attack appeared to have stalled, now might be the moment for the British to recover the Causeway Heights. In fact, the Duke of Cambridge's 1st Division had reached the track through the Sapoune Heights known as The Col in time to witness the charge of the Heavy Brigade. Cathcart, still showing no urgency, was some thirty minutes further behind even though the 4th Division had less ground to cover than the 1st. The two French brigades ordered forward by Canrobert had already debouched into the South Valley. The Allied force was growing ever stronger. Campbell, Scarlett and Brandling had bought Raglan the time he needed.

As a result, the British Commander-in Chief decided to try and push the Russians off the Causeway Heights, despite the fact they were occupied in considerable strength. Liprandi's men had already abandoned Redoubt No.4, after having demolished its parapets, 'as it was too much advanced, and I ordered its guns to be spiked, and their wheels and carriages to be broken, and the guns themselves to be thrown down the mountain.'[2]

Raglan therefore instructed his Quartermaster-General, Sir Richard Airey to send a message down to Lucan. This, the third order that had been sent to the cavalry commander, was delivered by Captain Edward Wetherall, Assistant Quartermaster-General, and read as follows:

> Cavalry to advance and take advantage of any opportunity to recover the Heights. They will be supported by infantry which have been ordered. Advance on two fronts.

This instruction was, as most commentators have declared, was nonsensical. What on earth did Raglan mean by 'Advance on two fronts'? The actual wording of this order was subsequently disputed, as will later be seen. According to Airey it read:

> Cavalry to advance and take advantage of any opportunity to recover the Heights. They will be supported by infantry which have been ordered to advance on two fronts.

This makes a little more sense. The infantry, in the form of the 1st and 4th Divisions, which would arrive separately, were to attack from the direction in which they would arrive on the battlefield, thus they would advance on two fronts. Lucan, quite understandably, therefore, waited for the arrival of the infantry. It would be reckless in the extreme for him to try taking the Heights which were held in considerable strength without infantry support. Obviously, if the Russians withdrew from the Causeway Heights, Lucan could 'advance' and take that 'opportunity' to recover the Heights. So, until such an opportunity came his way, or until the infantry arrived, Lucan could do little other than prepare. Which is what he did, as detailed by Private James Wightman of the 17th Lancers who was at the forefront of the Light Brigade:

> After the Heavies' charge the Light Brigade was moved a little way 'left back' and then forward, down into the middle of the upper part of the outer valley, and fronting straight down it, the Heavies remaining a little in advance to the right about the crest of the Causeway Ridge. We stood halted in these positions for about three quarters of an hour, Lord Cardigan in front of his brigade, Lord Lucan on our right front about midway between the two brigades ... On the right were the 13th Light Dragoons (now Hussars) in the centre of the 17th Lancers, on the left of the 11th Hussars, which latter regiment before the charge began was ordered back in support, so that during the charge the first line consisted only of the 13th Light Dragoons and the 17th Lancers. All three regiments were but of two squadrons each; the formation of course was two deep.[3]

Lucan received this order at around 09.50 hours. In his own words, 'The division took up a position with a view of supporting an attack upon the heights'. Whilst he waited for the arrival of the infantry, the division was allowed to dismount. This gave Private Albert Mitchell a chance to assess the situation around him though whether or not he could actually see as much as he claims is debatable:

> We were now dismounted, and soon we could see the enemy had placed a number of guns across the lower part of the valley a mile and a half from us. At the same time a field battery ascended a hill on our left front, where it was placed in a position facing us. They also placed a field battery on the slope between the redoubts and the valley on our right. The rest of the enemy's troops were placed in rear of his guns, except those who held the captured redoubts, and some others who were at the time employed in carrying off the guns lost by the Turks, as also a battalion or two of infantry, who were extended along the slope towards the lower end of the valley.[4]

It seems evident that Liprandi was not retreating but had, nevertheless, adopted a defensive stance. Raglan, meanwhile, was waiting for the attempt to recover the Causeway Heights. The Cavalry Division still showed no signs of movement but, according to Kinglake, Cathcart's division had at last reached The Col:

> When Cathcart had reached the Col, General Airey rode up to him, and said 'Sir George Cathcart, Lord Raglan wishes you to advance immediately and recapture the redoubts.' The order was given very plainly, and Airey, after having delivered it, turned to the staff-officer who had carried Lord Raglan's original orders to Cathcart, and said: 'You are acquainted with the position of each redoubt, remain with Sir George Cathcart and show him where they are.'[5]

The 4th Division moved with 'exasperating slowness', marching past the ground on which the Heavy Brigade had fought, towards the empty redoubts. After occupying the first two redoubts Cathcart halted, ordering his divisional artillery to fire on the redoubts still occupied by the Russians.[6]

The Duke of Cambridge's division was moving up through the South Valley whilst the French 1st Division had already reached Colin Campbell's position in front of Kadikoi along with two squadrons of the recently-landed Chasseurs d'Afrique.

General Bosquet's aide-de-camp, Captain Charles Alexandre Fay, described the dispositions of the Allied forces from his position on the Sapoune Heights:

> The Allied troops ordered to reinforce had arrived on the plain; they were established in two lines: the first, formed by the English cavalry, was between Redoubts No. 4 and 5, and directed to the right, towards Balaklava; our Chasseurs d'Afrique formed the left, to the north of the redoubts, in the plain of the Tchernaya. The second line is composed of infantry; the English (the First Division, with the Fourth in reserve, behind their cavalry, and the first brigade or our first division to their left, at the height of Redoubt No. 5. During this time, the Brigade of General Vinoy (second brigade of the first division) followed to the south, to the pass of Balaklava, and occupied Kadikoi.[7]

Liprandi had not renewed his assault upon Balaklava and now with the Allied force increasing in strength his chance had gone. It would seem that the Russian general realised this and was about to withdraw his most advanced troops. This was spotted by Raglan and his staff, including Lieutenant Calthorpe who was the aide-de-camp in line to carry the Commander-in-Chief's next order:

> It was now shortly after 11 a.m.: Lord Raglan, from the place that he occupied, commanding as it did so extensive a view of the whole of the valley of Balaklava and the position of the Russian forces, thought that he perceived a retrograde movement on the part of the enemy.
>
> Upon a closer examination with our glasses it appeared pretty evident that the Russians were removing our guns which they had captured in the forts. Lord Raglan, wishing, therefore, to prevent their object being attained, sent an order to Lord Lucan.[8]

Raglan, it has been said, was determined not to lose any of his cannon to the enemy, as this would indicate that the Russian attack had been, at least to some degree, a success. It would only take a few minutes for the Russians to start hauling away the guns from the redoubts. By the time Cathcart moved along the Heights or Cambridge had marched across the valley it would be far too late. The only chance Raglan had of saving his guns was to send his cavalry immediately. The order he sent to Lord Lucan was the one that would launch the Light Brigade into the 'Valley of Death'.

However, it would not be Calthorpe who carried that order. It would take at least fifteen minutes (some sources state as long as twenty or thirty) for a horseman to gallop down from the Sapoune Heights, by which time the Russians might well have already removed the guns. With no time to lose another aide, a noted horseman, was called forward, whilst Airey wrote down Raglan's instructions, which read:

> Lord Raglan wishes the cavalry to advance rapidly to the front – follow the enemy and try to prevent the enemy carrying away the guns – Troop of Horse Artillery may accompany – French cavalry is on your left – R. Airey
> Immediate

It was another imprecise order. But this one made no mention of the infantry and unlike the previous three included two significant words, that of 'rapidly' and 'immediate', indicating that Lucan should act without delay and without waiting for the infantry. It also stated that Lucan was to 'follow' the enemy. This can also be construed to mean that Raglan believed the Russians were already removing the guns from the redoubts or that they would be doing so by the time Lucan received the order: hence the need for speed.

Baron de Bazancourt retold the event only slightly differently:

> Lord Raglan, from his elevated position, which enables him to embrace all the operations in one view, and appreciate their results, seeing the enemy retreat from the ground which he had for a short time occupied, ordered the cavalry, supported by the 4th Division under the command of Lieut.- General Cathcart, 'to advance and take advantage of every opportunity to recapture the heights.' 'The enemy,' writes Lord Raglan in his despatch, 'seemed attempting to carry off the cannon which had been taken. Lord Lucan received orders to advance rapidly, to follow him in his retreat, and to endeavour to hinder the accomplishment of his purpose.'[9]

Calthorpe moved forward to take the order from Airey, but Raglan said that he wanted a more accomplished rider: 'This order was entrusted to Captain Nolan,' recalled Cathorpe, 'aide-de-camp to General Airey, a cavalry officer of great experience. Previous to his departure he received careful instructions from both Lord Raglan and the Quartermaster-General.'

General Canrobert was also on the Heights with the British staff and recorded what he witnessed:

> Lord Raglan was anxious: he first sent an aide-de-camp, Commandant Witherall [sic], of his staff, to Lord Lucan, then after he called General Airey and spoke with him. We saw the latter taking his sabretache, using it as an improvised desk, to write a note in crayon. With the note written, the two Generals exchanged some further words, and Lord Raglan, calling Captain Nolan, of the 15th Hussars, aide-de-camp of General Airey, entrusted him with the paper to carry to Lord Lucan.[10]

Wishing to stress the urgency of the situation, as Nolan turned to gallop away, Raglan called after him, 'Tell Lord Lucan the cavalry is to attack immediately.' According to General Patrice de MacMahon, Raglan addressed Nolan, 'You will order him,' he said, 'to charge the Russians. The orderly officer galloped off without a word.'[11]

With these instructions Nolan set off down the Heights, not picking his way carefully down the easiest path but straight down the steep slope, his horse slithering and stumbling. Reaching the valley floor safely, Nolan galloped the mile or so to where the Cavalry Division was posted.

Being in the front rank of the 17th Lancers, Private Wightman was well placed to observe the unfolding drama:

> As we stood halted here, Captain Nolan, of the 15th Hussars, whom we knew as an aide-de-camp of the head-quarter staff, suddenly galloped out to the front through the interval between us and the 13th, and called out to Captain Morris, who was directly in my front, 'Where is Lord Lucan?' 'There,' replied Morris, pointing – 'there, on the right front!' Then he added, 'What is it to be, Nolan? – are we going to charge?' Nolan was off already in Lord Lucan's direction, but as he galloped away he shouted to Morris over his shoulder, 'You will see! you will see!'

Nolan spurred his horse onwards again, reining in by the cavalry commander, and handing over Airey's note. Typical of Raglan's and Airey's orders it was hopelessly vague. What was mean by 'French cavalry is on your left'? It implied, though it certainly did not make it clear, that the Chasseurs d'Afrique were to support the attempt at preventing the Russians from removing the guns, but had the French been informed of this, or was Lucan supposed to arrange this with the Chasseurs?

Secondly, and more crucially as events would unfold, the order did not state which guns, though it was fairly obvious that Raglan was referring to the guns in the redoubts. 'After carefully reading this order,' Lucan later declared:

> I hesitated and urged the uselessness of such an attack, and the dangers attending it. The aide-de-camp [Nolan], in a most authoritative tone, stated that they were Lord Raglan's orders that the cavalry should attack immediately. I asked, 'Where, and what to do?' neither enemy nor guns being in sight. He replied in a most disrespectful but significant manner, pointing to the further end of the valley, 'There, my Lord, is your enemy; there are your guns!'[12]

As has been said many times, it was part of an aide-de-camp's duty to explain the orders he carries to the recipient. Equally, it is the responsibility of the chief of staff, in this case General Airey, to correctly interpret his commander's instructions. If it is assumed that both men understood fully what Raglan required, and there is nothing to indicate otherwise, then, on the face of it, both failed to communicate the Commander-in-Chief's wishes adequately or accurately – the one by written means and the other verbally.

Lucan claimed that he told Nolan he could not see any guns and in response the young captain had pointed somewhat imprecisely down the North Valley. Much has been made of exactly where Nolan had indicated, and it has been decided that there was just a difference of twenty degrees between the far redoubts on the Causeway Heights and the end of the North Valley. But it can hardly be imagined in the heat of the moment that Lucan could deduce this. Nolan pointed in the general direction of the Russian army. The Heights and the valley are contiguous, and the enemy occupied both, as related by Baron de Bazancourt:

> In fact, the Russian cavalry had retired upon the Jalta roa; the enemy was again in order of battle, and presented a dense mass, protected by a formidable artillery. At the bottom of the valley, was the main-body of Liprandi's Division, and, considerably in advance, crossing their fires, the two first redoubts, and that on the heights of the Tchernaya. Besides which, the hill-sides, thickly wooded, were very favourable for sharpshooting, and at the same time hid and protected strong columns of infantry.[13]

We know that Lucan considered Nolan's attitude to be insolent, yet his words, 'There, my Lord, is your enemy; there are your guns!' do not in themselves sound at all disrespectful. What Lucan must have meant was that Nolan was pointing towards the Russians meaning that it was blindingly obvious where the enemy was, there were, after all about 25,000 of them. The battle so far had centred on the Causeway Heights and Kadikoi, and the previous order, the third order, had instructed Lucan to try and recover the Heights if the opportunity arose. The probability was that it was the guns in the redoubts that Raglan was referring to. But whereas when Lucan received the first of Airey's ambiguous orders Lucan kept the aide who had delivered the order with him to make sure he had understood it correctly, Nolan's 'disrespectful' attitude angered Lucan so he did not ask for further elucidation, as Sir John Blunt, the Earl's civilian interpreter, noted: 'Surprised and irritated at the impetuous and disrespectful attitude and tone of Captain Nolan, Lord Lucan looked at him sternly, but made no answer.'

Lucan could not demean himself by speaking to the aide-de-camp again nor could he have sent his own man up to the Commander-in-

Chief to question the instructions he had received. For someone to ride up the steep hill to Raglan's position and back again would have taken at least thirty minutes and, in the midst of a battle, such a length of time might prove critical, particularly as he had been instructed to act immediately. As he later told Lord Raglan, 'So distinct, in my Opinion, were your written Instructions, and so positive and urgent were the Orders delivered by the Aide-de-Camp, that I felt it was imperative on me to obey.'

> My lord, I considered at the time—I am still of the same opinion— that I followed the only course open to me. As a lieutenant-general, doubtless I have discretionary power; but to take upon myself to disobey an order written by my commander-in-chief within a few minutes of its delivery, and given from an elevated position, commanding an entire view of all the batteries and the position of the enemy, would have been nothing less than direct disobedience of orders, without any other reason than that I preferred my own opinion to that of my general, and in this instance must have exposed me and the cavalry to aspersions, against which it might have been difficult to have defended ourselves.[14]

Lucan was right in that he really did not have much choice in the matter. The Light Brigade had not yet been employed so he decided to give Cardigan the chance he had so evidently wanted. According to Cardigan, the order to charge was given to him in what can only be described as an entirely unsatisfactory fashion. The following was written by Cardigan on 27 October:

> On the afternoon of the 25th Inst. when in sight of the Russian Army, I perceived that our Cavalry were on the point of being employed, I sent my Aide de Camp Lt F Maxse to the Lt General Comg the Division to say that the heights which flanked the valley leading to the Russian battery of heavy guns was covered with Artillery & Riflemen. The answer was we were going to attack. A few minutes afterwards the Lt General came in front of the Brigade, ordered the 11th Hussars to fall back in support and told me to attack the Russians in the Valley, about ¾ of [a] mile distant with the 13th Lt Dragoons & 17th Lancers. I answered 'certainly but allow me to point out to you that the hills on either side are covered with Artillery & Riflemen.' The Lt General replied 'I cannot help it, you must attack, Lord Raglan desires the Lt Brigade immediately to attack the enemy'.[15]

Lucan's recollection differed quite significantly, in light of the recriminations that later followed:

> With General Airey's order in my hand, I trotted up to Lord Cardigan, and gave him distinctly its contents so far as they concerned him, I would not on my oath say that I did not read the order to him. He at once objected, on the ground that he would be exposed to a flanking battery. When ordered to take up his then position, he had expressed, through his aide-de-camp, the same apprehensions. I told him that I was aware of it. 'I know it,' but that 'Lord Raglan would have it,' and that we had no choice but to obey. I then said that I wished him to advance very steadily and quietly, and that I would narrow his front by removing the 11th Hussars from the first to the second line. This he strenuously opposed; but I moved across his front and directed Colonel Douglas not to advance with the rest of the line, but to form a second line with the 4th Light Dragoons.[16]

Of course, so poor was the relationship between the two earls, they were unable to discuss Raglan's instructions properly. Angered by Nolan's attitude, which had implied that Lucan was being deliberately obtuse by asking which guns he was supposed to attack, and contemptuous of his brother-in-law, Lucan merely passed on the order with little elaboration. Cardigan, in all fairness, pointed out the impracticality of the order to attack. But after his objections had been dismissed by Lucan, he was too proud to protest further. He would never allow his hated relation to accuse him of challenging one of his orders.

The Special Correspondent of the *Morning Chronicle* relayed these crucial exchanges to his readers from outside Sevastopol on 28 October:

> A little after nine o'clock, Captain Nolan of the 15th Hussars, aide-de-camp to General Airie [*sic*], arrived at full gallop before Lord Lucan, and handed him a written order to attack the enemy … The Earl Lucan, it is now said, hesitated at the madness of the instructions given to him; but certain it is orders were given by him to his Brigadier, the Earl of Cardigan, to prepare to charge.[17]

The dye, then, was cast. According to Lucan, 'Having decided, against my Conviction, to make the Movement, I did all in my Power to render it as little perilous as possible. I formed the Light Brigade in Two Lines, and led to its Support Two Regiments of Heavy Cavalry, the Scots Greys and Royal Dragoons.'[18]

Cardigan now had to explain what was about to happen to Lord George Paget, second-in-command of the Light Brigade:

> The first intimation I received of our intended attack was conveyed by Lord Cardigan riding up to me and saying, 'Lord George, we are ordered to make an attack to the front. You will take command of the second line, and I expect your best support, *mind, your best support,*' this last sentence being repeated more than once, and perhaps with rather a marked emphasis, as I thought, though it was probably more the result of excitement than anything else. But it caused me to answer with equal emphasis, 'Of course, my Lord, you shall have my best support.' He then galloped back to his troops.[19]

Private Henry Naylor of 'D' Troop, 13th Light Dragoons recounts the events of that morning after the repulse of the Russian cavalry by the Heavy Brigade:

> We had been dismounted about a half of an hour when we saw an aide-de-camp coming up towards us at a gallop, which turned out to be Captain Nolan. When he gave his last order, we had not long to wait, we soon knew what it was, we were ordered to mount and form in two lines, the 17th, 13th and 11th in the front line, the 4th and 8th in the second line.[20]

As he was already present with the cavalry, Nolan sought permission from Lord Cardigan to ride with the Light Brigade in the attack. This was seen by James Wightman:

> I distinctly remember that Nolan returned to the brigade, and having a mere momentary talk with Cardigan, at the close of which he drew his sword with a flourish, as if greatly excited. The blood came into his face – I seem to see him now; and then he fell back a little way into Cardigan's left rear, somewhat in front of and to the right of Captain Morris.[21]

Though there has been speculation over what was said in this exchange between Cardigan and Nolan nothing is known for certain, other than the latter took up the position described by Wightman.

It might be noted at this time that although Lucan had been told that he could use the horse artillery troop that was attached to the Cavalry Division as well as the French cavalry, Lucan appeared to have failed to involve either. This, it will shortly be seen, may not have been the case, but it was remarked on by Regimental Sergeant-Major George Loy Smith:

> Strange as it may seem, although 12 Horse Artillery guns were at this moment close at hand, the divisional general made no use of them before he ordered the attack. It had been the custom on brigade field days for artillery fire to precede a cavalry attack. Had this simple rule been followed out on the Causeway Heights for a few minutes before we moved off, it would have been of the greatest advantage to us, for it was the enemy's guns and infantry posted there that caused us the greatest losses – both going down the valley and returning. This was a most unfortunate omission for us.[22]

After muttering 'Here goes the last of the Brudenells', Cardigan turned his horse to face his men: 'He threw a look of profound sadness (we have been told by one who was near him) over the splendid squadrons whom an inevitable death was about so soon to decimate,' wrote Baron de Bazancourt.[23] The major general then issued the order, 'The brigade will advance. First squadron of the 17th Lancers direct.' Billy Britten was told to sound the advance, and the Light Brigade moved off at a walk into the Valley of Death.

Chapter 9

'Magnificent But Not War'

In a charge, it is essential that the cavalry retains formation so that it can crash into the enemy in one solid mass. It is also important that the horses are at full gallop during the crucial final stages of the charge to have the greatest impact. These two requirements mean that the early stages of a charge are conducted in a very measured and controlled manner, first at a walk then a trot. The 17th Lancers, their nine-foot long lances certain to have a devastating effect upon the Russians, were on the left-centre of the front line, with Captain Robert White's squadron the squadron of direction. To the right of the lancers was the 13th Light Dragoons. In front rode their brigadier, controlling the pace of the advance, as watched by James Wightman:

> Cardigan looked the ideal cavalry leader, with his stern firm face, and his quiet soldierly bearing. His long military seat was perfection on the thoroughbred chestnut 'Ronald' with the 'white-stockings' on the near hind and fore, which my father, his old riding-master, had broken for him. He was in the full uniform of his old corps, the 11th Hussars, and he wore the pelisse, not slung, but put on like a patrol jacket, its front one blaze of gold lace. His drawn sword was in his hand at the slope, and never saw I a man fitter to wield the weapon.[1]

According to Private Dennis Connor of the 4th Light Dragoons, the men were all 'perfectly cool and collected:

> When the order was given I heard the men chaffing each other. One would tell another that he 'would lose the number of his mess that day', meaning that he would be shot; others said, 'Here goes for victory!' whilst others declared they would have Russian biscuits for dinner.[2]

William Russell's account of the charge printed in *The Times* on 14 November, gives details of the numbers involved, though the general consensus is that the total was a little under 670. 'The whole brigade,' he wrote, 'scarcely made one effective regiment, according to the numbers of continental armies; and yet it was more than we could spare':

> At 11.10 our Light Cavalry Brigade rushed to the front. They numbered as follows, as well as I can I ascertain: -
> Men
> 4th Light Dragoons 118
> 8th Irish Hussars 104
> 11th Prince Albert's Hussars ... 110
> 13th Light Dragoons 130
> 17th Lancers ... ... <u>145</u>
> Total 607 sabres.

According to Lord George Paget the second line, under his command, was formed up about 100 yards behind the first line. When the brigade moved off the second line did so at a somewhat reduced pace to allow the first line to stretch the space between the lines to the regulation 200 yards. He wrote that the 13th Light Dragoons and 17th Lancers advanced in one line down the right of the valley, with the 11th Hussars 'in rather an oblique direction towards the left of the valley'. The 4th Light Dragoons were somewhat behind and to the right of the 11th. The 8th Hussars were to the right of the 4th.

Private Joseph Grigg, of the 4th Light Dragoons, explained the reason for the gap between the two lines: 'The lines were about a hundred yards apart, so that when a man went down with his horse, the man behind him had time to turn his horse on one side or jump over the obstacle.'[3]

It was as the second line was moving off down the valley, 200 yards behind the front line, when the first shot was fired at the Light Brigade. It came from Fedioukine Heights where two batteries from Major General O.P. Zhabokritski's division were posted.[4]

That first shot was spectacularly accurate: 'After advancing about eighty yards,' Cardigan said after the battle, 'a shell fell within reach of my horse's feet, and Captain Nolan, who was riding across the front, retreated with his arm up through the intervals of the brigade.'[5] The incident was witnessed by many, including Private Wightman:

> We had ridden barely 200 yards, and were still at the trot, when poor Nolan's fate came to him. I did not see him across Cardigan's front,

but I did see the shell explode of which a fragment struck him. From his raised sword-hand dropped the sword, but the sword-arm remained erect … but all the other limbs so curled in on the contorted trunk as by a spasm, that we wondered how for the moment the huddled form kept the saddle. It was the sudden convulsive twitch of the bridle hand inward on the chest, that caused the charge[r] to wheel rearward so abruptly. The weird shriek and the awful face haunt me now to this day, the first horror of that ride of horrors.

Another trooper, Private Henry Naylor, rode with the 13th Light Dragoons:

The first shell burst and killed poor Nolan. I shall never forget the shriek that he gave; it rung in my ears above the roaring of the cannon; when his horse turned and passed through the interval of squadrons and fell; that was the last I saw of Capt. Nolan.[6]

Kinglake provided a more detailed account based on interviews with survivors:

But a Russian shell bursting on the right front of Lord Cardigan now threw out a fragment which met Nolan full on the chest, and tore a way into his heart. The sword dropt from his hand; but the arm with which he was waving it the moment before still remained high uplifted in the air, and the grip of the practised horseman remaining as yet unrelaxed still held him firm in his saddle.

Missing the perfect hand of his master, and finding the accustomed governance now succeeded by dangling reins, the horse all at once wheeled about, and began to gallop back upon the front of the advancing brigade. Then from what had been Nolan—and his form was still erect in the saddle, his sword-arm still high in the air—there burst forth a cry so strange and appalling that the hearer who rode the nearest to him has always called it 'unearthly.' And in truth, I imagine the sound resulted from no human will, but rather from those spasmodic forces which may act upon the bodily frame when life, as a power, has ceased.

The firm-seated rider, with arm uplifted and stiff, could hardly be ranked with the living. The shriek men heard rending the air was scarce other than the shriek of a corpse. This dead horseman rode on till he had passed through the interval of the 13th Light Dragoons. Then at last he dropt out of the saddle.[7]

Lieutenant Calthorpe, the man whose turn it had been to carry the order to Lucan, watched the drama unfold from the Sapoune Heights:

> It [the Light Brigade] consisted of scarce 700 horses, although composed of no less than 5 different regiments. In the first line were 4 squadrons of the 13th Light Dragoons and 17th Lancers; in the second were 4 squadrons of the 4th Light Dragoons and 11th Hussars. Again, in their rear was 1 squadron of the 8th Hussars, as a sort of reserve. As they started into a trot, poor Nolan galloped some way in front of the brigade, waving his sword and encouraging his men by voice and gesture. Before they had gone any distance the enemy's guns opened on them at long range. Nolan was the first man killed; some grape-shot hit him in the chest: his horse turned and carried him to the rear through our advancing squadrons. His screams were heard far above the din of battle, and he fell dead from his saddle near the spot where the order had been given for the charge.[8]

James Lamb of the 13th Light Dragoons, writing in *Strand Magazine*, recalled:

> I was riding together with Captain Nolan when he was mortally wounded. The next discharge tore wide gaps through our ranks and many a trooper died. Owing to the dense smoke I lost sight of him.[9]

Captain The Honourable Godfery Charles Morgan of the 17th Lancers had a clear view of the incident:

> We had not gone many yards before we were under fire of the first heavy battery on our left – the first shot from which killed poor Nolan, a splinter going right through his heart. He was a dashing young fellow, and, with a smile on his face, was riding about twenty yards in front of us.[10]

Lastly, we have the version related by Corporal James Nunnerley, also of the 17th Lancers. Being in the first line of the right squadron he saw Nolan ride up to Cardigan who was in front of the left squadron. After delivering the order, and being granted permission to join the Lancers in the advance, he heard Nolan say to Captain Morris 'Now, Morris, for a bit of fun!'. Scarcely had he uttered these words, according to Nunnerley, than he was struck:

After giving a kind of yell which sounded very much like 'Three right', and throwing his sword hand above his head, his horse wheeled to the right and he fell to the rear. As though obeying this death-like order, part of the Squadron wheeled, 'Threes right'. I immediately gave the order 'Front forward' and so brought them into line again.[11]

Private Wightman continued his detailed account of the charge which appeared in *The Nineteenth Century* magazine in May 1892:

As the line at the trumpet sound broke from the trot into the gallop, Lord Cardigan, almost directly behind whom I rode, turned his head leftward toward Captain Morris and shouted hoarsely, 'Steady, steady, Captain Morris!' The injunction was no doubt pointed specially at the latter, because he, commanding the regiment one of the squadrons of which had been named to direct, was held in a manner responsible to the brigade commander for both pace and direction of the whole line. Later, when we were in the midst of our torture, and, mad to be out of it and have our revenge, were forcing the pace, I heard again, high above the turmoil and din, Cardigan's sonorous command, 'Steady, steady, the 17th Lancers.'

Corporal Thomas Morley was one of those Lancers:

If we had been moving over uneven ground we should have had some slight protection in the necessary uncertainty of aim of the guns, but moving as we did in compact bodies on smooth ground directly in range, the enemy gunners had an admirable target and every volley came with terrible effect.

There is a natural instinct to dodge cannon balls. In such fire as we were under it changed to an impulse to hurry. There was no time to look left or right, and the guns in front were what I looked out for. They were visible as streaks of fire about two feet long, and a foot thick in the centre of a gush of thick white smoke, marking about every three hundred yards of the way, as they would reload in 30 or 40 seconds.[12]

Captain Morgan of the 17th Lancers wrote that he did not recall hearing any instructions to increase speed as the noise of the men and horses being struck by shells and round shot was deafening, but the brigade gradually broke from a trot to a canter, and 'the dust and gravel struck up by the round shot that fell short was almost blinding, and irritated my horse so that I could scarcely hold him.'

As always William Russell of *The Times* provides one of the liveliest reports of the charge:

> As they passed towards the front, the Russians opened on them from the guns in the redoubt on the right, with volleys of musketry and rifles. They swept proudly past, glittering in the morning sun in all the pride and splendour of war. We could scarcely believe the evidence of our senses! Surely that handful of men are not going to charge an army in position? Alas! it was but too true – their desperate valour knew no bounds, and far indeed was it removed from its so-called better part-discretion.
>
> They advanced in two lines, quickening their pace as they closed towards the enemy. A more fearful spectacle was never witnessed than by those who, without the power to aid, beheld their heroic countrymen rushing to the arms of death. At the distance of 1,200 yards the whole line of the enemy belched forth, from 30 iron mouths, a flood of smoke and flame, through which hissed the deadly balls.
>
> Their flight was marked by instant gaps in our ranks, by dead men and horses, by steeds flying wounded or riderless across the plain.

As Cardigan led his men forward more Russian guns were brought to bear on the Light Brigade including those of the Heavy Battery No.1 and Light Battery No.2 on the Causeway Heights, which were covered by a line of carabineers of the Odessa Chasseur Regiment and the riflemen of Colonel A.P. Skiuderi's detachment. The composition of the Russian force at the head of the valley was given by Staff-Captain Yevgenii Arbuzov:

> In our rear was the canal [River Tchernaya] and the bridge over it, and in front was Sapoune Hill. In this position we were deployed in the following manner: in front of everyone, across the whole width of the valley, were placed Light No. 12 Horse Battery, the Don Cossack heavy battery, and a heavy foot battery; forty paces from the artillery, in the first line, was the Ural Cossack Regiment with an extended front; in the second line, at the same distance [i.e. forty paces] from the first line, was the Kiev Hussar Regiment in attack columns; forty paces from them, in the third line, in an extended front, were deployed five badly hurt squadrons of our

Ingermanland Hussar Regiment. Behind us in the bushes, a little to the left, stood the combined regiment of Lancers, which had not been in the fighting, under the command of Colonel Yeropkin; on the Ural Cossacks' right flank, at a right angle both to them and to the attacking enemy, was placed our regiment's 7th Squadron.[13]

Ahead of the Light Brigade therefore was Colonel Prince Obolensky's Don Cossack No.3 Battery of four 6-pounders and four 9-pounder howitzers and, it would seem another half battery, Light Horse Battery No.12, though this is disputed by most British historians.[14] The disposition of the Russian force was also described by an unknown officer of the Don Cossack Battery, which appears to confirm the dispositions given by Arbuzov, though with some notable irregularities:

> The artillery battle ended with the taking of Redoubt No. 3, and Don Heavy No. 3 Battery withdrew to Redoubt No. 1 to deploy with an extended front across the Balaklava Valley. On its right it had the Fedioukine Heights on which were deployed General Zhabokritski's infantry, while on the left, in the redoubts, was the infantry of General Liprandi. In the battery's rear were the two hussar regiments: in echelon behind, on the right flank – the Leuchtenberg, and on the left – the Weimar in columns by squadron. Ural Cossack No. 1 Regiment stood at the foot of the Fedioukine Heights, with a squadron of Aleksandrin's Regiment to its left, under the command of Voiskovoi Starshina Porfirii Kon'kov. To the right of the Don battery was deployed Colonel Brombeus' Horse Artillery No. 12 Battery.[15]

Though Raglan had wanted the cavalry to recapture the guns from the Causeway Heights' redoubts, it was the guns at the end of the valley that the Light Brigade was now moving inexorably towards. Lucan ordered the Heavy Brigade to support the charge of Cardigan's men and it was Sergeant John Louden who sounded the advance of the Heavies:

> I was alongside General Scarlett when he gave the order, 'The Heavy Brigade will support the Lights.' These were, I believe, his exact words. The Lights had then broken into a gallop, and were close to 'The Valley of Death.' I sounded, and soon myself and General Scarlett were some 30 yards in front of the advancing squadrons.[16]

Troop Sergeant-Major Henry Franks of the 5th Dragoon Guards also related the advance of the Heavy Brigade in support of the Light Brigade:

Three of us were riding close together – Troop Sgt Major Russell on the right, myself in the centre, and Trumpeter Baker on the left of the three. We were moving at a trot, when a shell from the Russians dropped and exploded close under the three Horses. The whole of the contents of the shell seemed to have entered into the body of Russell's horse and literally shattered him to pieces. Russell was shot over the horses' head and was on his feet again in a moment none the worse for his sudden flight. The shock of the shell exploding actually lifted both my horse and Baker's off their feet, but that was all the injury we sustained. Russell caught hold of my right foot stirrup and ran along for a few yards, until he caught a horse that had lost its rider, and then joined us again.[17]

The leg of one of the 2nd Dragoons, Private Alexander Gardiner, was shattered by a round shot and he fell to the ground, lying helpless amidst the crossfire of the enemy artillery on the heights. Another dragoon 'dashed' to Gardiner's help and carried him back to safety. That dragoon was Sergeant Henry Ramage who had already distinguished himself in the Heavy Brigade charge and who would see the saving of Private Gardiner added to his citation for the awarded the Victoria Cross.

Lucan, it would appear had failed, or forgotten, to inform the artillery troop to accompany the Light Brigade, so Captain J.W. Shakespear took it upon himself to support Cardigan's men:

It is well known that on Major Maude falling seriously wounded early in the day I, who had been with him in four previous actions and affairs, succeeded to the command of his troop. Passing over all previous occurrences of that day, I had brought my guns up at a gallop on the left flank of the Heavy Cavalry, while reforming after their charge. The light Cavalry, having passed along my rear, were on my left flank.

It must, now be remembered that the whole cavalry brigade were in the plain on the Balaklava side of the heights on which were the redoubts. My troop would be about 600 yards from the crest of those heights. Considering all immediate action over, if not, indeed, the whole thing for the day, I rode over the heights to reconnoitre. I there met Lieutenant-Colonel McMahon, the Quartermaster-General of Cavalry. We were alone, and with our telescopes were examining the Russian Artillery in the bush on the opposite heights across the second plain. The distance would be about 1,500 yards. I had counted 10 guns; there were other guns further on to the left of these. There was cavalry, infantry, and artillery in the plain, nearly a mile away. I knew that the Russians held Nos. l, 2, and 3 redoubts, which, it must be remembered, faced the bush I have before, mentioned.

Captain Charteris rode up to us: he was accompanied, I think, by Captain Methuen, of the screw steam ship *Colombo*. The former said, 'You will see something now; the Light Cavalry are going to attack down the plain.' I exclaimed, 'You will all be destroyed. I will go and bring up the troop and try and give assistance. I galloped back; I could not see Lord Lucan; but, Major-General Scarlett being close at hand, I said, 'Will you allow me to go to the support of the Light Cavalry?' His answer was, 'Certainly.'[18]

Though Shakesper tried his best to join the Light Brigade, it had moved too far down the valley for him to catch it up: 'I moved off at a smart trot, seeing the rear regiments of the Light Cavalry just slip out of sight over the heights. My horses were tired and reduced in numbers, several having been killed in the early part of the day; so I soon came to a walk.'

It has often been remarked upon that Lucan's failure to include the horse artillery was a serious mistake. There is, however, a slightly different story to this, as Shakesper himself acknowledged:

The Scots Grays [*sic*] had moved before me, and had halted in line, just at the foot of the heights. I passed through their squadron at intervals. At this time Major Walker, Lord Lucan's aide-de-camp, rode up to me, and, in a conversation I had with him afterwards, he said, 'with an order for me to advance.' I perfectly remember his being with me, but have no recollection of this order. Had he brought me directions to do otherwise than I was doing, I should, probably have paid more attention. Major Walker in speaking to me on the subject afterwards said, 'My life war probably saved by being sent back for you.' I passed on over the heights with the troop; a heavy fire was immediately opened on me, happily without effect, from the artillery in the bush on the opposite heights; to this I could not reply, the range being too great for my light guns. I at once 'wheeled to the right,' and endeavoured to pass along the Balaklava side of the heights immediately below their crest, screened from the enemy's fire, and so come over, if possible, on the right rear of our Light Cavalry but a cut down into the Woronzoff road, past which I could not get my guns, prevented me. I wheeled about and followed the Heavy Cavalry, which had now come up, down into the plain in support of the Light Cavalry.

The fire at this time from the Russian front and flanks was tremendous. I halted for a moment in the rear of the Heavy Cavalry, but, not being able to make my guns of any use, seeing the disaster and knowing from previous observation that descending further into the plain was taking the troop to certain destruction and giving the guns intrusted to my care into the hands of the enemy, I retired at a walk to the crest of the heights on my own responsibility

John Louden, who had sounded the advance of the Heavy Brigade, also related the circumstances of the brigade being halted:

Suddenly he [Scarlett] turned around in the saddle and exclaimed, 'Why! The Heavies are retiring! Have you sounded retire?' He was very much excited. I replied, 'No, General.'

We galloped back and met Lord Lucan. It was he who had stopped the Heavies. As near as I can recollect, Lord Lucan said to General Scarlett, 'We've lost the Light Brigade and we must save the Heavies'.

Lieutenant Colonel Charles Beauchamp Walker, although an aide on the staff of Lord Raglan, rode with the Heavy Brigade in support of Cardigan's men. His letter, written on the 29th, shows how severely affected the heavies were by the Russian guns before they were halted by Lucan.

Lord Lucan immediately ordered the Light Cavalry to attack down the valley, a distance of a mile and a half, as it proved into a terrain which was completely swept by the Russian artillery. As soon as we came within range, they opened on us from a line of guns formed right across the valley, from some more guns very well placed on their left, but which were partially occupied by the fire of our artillery, and on our left by a line of guns planted on the ridge of hills near the Black River. Before they opened fire I saw these guns or rather saw the horses and I pulled out my glass, and in a moment saw what they were, and how completely they swept the whole length of our advance. I would not live over that moment for a kingdom. My only consolation was seeing two squadrons of Chasseurs d'Afrique stealing on them up the hill, and after they had pounded us for about ten minutes they did succeed in dislodging them, but were themselves repulsed with some loss by a body of Russian infantry which was in support. I thought the fire on the 17th was pretty heavy, but it was a joke to this, which certainly for eight or ten minutes exceeded my liveliest conception. I hope I shall not again get such a pelting.[19]

Private John Vahey, the regimental butcher of the 17th Lancers, was actually under guard for being drunk on duty the night before with a Paddy Hefferman of the 1st Royals. The cannonading in the morning woke the two prisoners who, when they peered out of the tent in which they were being held, found that not only was there no-one guarding the tent, but that the entire cavalry camp was deserted. Realising that something 'big' was afoot, the two men were determined not to miss the action. So they went on foot up the South Valley, reaching there just after the charge of the Heavy Brigade. They saw a number of rider-less Russian horses running around and managed to capture two of them. The two men then rode up to the where the Heavy Brigade was posted.

'I was bareheaded, and my hair was like a birch-broom in a fit,' wrote Vahey, 'I was minus a coat, with my shirt-sleeves turned up to the shoulder, and my shirt, face, and bare hairy arms were all splashed and darkened with blood, which I had picked up at the butchering the day before, and had never wiped off. A pair of long, greasy jack-boots came up to the thigh, and instead of a sword I had an axe over my shoulder.'

The two men formed up with the 1st Royal Dragoons as the Heavy Brigade prepared to support the Light Brigade, but was 'ordered off'. So, seeing the plumes of the lancer-caps of his regiment bobbing ahead, and being determined not to miss the action, Vahey made up his mind to join his comrades, and he galloped forward and managed to catch up with the 17th just before they set off down the valley:

> Just as I came up in line with the flank sergeant of the front rank, who looked sideways at me as if I had been a ghost, Cardigan turned round in his saddle to say a word to the trumpeter riding at his heels, and then with a wave of his sword went off at score out to the front.[20]

According to Troop Sergeant-Major Joseph Pardoe of the 1st Dragoons, Vahey had somewhat over-elaborated his story when he related it after the charge. 'I can at this point retell the true story of Butcher Jack,' Pardo later declared:

> He came up between two squadrons of the 1st Dragoons and joined us as we advanced, in fact he was on my right hand. Colonel Yorke

looked round and said to me, Sergeant that man does not belong to my regiment, who is he? The man answered, I belong to the 17th Lancers, sir. Colonel Yorke replied, I admire your spirit my man, but you had better join your own regiment. He replied, all right sir, and galloped away ... He was not mounted on a grey horse, nor had he an axe in his hand, he had no coat on and his shirt sleeves were turned up. He had one sword in his hand and one in a scabbard buckled round his waist.[21]

Vahey did reach the Light Brigade which, alone and only supported by the Heavy Brigade at a distance, moved steadily down the valley. *'C'est magnifique, mais ce n'est pas la guerre: c'est de la folie'*; 'It is magnificent, but it is not war: it is madness', declared General Pierre Bosquet from the Sapoune Heights.

Amid all that madness, riding with the 8th Hussars, was Lieutenant Edward Seagar on his horse 'Malta':

On the hills on each side of the Valley, the Russian guns, and also on our right a line of Infantry, armed with Minié Rifles. The whole of this force we had to pass before we got to their cavalry. We advanced in three lines, the 8th the last line went in support. There were about 100 of our regiment in the field. We advanced at a trot and soon came within the Cross fire from both hills, both of cannon & rifles; the fire was tremendous, shells bursting amongst us, Cannon balls tearing the earth up and Minié balls coming like hail. Still on we went, never altering our pace or breaking up in the least, except that our men and horses were gradually knocked over. Our men behaved well. Poor [Lieutenant John Viscount] Fitzgibbon was shot through the body and fell, he was supposed to be dead. [Cornet George] Clowes' horse was shot under him and that was the last that was seen of him, he was walking towards where he started from and we suppose he was taken prisoner or killed. Up to this time I was riding in front of the men and on the right of the line of officers ... [Captain Edward] Tomkinson who commanded the squadron had his horse shot under him. I then took command of the squadron and placed myself in front of the centre. Malta had just previously got a ball through her neck, just above the windpipe, but went bravely on.[22]

Private, later Troop-Sergeant, Berryman was at the front of the brigade with the 17th Lancers:

'Gallop' was the order as the firing became general. A discharge from the battery to our front, whose guns were double-shotted, first with shot or shell, then with case, swept away Captain Winter and the division on my right. The gap was noticed by Captain Morris who ordered 'Right Incline' but a warning came from my coverer, Corporal John Penn, 'Keep straight on, Jack'. He saw what I did not, that we were opposite the intervals of the guns and thus we escaped. My attention was attracted by James Melrose, a Shakespearian recite, calling out, 'What man here would ask another from England?' Poor fellow, the next round killed him and many others. This round broke my mare's off-hind leg and caused her to stop instantly.[23]

Private Robert Ashton was with the 11th Hussars:

My first horse was shot under me a very short time after we started. After being dismounted, Sergeant Fleming was near me, and I caught hold of the bridle of his horse. He said, 'Leave go, or we shall both be killed.' The bridle slipped out of my hand, and as the horse passed me I managed to catch his tail, to which I held on for a few yards; but the pace at which he was going was too much for me, and I was obliged to let go. Shortly afterwards I saw a horse belonging to the 4th Light Dragoons coming towards me, which, after some difficulty, I succeeded in catching, and, mounting it, I proceeded down the valley.[24]

A soldier of the 4th Light Dragoons wrote a letter to his mother, which was printed in the *Bath Chronicle and Weekly Gazette* of Thursday, 23 November 1854:

I shall never forget the 25th of October–shells, bullets, cannon balls and swords kept flying all about us. I escaped them all, and except a scar on my nose, from the bursting of a shell, and a slight touch on my shoulder from a cannon ball, after it killed one of our horses; but God be thanked, it did not disable me. The Russians fight hard and well, but we will make them yield yet. Dear mother, every time I think of my poor comrades it makes my blood run cold, to think how we had to gallop over the poor wounded fellows lying on the field of battle, with anxious looks for assistance–what a sickening scene! In one part of the battle I lost my horse, owing to the one in front of me being shot dead, and my poor horse fell over it, and I was unhorsed; in getting up my horse took fright and got from me;

but fortunately for me, I saw another that some poor fellow of the 8th Hussars had been killed from; I mounted it in a moment, and was in the rank again.

On our return from the charge I got my own horse again; he had galloped back to the camp, and, dear parents, I was as glad when I saw him there as if I had half the whole world [had been] given to me.

Private Lamb of the 13th Light Dragoons continued with his description of the charge up to the point where he was hit:

We still kept on at a gallop ... the crossfire of the battery on our right opened a deadly crossfire with canister and grape, causing great havoc amongst out men and horses, mowing them down in heaps. I myself was rendered insensible.

Baron de Bazancourt, who asserted that he related the charge 'in all its details, with the most scrupulous and impartial exactitude,' wrote as follows:

The troops, placed in successive lines, on the summit and on the slopes of the hills, saw, with the most painful sensations, that superb brigade dash across the plain to an impossible attack, the madness of which could be equalled only by its heroism. All hearts throbbed, all eyes followed them, till they were lost in clouds of smoke. Amidst the iron hail which showered upon them, they passed rapid as lightning, dashing on towards those murderous batteries which vomited upon them. This hurricane, which the fire of cannon could not check, greatly astonished the enemy. The horsemen bounded up the hills, dashed past the batteries, and cut their way through dense columns, opening wide gaps, in their deadly career.[25]

Lord George Paget was trying to keep the second line together, and to give Cardigan the support he had promised:

We rode on in this disposition for perhaps a third of a mile, when the 8th Hussars would gradually incline away to our right, though I continually holloaed to them to keep to us. During the advance, however, the 11th dropped in rear of the 13th, which brought the former and the 4th into action with the enemy about the same time, the 8th having gradually fallen to our rear. When I, with the 11th and 4th, got to the guns, and saw all their host advancing, I looked

in vain for the first line, and could never account for them, till I came
back and said, 'I am afraid the 13th and 17th are annihilated, for I
saw nothing of them;' when I found that the few of them remaining
had returned, unobserved by me, by ones and twos, and that they
had got back first; so that in fact, when we had got to the end of this
horrid valley, the 11th and 4th were the last left there ...

Oh, how nobly the fellows behaved! At one time we were,
between four fires, or rather four attacks — right and left, front and
rear. That is, a heavy fire from right and left, and cavalry in front
and rear; and during all this time the fellows kept cheering.[26]

Up on the Sapoune Heights Raglan and his staff watched on in dismay
as, instead of moving up to intercept the Russians withdrawing from
the Causeway Heights, the Light Brigade continued down the North
Valley. Lieutenant Calthorpe continued his narrative:

The pace of our cavalry increased every moment, until they went
thundering along the valley, making the ground tremble beneath
them. The awful slaughter that was going on, from the fire the
enemy poured into them, apparently did not check their career. On
they went, headlong to the death, disregarding aught but the object
of their attack.[27]

Henry Clifford, aide-de-camp to Sir George Brown, watched the charge
which he described as 'the most useless and shocking sacrifice of the
lives of hundreds of brave men that was ever witnessed.' Though it is
not possible to state exactly where he was positioned at the time, he did
mention that he saw both Raglan and Canrobert with their staff, so it is
possible that he was also on the Sapoune Heights:

From the commanding position in which I stood by the side of
General Brite [Bosquet] we saw the Light Brigade of Cavalry moving
forward at a trot, in face of the Russian Army. '*Mon Dieu*!!' said the
fine old French General, '*Oue vont-ils faire?*' They went steadily on,
as Englishmen only go under fire. Artillery in front, on the right and
left. When some thousand yards from the foremost of the enemy, I
saw shells bursting in the midst of the Squadrons and men and
horses strewed the ground behind them; yet on they went, and the
smoke of the murderous fire poured on them, hid them from my
sight.

The tears ran down my face, and the din of musketry pouring in
their murderous fire on the brave gallant fellows rang in my ears.

'Pauvre garcon,' said the old French General, patting me on the shoulder. '*Je suis vieux, j'ai vu des batailles, mais ceci est trop.*' Then the smoke cleared away and I saw hundreds of our poor fellows lying on the ground, the Cossacks and Russian Cavalry running them through as they lay, with their swords and lances.[28]

Private Thomas Dudley of the 17th Lancers stated that when they received the order to charge, 'not a man seemed to believe it'. However, as he wrote to his parents on 18 December, on they went:

During that ride what each man felt no one can tell. I cannot tell you my own thoughts. Not a word or a whisper. On – on we went! Oh! If you could have seen the faces of that doomed 800 men at that moment; every man's features fixed, his teeth clenched, and as rigid as death, still it was on – on! At about 300 yards I got my hit, but it did not floor me. Clash! And oh God! What a scene! I will not attempt to tell you, as I know it is not to your taste, what we did; but we were Englishmen, and that is enough. I believe I was as strong as six men – at least I felt so; for I know I had chopped two Russian lances in two as if they had been reeds.[29]

Riding with the 4th Light Dragoons was Sergeant John George Baker. He wrote about the charge to his parents and the letter was printed in the *Leeds Mercury* under the heading 'Soldier's Letter from the Crimea' on 2 January 1855:

At this time, the Light Brigade formed up on the left, on some ground which commanded a long valley about two miles long, at the end of which the enemy retired. By some misunderstanding, we were ordered to advance and charge the guns, which they had formed up full in our front at the extreme end, and here took place a scene which is unparalleled in history. We had scarcely advanced a few yards, before they opened on us with grape, shot and shell. It was a perfect level, the ground only enough for the 17th and 13th to advance, the rest of the brigade following. To our astonishment, they had erected batteries on each side of the hills, which commanded the whole valley: consequently, a dreadful cross-fire opened on us from both sides and in front, but it was too late to do anything but advance, which we did in a style truly wonderful, every man feeling certainly that we must be annihilated.

According to Lieutenant General Ryzov, the Don Cossack gunners,

Cheered as they realised that these insane cavalrymen were riding straight at the muzzles of their guns. As the enemy came within range, the order to fire was given … The Don Cossack gun crews were loading and firing every thirty seconds. A thick bank of smoke rolled over the battery at each volley and for a time the gunners lost sight of the target, then just before they fired again there the British were – the roundshot and shell was wreaking havoc …

At close range the deadly contents of the [canister] shot from each gun would have a spread of ten yards, and every man and horse within that arc would be hit … [and] by loading a roundshot on top of the canister it was possible to fire double-shotted. No force of cavalry could ride through such an iron storm and live to tell of it.[30]

Yet many did live to tell of it, including Private Mitchell, who continues his story of the charge from immediately after the death of Nolan:

In a few minutes several casualties occurred, for by this time the guns in our front were playing on us with round shot and shell, so the number of men and horses falling increased every moment. I rode near the right of the line. A corporal who rode on the right was struck by a shot or shell full in the face, completely smashing it, his blood and brains bespattering us who rode near. His horse still went with us. By this time, the ranks being continually broken it caused some confusion. Oaths and imprecations might be heard between the report of the guns and the bursting of the shells, as the men crowded and jostled each other in their endeavour to close to the centre. This was unavoidable at times, especially when a shell burst in the ranks, sometimes bringing down three or four men and horses, which made it difficult to avoid an unpleasant crush in the ranks. We were now fully exposed to the fire from all three batteries – front, right, and left – as also the infantry on our right, who were now able to reach us. As we drew nearer the guns in our front supplied us liberally with grape and canister, which brought down men and horses in heaps.[31]

A Private of the 11th Hussars, Robert Martin, gave an interview recounting his 'reminiscences' of the charge to the *Birkenhead and Cheshire Advertiser and Wallasey Guardian* on 28 October 1899:

The fire from the enemy then became most murderous from the flank batteries on our right and left, while the guns in front were belching forth their deadly missiles and making complete streets through our ranks. [Private David] Ward in front of me was blown to pieces, [Private George] Turner on my left hand side had his right arm blown off and afterwards died, and [Private Richard] Young, on my right also, had his right arm blown off. Just at that moment my right arm was shattered to pieces. I gathered it up as well as I could and laid it across my knees.

Private Edward Woodham of the 11th Hussars recalled how the brigade 'increased speed at every stride', and went down the valley 'at a terrific rate', though this is most certainly hyperbolic:

The scene that presented itself as we proceeded was indescribable; from all sides the bullets came flying, and many a men had his arm shot off, while our gallant comrades were falling from their horses in all directions. A battery on our right was firing shell, but we were galloping at such a pace that we had time to get away before the shells burst, and of course that, in a great measure, saved many of us from being wounded or killed.'

Sergeant Seth Bond was also with the 11th Hussars:

The smoke was almost too blinding. Horses and men were falling in every direction, and the horses that were not hurt were so upset that we could not keep them in a straight line for a time. A man named Alfred who was riding on my left fell from his horse like a stone. I looked back and saw the poor fellow lying on his back, his right temple being cut away and his brain partly on the ground.[32]

Lord George Paget remarked on one particular aspect of the charge which, he wrote, struck him forcibly, that of the numerous rider-less horses that galloped along with the rest of the brigade:

I was of course riding by myself [at the head of his regiment] and clear of the line, and for that reason was a marked object for the poor dumb brutes, who were by this time galloping about in numbers, like wild beasts. They consequently made dashes at me, some advancing with me a considerable distance, at one time as many as five on my right and two on my left, cringing in on me, and positively squeezing me, as the round shot came bounding by them, tearing the earth under their nostrils, my overalls being a mass of blood from their gory flanks.[33]

Private Robert Grant rode with the 4th Light Dragoons, relating details of the charge in the *Illustrated London News* of 30 October 1875:

> In the early part, a peculiar thing happened. A shot came over the hill and dropped on the neck of the horse of a man named Gowens [actually Private George Gowings]. The shot cut off the head as cleanly as with a knife. The horse stood still for a moment, and then dropped. Gowens got on a spare horse running by, and in a few minutes this horse's head was also shot clean away. On being asked if he was hurt, Gowens replied, 'Not a bit of it.'

It had taken only a few minutes for the Light Brigade to reach the point where the horses could be allowed full rein and, after the restrained discipline of the advance, the men could at last charge the Don Cossack battery stretched out across the valley. 'At length they arrived at the guns,' wrote Lieutenant Calthorpe, 'their numbers sadly thinned':

> But the few that remained made fearful havoc amongst the enemy's artillerymen. Scarce a man escaped, except those who crept under their gun-carriages, and thus put themselves out of the reach of our men's swords. This was the moment when a general was most required, but unfortunately Lord Cardigan was not then present. On coming up to the battery (as he afterwards himself described it) a gun was fired close to him, and for a moment he thought his leg was gone. Such was not the case, as he remained unhurt; however, his horse took fright—swerved round—and galloped off with him to the rear, passing on the way by the 4th Light Dragoons and 8th Hussars before those regiments got up to the battery.[34]

Calthorpe's words concerning the conduct of Lord Cardigan would, as shall later be seen, have serious repercussions. Corporal John Daniel Robinson of the 13th Light Dragoons had no doubt where Cardigan was, and even claimed to have saved the Earl's life:

> I did not ride many yards further before I saw our commander, Lord Cardigan, very nearly thrust off his horse and if it had not been for me the old boy's life would not be worth a row of pins. I saved him for I directly saw a Russian had marked him for he drew his lance and made at his Lordship, but I was too expert for the rascal, I parried, whilst the man struck, and then he bolted as if Old Nick were after him.[35]

William Russell watched the light cavalry as it crashed into the battery:

> The first line is broken, it is joined by the second, they never halt or check their speed an instant; with diminished ranks, thinned by those 30 guns, which the Russians had laid with the most deadly accuracy, with a halo of flashing steel above their heads, and with a cheer which was many a noble fellow's death-cry, they flew into the smoke of the batteries, but ere they were lost from view the plain was strewed with their bodies and with the carcasses of horses. They were exposed to an oblique fire from the batteries on the hills on both sides, as well as to a direct fire of musketry. Through the clouds of smoke we could see their sabres flashing as they rode up to the guns and dashed between them, cutting down the gunners as they stood.[36]

The 11th Hussar's Troop-Sergeant-Major Loy Smith, saw how well his troop had kept together despite the heavy fire and losses the regiment had sustained:

> We swept down the valley much nearer the Fedioukine Hills than any other regiment. The round shot passed through us and the shells burst over and amongst us, causing great havoc. The first man of my troop struck was Private Young, a cannon ball taking off his right arm. I, being close to his right ear, fancied I felt the wind as it passed me, I afterwards found I was bespattered with his flesh ... The [Russian] infantry kept up a continuous fusilage as we came opposite them, but the men hung well together, keeping their line and closing in as their comrades fell back wounded or killed. Many riderless horses of the first line were now galloping along with us, forcing their way into the ranks.[37]

In his memoirs, Cardigan proudly relates how he led his brigade into the guns:

> On coming at a steady pace within about eighty yards of the battery, consisting of about twelve or fourteen pieces of heavy ordnance, a fire was opened along the whole line of the battery. This was a very exciting moment, and one or two of the squadron leaders became much excited; but I succeeded in keeping them back, and we reached the battery in a very good line, and at the regulation pace.[38]

'Oh, such a charge,' wrote one of the 'Six Hundred':

140

From the moment we dashed at the enemy I knew nothing but that I was impelled by some irresistible force onward, and by some imperceptible influence to crush every obstacle which stumbled before my good sword and brave old charger. I never in my life experienced such a sublime sensation as in the moment of the charge. I know this, that it was such as made me a match for any two ordinary men and gave me such an amount of glorious indifference as to life as I thought it impossible to be master of. Forward – dash – bang – clank – and there we were in the midst of such smoke, cheer and clatter as never before stunned a mortal ear. It was glorious, I could not pause. It was all push, wheel, frenzy, strike, and down they went.[39]

The 11th Hussars, in the second line, now reached the guns:

As we neared the battery, a square of infantry gave us a volley in flank. The very air hissed as the shower of bullets passed through us; many men were killed or wounded. On looking down I saw that a bullet, which must have passed close in front of my body, had blackened and cut the lace on my cuff. Private [James] Glanister had his lower jaw shattered by a bullet entering on the right side, and a bullet passed through the back of Private Humphries' neck, just missing the spinal cord. At this time we were a sweeping gallop.[40]

We are fortunate to have the memoirs of an unnamed member of the Don Cossack battery. Though it contains a number of obvious errors regarding the Allied forces, his account provides us with a unique view from someone on the receiving end of the charge. Even he could admire the determination of the light cavalrymen, describing the attack having been carried out with 'courage and daring':

In order to counter our success in occupying the three redoubts, the enemy prepared a cavalry attack on our forces. For this he sent forward a regiment of French dragoons and Queen Victoria's Guards Cuirassier Regiment, under the command of Lord Cardigan. Upon noticing the movement of the enemy cavalry, General Liprandi sent his adjutant to tell our battery to prepare to receive a cavalry attack. In fact, as soon as the adjutant galloped off, the English cavalry passed by the redoubts at a trot in orderly formation and then at a gallop fell onto the right flank of Don Heavy No. 3 Battery, which opened up with rapid canister shell fire. The cavalry closed up its torn-open files and pressed forward, as brave as a whirlwind, with all the officers in front. The battery started canister fire, managing to fire some 32 rounds, which tore out whole files from the regiment, so that barely a third of the Englishmen reached the battery. Lord Cardigan on a white horse was far ahead of the regiment, and he galloped up to the battery and brandished his sabre at the guns.[41]

James Wightman was relieved that the 17th Lancers had run the gauntlet of fire from the Russians on the flanking hills:

Well we were nearly out of it at last, and close on those cursed guns. Cardigan was still straight in front of me, steady as a church but now his sword was in the air, he turned in his saddle for an instant, and shouted his final command, 'Steady! Steady! Close in!' Immediately afterwards there crashed into us a regular volley from the Russian cannon. I saw Captain White go down and Cardigan disappear into the smoke. A moment more and I was within it myself. A shell burst right over my head with a hellish crash that all but stunned me. Immediately after I felt my horse under me take a tremendous leap into the air. What he jumped I never saw or knew; the smoke was so thick I could not see my arm's length around me. Through the dense veil I heard noises of fighting and slaughter, but saw no obstacle, no adversary, no gun or gunner, and, in short, was through and beyond the Russian battery before I knew for certain that I had reached it.

The Russian artillerymen worked their cannon until the last moment, then, as the Light Brigade reached the battery, the gunners tried to defend themselves with anything at hand. It was an unequal contest, with the dragoons and hussars able to slash down upon the gunners from high in their saddles. In close combat the long primary weapons of the 17th Lancers were an encumbrance and after the initial assault many would have thrown away their lances and drawn their sabres. The anonymous Don Cossack gunner continued with his narrative:

Although the First Division limbered up in time, Sotnik Rebinin used the command, 'Pull back' instead of 'Limbers back', and the gun trails plowed into the ground and the tired horses halted. Surrounded by the English, the division defended itself as best it could. All the crew members with ramrods worked them with a will, defending themselves and the guns. In this hand-to-hand fight the first ramrod number, Cossack Studenikin, especially distinguished himself. Of great physical strength, he struck the English with terrible blows of his ramrod, felling eight men and saving Sotnik Rebinin when several cavalrymen rushed at him, wounding him twice in the neck and stabbing him once in the right side with a broadsword. The rear driver of the first gun, Cossack Nikulin of the Veshenskaya Settlement, had his throat run through by an Englishman's lance; he lost his voice, but is still alive today.

In the meantime, the Second Division successfully limbered up on the command 'Limbers back!, and rode off in time, except for the fifth gun, whose horses got tangled in their harness. I was with the gun, and after the horses were freed and the guns hooked onto the limber, I took hold of the lead horse's traces and shouted, 'Go!' The gun drew away at a full trot, but after withdrawing about 100 yards, it was surrounded by enemy cuirassiers. One of them even swung his long straight sword over my head, but Cossack Popov covered me with his shashka sword [a form of semi-curved sword], and Cossack Sherstyugin, a ramrod number, wounded my attacker in the arm with a pistol shot. I picked up the wounded man's sword and struck his horse's nose so hard that it reared up and threw its rider onto the ground, where the Cossack ran him through.

Behind the first line came the 4th Light Dragoons, a member of which was Private Joseph Grigg:

I remember as we neared the guns, Captain [John] Brown, who was in command of our squadron, called out to the men in the second line, who were getting too near the front 'Steady, men, Steady! You shall have a go directly.' Just before we got to the guns we gave three loud cheers, and then in a moment, we were amongst the enemy.[42]

Lord George Paget, leading the support line, could see little of what was happening ahead of him:

This battery, owing to the dust and confusion that reigned, had not been perceived by us (by me at least) until we got close upon it, though we had of course been suffering from its fire on our onward course. The first objects that caught my eyes were some of these guns, in the act of endeavouring to get away from us, who had by this time got close upon them. They had, I fancy, ceased to fire on our near approach, and the men were dragging them away, some by lasso-harness but others with their horses still attached. Then came a 'View Holloa!' and a sort of simultaneous rush upon them by the remnants of the 4th and cut and thrust was the order of the day.[43]

The anonymous Don Cossack gunner also described the efforts of the artillery to escape before the Light Brigade was upon them, but the brave gunners had kept on firing until it was too late. Again, his account contains errors concerning the British, most notably describing the death of Lord Cardigan:

> At this time, on Sotnik Ponomarev's command, the horse tenders led the horses to the guns, the crew numbers quickly jumped onto them, and along with the Second Division's remaining crew that had galloped up, they threw themselves to the rescue of the First Division, shashkas [curved sword] in hand and commanded by Ponomarev and myself. Now a desperate hand-to-hand fight ensued. Under the command of Voiskovoi Starshina Porfirii Kon'kov, the sotnia from Colonel Aleksandrin's Regiment hurried to aid the artillerymen, and from this moment there began a general slaughter of the English, who would lose consciousness and be dragged along the ground and perish. Lord Cardigan, seeing the destruction of the cavalry he was leading, turned back and was quickly carried toward the redoubts by his thoroughbred steed, but he was not destined to reach them. His horse was hit by crossfire from the infantry and fell down while galloping at full speed, killing the earl. The next day his body was turned over to the allies and buried with great honour.

The Russians were not alone in believing that Cardigan had been lost, this also being reported in the *Chester Chronicle* of Saturday, 18 November:

> The Light Brigade still kept sweeping on till they were right in front of them [the Russian guns], when a 32-pounder went off within two feet of Lord Cardigan's horse, quite lifting him off the ground, but he got in among them, and was, where he always will be when it comes to the point, in the first rank. It seems they rode right through the guns and turned, after killing the men who were serving them. His Lordship's extra aide-de-camp, it is supposed, was wounded and taken prisoner, for he has not since been heard of.

Regimental butcher John Vahey was still feeling the effects of the previous night's drinking session:

> On still, on we went, faster and faster as our horses got excited and warmed to their work, heedless of the torrent of shot that came

tearing through us, and stopping for ever many a bold rider. As for myself, what with the drink in me, and the wild excitement of the headlong charge, I went stark mad, and sent the plucky Russian horse ahead at a pace which kept me in line with the very foremost. Nearer and nearer we came to the dreadful battery, which kept vomiting death on us like a volcano, till I seemed to feel on my cheek the hot air from the cannon's mouth. At last we were on it. Half a dozen of us leaped in among the guns at once, and I with one blow of my axe brained a Russian gunner just as he was clapping the linstock to the touch-hole of his piece. With another I split open the head of an officer who was trying to rally the artillery detachment in the rear; and then what of us were left went smack through the stragglers cutting and slashing like fiends, right straight at the column of cavalry drawn up behind the battery.

Private William Henry Pennington of the 11th Hussars wrote to his father from his hospital bed in Scutari and his letter was published in the *Oldham Chronicle* of 30 December:

We advanced at a gallop to these guns, amid a fearful fire from the front, with 'ditto' on the right and left flanks, of grape, shell, and canister, and infantry also pouring in a tremendous fire. The effect was that horses and men fell thick and fast; but even this did not check our onward rush. All the Russian artillerymen were sabred, and for an instant, we were masters of the guns, but, having no support, could not keep them.

Joseph Grigg continued his story as he charged into the battery:

As I passed the wheel of the gun-carriage the gun was fired and I suppose some of the 8th Hussars [behind] got that shot, or shell or whatever it was. The wind was blowing from behind us, and the smoke from the guns prevented us seeing very well what work there was to do. The first man I noticed was a mounted driver. He cut me across the eyes with his whip which almost blinded me, but as my horse flew past him, I made a cut at him and caught him in the mouth so that his teeth all rattled together as he fell from his horse. I fancy I can hear the horrible sound now. As he fell I cut him once again; and then I made for another driver, and cut him across the back of his neck, and gave him a second cut as he fell. A few gunners stood in a group with their rifles, and we cut at them as we went rushing by.[44]

A large proportion of Ryzhov's cavalry had withdrawn behind the Don Cossack battery, and was placed in three ranks, fifty metres apart. The first rank was composed of the Ural Cossack Regiment No.1, the second was formed of the Kiev Hussar Regiment of His Highness the Duke of Leuchtenberg, with the third rank consisting of five squadrons of the Hussars of the Grand-Duke of Saxe-Weimar (Ingermanland Regiment). The 6th Squadron of the Ingermanland Regiment was in the front rank on the right flank of the Ural Cossacks, and three squadrons of the Composite Uhlan Regiment commanded by Colonel V.M. Eropkin was placed on the left flank.[45]

Many of the Russian horsemen, seeing the Light Brigade charging towards them did not wait around, as General Ryzhov was forced to admit:

> I was with the Don heavy battery, talking with Colonel Prince Obolenskii about the way the affair went, when the sharp eyes of the Don men noticed that enemy cavalry was descending the heights. In not more than two minutes they would already be moving back. Our artillery at first met them with shell and round shot and then with canister. I ordered the first line forward to meet the enemy, but just then it became clear how much loss we had suffered in division and squadron commanders, whose places were perforce taken by junior, inexperienced officers ... They started off slowly. Having moved no more than 150 paces, the front division of the Leuchtenberg Regiment was the first to turn back, and with a deafening cry of 'Ura!' and not allowing themselves to be halted or given orders, they collided with the second line, part of which I wanted to take to strike the enemy flank. This could no longer be done. The second line was drawn away by the first, and in this state they galloped back for more than a quarter mile with the enemy on their horses' tails.

A letter from Trumpet Major William Grey of the 8th Hussars was published in the *Nottingham Guardian* on 8 December:

> On going down on the charge I was wounded in my right shoulder, but thank God, not dangerously, as soon as we got down about a mile in the valley, we had to meet a regiment of Polish Lancers, about 2,000 in number, we broke our way through them manfully and left many of them dead alongside our poor fellows that had been killed by their cannon.

Grigg, of the 4th Light Dragoons, also went through the battery:

A few gunners stood in a group with their rifles, and we cut at them as we went rushing by. Beyond the guns the Russian cavalry, who should have come out to prevent our getting near the gunners, were coming down upon us howling wildly, and we went at them with a rush. I selected a mounted Cossack, who was making for me with his lance pointed at my breast. I knocked it upwards, pulled up quickly, and cut him down across the face. I tried to get hold of his lance, but he dropped it.

As he was falling, I noticed that he was strapped to the saddle, so that he did not come to the ground, and the horse rushed away with him.[46]

Lieutenant Stefan Kozhukhov, of the Russian 12th Artillery Brigade's 8th Light Battery, described the charge in an article published in 1869:

The English cavalry—what was left of it after canister and battle fire—galloped through our line of troops, coming madly on the heels of our cavalry. At the medical aid point all these masses came to a halt, since it was impossible to retreat any further. The Ukraine Regiment and our artillery, which was covering the Chorgun Ravine, were energetic in not allowing any further withdrawal. Four regiments of hussars and cossacks crowded into that small area right at the entrance to the Chorgun Ravine where the medical aid post was set up. Among them, like infrequent specks, one could see the red coats [sic] of the English, no doubt not any less surprised than ourselves by what had unexpectedly happened.[47]

Likewise, the anonymous member of the Don Cossack battery admitted to the flight of the Russian cavalry:

The notable English cavalry attack was carried out with such courage and daring that our cavalry under General Ryzhov and the battery under Baron Brombeus turned around long before coming into contact and only halted at the Chernaya River. This circumstance made it possible for the English to charge onto the Don Heavy No. 3 Battery.

Once through the guns, continued Kozhukhov:

the enemy moved quickly and bravely at a gallop towards our cavalry. This was so unexpected that before anyone realized it our cavalry had broken … it was chaos. Our cavalry outnumbered the enemy five times over, and yet it fell back in total disorder to the Chernaya, with the English coming hotly forward at the hooves of our horses.

Evelyn Wood, who served as a midshipman with the Naval Brigade, related one remarkable story of the charge from an officer in the 13th Light Dragoons. This was the regiment Wood joined after transferring from the Navy to the Army:

> Lieutenant Percy Smith … from an accident to his right hand, carried merely a dummy sword in the scabbard. While leading his men on the far side of the Russian battery, a Russian soldier, perceiving he had no sword, galloped up alongside and resting his carbine on the left arm, pressed the muzzle close to Smith's body as the two horsemen galloped, locked together. Smith presently, finding the suspense intolerable, struck with his maimed hand at the Russian's face, and the carbine going off, the bullet passed over Smith's head, his opponent then leaving him alone.[48]

Though the Heavy Brigade and the Horse Artillery had been reined in, the French cavalry, in the form of the 1st and 4th Regiments of the *Chasseurs d'Afrique*, which Lucan had been told he could use to help recover the guns, now made its presence felt:

> The brigade of African Chasseurs had hardly arrived to support the left of the English cavalry, when the light brigade rushed upon the Russian redoubts. General Morris, who knew nothing of the order sent to Lord Lucan, could not comprehend this movement. Nevertheless, seeing the disaster which menaced the Cardigan brigade, he could not remain inactive. He pushed his ranks forward at once; and with two squadrons of the 4th African Chasseurs, supported by two other squadrons of the same regiment, attacked without hesitation the Russian battery which crowns the large wooded mamelon [rounded hill].
>
> These brave troops, commanded by General Allonville and Colonel Champeron, dash forward and ascend the steep sides of the hill at a gallop. The Russian battery towards which they are hastening, observes this movement and throws some shells among them, but without effect; they are already on the summit of the mamelon, and are advancing directly upon the guns, which, horsed in haste, are withdrawn at the very moment that the 4th squadron reaches the place that they had occupied.[49]

Above: The view from the Sapoune Heights looking into the 'Valley of Death'. The Fedioukine Heights are to the left with the North Valley and the Causeway Heights in the centre and right of the photo. The Russians troops were occupying both heights and the valley when Raglan ordered Lucan to attack. It is said that the Light Brigade commenced its charge in the approximate position of the white buildings seen in the middle distance. (Courtesy of David Rowlands)

Below: A View looking south-west from the Causeway Heights across South Valley. The Heavy Brigade charged toward this viewpoint. (Courtesy of David Rowlands)

Above: Looking south-south-west across the North Valley from lower slope of Fedioukine Hills. The Causeway Heights are in the distance. (Courtesy of David Rowlands)

Below: In the North Valley, looking north to Fedioukine Heights. (Courtesy of David Rowlands)

Above: A little local knowledge – the author and a guide in the North Valley, looking west-south-west. The Sapoune Heights are in the distance. (Courtesy of David Rowlands)

Below: The old Woronzoff road can be seen winding its way along the Causeway Heights. (Courtesy of David Rowlands)

Above: Looking eastwards along crest of the Causeway Heights, towards the Light Brigade monument. The rough and broken nature of the ground can be fully appreciated in this photograph. (Courtesy of David Rowlands)

Below: The military artist David Rowlands and the author at the Light Brigade memorial on the Causeway Heights. (Courtesy of David Rowlands)

Above: One of those men whose voices from the past we are privileged to still read – in this instance Captain Robert Portal of the 4th Light Dragoons. (US Library of Congress)

Below: Lieutenant John Yates, 11th Hussars. (US Library of Congress)

Above: Brigadier General Lord George Paget CB. (US Library of Congress)

Below: The man who possibly emerged from the charge with the greatest credit, Lieutenant Colonel Frederick Shewell of the 8th Hussars. It was Shewell who rallied the men after the charge and led them through the Russian cavalry which attempted to cut off the retreat of the Light Brigade. (US Library of Congress)

Above: A camp of the 5th Dragoon Guards, looking towards Kadikoi. (US Library of Congress)

Below: A view of the lines of Balaclava with Canrobert's Hill in the distance. (US Library of Congress)

Above: In the North Valley with the Fedioukine Heights on the left. (Courtesy of David Rowlands)

Below: In the North Valley, looking east-north-east. (Courtesy of David Rowlands)

The *Chasseurs* chased after the retreating artillery but in doing so galloped right into a line of waiting infantry, as the anonymous Don Cossack gunner saw:

> The French dragoons attacked General Zhabokritski's troops on the Fedioukine Heights, but their attack ended even less successfully that that of the English. Rushing onto riflemen deployed behind cover, the dragoons were met by such a murderous fire that they could not endure it and turned back.

In Bazancourt's words: 'a dense line of sharp-shooters, and two Russian squares crouching on the ground, and hidden in a jungle of thick brushwood, suddenly start up, and salute the Chasseurs with a terrible fire.' But behind the *Chasseurs* came a battalion of French infantry, and the French cavalry was able to withdraw and, as Bazancourt makes clear, 'the object was attained. The most important and the most murderous of the enemy's batteries had ceased to pour its fire upon the English cavalry.' There bold intervention certainly silenced the guns on the Fedioukine Heights and saved many lives in the Light Brigade. It cost the *Chasseurs* twenty men, thirteen of whom were killed.

Private Henry Naylor's horse was hit but it still carried him into the battery:

> My horse began to limp and I could not manage him. My off reins were cut in two. I managed to tie them; my curb was gone likewise, I received a stinging sensation about my left shoulder. I got to the guns and passed through and got a tremendous blow with a sponge staff as I passed through. Then it was our turn. We drove the enemy into the river Tchernaya.[50]

Private Robert Martin, despite his shattered arm, continued onto the battery. It will be seen that Martin gives a substantially different account of the injury to Private Glanister:

> While fighting in the midst of the guns Glanister unfortunately broke his sword off short at the hilt by striking a Russian on the top of his helmet. The order to retire was given by Lord George Paget, and on turning I perceived a Cossack close to us. He immediately levelled his pistol and fired at Glanister and myself. The bullet whizzed by my face and struck Glanister, shattering his lower jaw and causing him to fall forward on his cloak, which was rolled up in front of him. The Cossack bolted at once, and I had the presence of

mind to grasp the reins of my horse and place them in my mouth, at the same time seizing those of Glanister's horse and turning it into the ranks. By this means, no doubt, his life was saved.

Though Martin had saved the life of his comrade, his shattered arm could not be saved and was later amputated.

James Wightman, who had charged through the Don Cossack battery without realising it, now found himself all but alone beyond the Russian guns:

> There was no longer any semblance of a line. No man of the Lancers was on my right, a group was a little way on my left. Lord Cardigan must have increased his distance during or after passing through the battery for I now saw him some way ahead, alone in the midst of a knot of Cossacks. At this moment Lieutenant Maxse, his Lordship's aide-de-camp, came back out of the tussle, and crossed my front as I was riding forward. I saw that he was badly wounded; and he called to me, 'For God's sake, Lancer, don't ride over me! See where Lord Cardigan is,' pointing to him, 'rally on him!' I was hurrying on to support the brigade commander, when a Cossack came at me and sent his lance into my right thigh. I went for him, but he bolted; I overtook him, drove my lance into his back and unhorsed him just in front of two Russian guns which were in possession of Sergeant-Majors Lincoln and Smith, of the 13th Light Dragoons, and other men of the Brigade. When pursuing the Cossack I noticed Colonel [George] Mayow deal very cleverly with a big Russian cavalry officer. He tipped his shako with the point of his sword and then laid his head right open with the old cut seven [there were actually only six official sabre cuts]. The chase of my Cossack had diverted me from rallying on Lord Cardigan; he was now nowhere to be seen, nor did I ever again set eyes on the chief who had led us down the valley so grandly.

Cardigan's aide mentioned above, Lieutenant Henry Fitzhardinge Berkeley Maxse, was by the earl's side during the charge:

> Lord C led gallantly right through the battery a gun going off between his horse's legs I was struck on the foot by a spent round shot or a bit of shell and though I managed to get on 40 or 50 yards past the batteries I was obliged then to cling to my horse's mane and was nearly fainting.[51]

Cardigan himself wrote of the moment he led the brigade into the guns:

> On leading into the battery a gun was fired close by my horse's head. I rode straight forward at the same pace, till I came near to a strong force of Russian cavalry. I was then attacked by two Cossacks, slightly wounded, and nearly dismounted ... I had difficulty in recovering my seat, and then in defending myself against several Cossacks.[52]

Exactly where Cardigan was after the brigade reached the battery, however, was to become one of the more contentious subjects of the charge, resulting in a court case, which will be examined later in this book. Amongst those who provided affidavits for the trial in June 1863, was Sergeant Frederick Short of the 4th Light Dragoons:

> On arriving at the guns the Russians were retreating with them from their original positions. The 4th endeavoured to take possession of these guns. Lieutenant Joliffe (now Captain, retired) was next to me. I was slightly in advance and attacked the drivers of the guns while Lieutenant Joliffe shot with his revolver the gunners sitting on the guns. I distinctly saw him do that. I state positively that I cut down at least six drivers.[53]

Cardigan himself wrote of the charge:

> I led the first line of the brigade, consisting of the 13th Light Dragoons and 17th Lancers, through the Russian battery, and that, being the first man into the battery, I pursued my course until I came up to the line of the Russian cavalry. That, being alone there, in consequence of the officers of my Staff being wounded or disabled, I was attacked by two Cossacks, slightly wounded, and nearly dismounted that, on being nearly surrounded by Cossacks, I gradually retreated until I reached the battery into which I had led the first line ... on arriving there, I found no part of the first line remaining there. Those which survived the charge had passed off to the left, short of the Russian gun limber carriages, or retreated up the hill.[54]

According to Private Edward Woodham, all the cavalry regiments were issued with spikes whenever there was the likelihood of a battle, which they kept in their pouches:

Well, as soon as we reached the guns the men [the Russian gunners] began dodging by getting under them, and for a time they defended with the rammers; but it was no contest – they had no chance with us, and we cut them down like ninepins. Of course we captured the battery and many of our men dismounted to spike the guns … We had no hammers, but drove the spikes in with the hilt of our swords or our hands – in any way we could.[55]

In the midst of the smoke from the incessant cannon fire which stretched across the valley, the majority of the 11th Hussars, riding closest to the Fedioukine Heights, galloped passed the battery without even seeing it.

Even Private Wightman in the first line with the 17th Lancers missed the Russian guns:

I could not see my arm's length around me. Through the dense veil I heard noises of fighting and slaughter, but saw no obstacle, no adversary, no gun or gunner, and, in short, was through and beyond the Russian battery before I knew for certain that I had reached it.

The statement by Woodham about spiking the guns is somewhat contradicted by that of Corporal R. Grant of the 4th Light Dragoons:

When we charged into the guns I dismounted and could have used some gun spikes had I had them, but unfortunately none had been issued. I never saw a gun spike. We then disabled as many gunners and drivers as we could, to prevent them taking away the guns, feeling they were ours.[56]

A Russian lancer, Lieutenant Koribut-Kubitovich of the Reserve Composite Uhlan Regiment, who was watching the drama unfold, largely agreed with Private Woodham:

The English then rode down the Don battery sabring a number of gunners as they passed through; but the majority of the gun crews made off, mounted on horse teams and limbers. The enemy spiked some of the guns, hoping to drag them off on his return, but most of the cavalry continued the headlong chase after the hussars, slashing at them without mercy. The horse teams and limbers of the Don battery together with 12 Horse Battery and all the cavalry were soon milling about at the river, all trying to get over the bridge, while the English chased them almost as far as the transport lines.[57]

Lieutenant Colonel George Wynell Mayow also stated that some of the 17th Lancers did indeed consider trying to take the guns away:

> I was Brigade Major, and accompanied it [the front line] in its advance; and it so happened that with the first line I was the next senior officer to Lord Cardigan. As the line approached the Russian artillery, the smoke became so dense that we could see little except the flashes of the guns, and I then lost sight of Lord Cardigan. At the part of the Russian line that I came in contact with, they were trying to limber up and carry off their guns, and I heard some of our soldiers propose to secure these guns; but at that moment I perceived a line of Russian cavalry in rear of the guns, I directed these men, who belonged to the 17th Lancers, to leave the guns to be dealt with by the second line, and to charge the Russian cavalry, this they did, and drove them in on their second reserve. We were then within sight of the bridge over the aqueduct, and I should think 500 yards or more in the rear of the Russian guns. Finding the enemy then too strong to be dealt with by the few men that remained, I called out to the men to halt; and perceiving the 8th Hussars advancing, I further directed and led the men back to that corps, which on the moment was wheeled about by Colonel Shewell.[58]

Private Connor of the 4th Light Dragoons likewise sought to try and take away the guns: 'I was one of those who tried to cut the traces of the Russian guns. I used my pocket-knife, but found that within the leather were chains of steel.'

Amongst those that had ridden straight through the Don Cossack battery was Private Wightman, along with Private James Mustard, of the 17th Lancers, and Private Thomas Fletcher of the 4th Light Dragoons:

> We were now through [the battery] and on the further side a considerable body of the Russian cavalry, and so near the bottom of the valley that we could well discern the Tcherbaya [Tchernaya] river. But we were all three wearied and weakened by loss of blood; our horses wounded in many places; there were enemies all about us, and we thought it was about time to be getting back.

153

Chapter 10

'To Do or Die'

The Light Brigade could do no more. It had charged down the North Valley, scattering the Russian light cavalry and overrunning the Don Cossack battery. But the few hundred men that had reached the guns were now in the heart of the Russian positions and in danger of being surrounded and annihilated. General Ivan Ryzhov saw the situation the British cavalry was in and he rallied his horsemen:

> Soon the English were cut off and realized what had happened to them. I managed to halt my hussars, and they expiated their guilt in that they threw themselves after the enemy and put him between two fires. From this moment the battle could be compared to a rabbit hunt. Those who managed to gallop away from the hussar sabres and slip past the lances of the uhlans were met with canister fire from our batteries and the bullets of our riflemen. A few of them were fortunate enough to manage to return whole and unharmed; only a reserve [the Heavy Brigade] which saw the misfortune playing out was able to turn back in time, without a thought to rendering help to their comrades.

Stefan Kozhukhov, of the Russian 12th Artillery Brigade, said that it was Liprandi who ordered the uhlans/lancers to counter-attack:

> At this time General Liprandi was close to the medical aid post and saw that the Odessa battalions were holding firm, so he became reassured regarding the outcome of this mad attack. He did not rely any more on the panicked hussars and cossacks, but immediately ordered the six squadrons of Yeropkin's combined lancer regiment, which were right there in reserve, to attack the English in the flank and cut off their retreat.

It looked as though there was nothing else for the English to do except lay down their arms, and everyone expected this. However, that is not at all what happened. For some reason the lancers' attack failed. It was said at that time that one of the Odessa battalions mistook the lancers for the enemy and opened fire on them. As a result, the lancers turned around after only going halfway. In the meantime, the English saw this unsuccessful attack and also that they were not in any danger of serious pursuit by the scattered hussars and cossacks, and they decided to do what had appeared to be impossible—they decided to break through our line of troops on the same route they had advanced on, and thus pass once again through the ranks, so to speak, of canister and battle fire.

In his report on the battle, Liprandi, who estimated the Light Brigade to have been 2,000 strong, described the charge of the Composite Uhlan Regiment:

at this moment three squadrons of the combined regiment of lancers attacked him [the enemy] in flank. This unexpected charge, executed with precision and vigour, was attended with brilliant success. The whole of the enemy's cavalry in disorder precipitated itself in retreat, pursued by our lancers and by the fire from our batteries. In this attack the enemy had more than 400 men killed and sixty wounded, who were picked up on the field of battle, and we made twenty-two prisoners, one of whom was a superior officer.

Kozhukhov believed that 'these mad cavalrymen' of the Light Brigade would not be able to escape the Russian forces that were closing in around them:

After already having lost at least a quarter of their strength during their advance, they somehow formed their depleted squadrons and quickly went along the original route, now strewn with dead and wounded, leaving new victims at every step. With a sort of brave despair, these mad daredevils flowed back along the path they had forced open, and not one of them, wounded or not, laid down his arms.

But for a long time the Cossacks and Hussars were unable to rally themselves. They were convinced that they were being pursued by nothing less than the entire enemy cavalry force and angrily refused to believe that they had been defeated by a comparatively tiny handful of brave men.[1]

A letter from Cornet Denzil Thomas Chamberlain of the 13th Light Dragoons to his father was printed in the *York Herald* of 16 November:

> I received a lance thrust in the stomach from the right, which fortunately just missed me, but broke my cap-pouch and ripped up my revolver case. I also received a sword cut on the arm, but felt it very lightly, as I shot the Russian dragoon through the head when his arm was raised. My poor charger Pimento was shot through two places in the flank with Minié balls, and one through the body on our retiring. He was only just able to carry me out of the range of the enemy's batteries when he fell to rise no more. The enemy's cavalry was in immense force. I had very many hairbreadth escapes ... Returning was the worst part of the business. I was nearly the last out of about 35 that started together to return, but I only saw nine when we got out of range. Men and horses fell like nine-pins; it was an awful sight.

Lord George Paget described the retreat in more detail than the actual charge:

> We had got beyond their guns, at the entrance of a sort of widish gorge, when, finding it useless to proceed, our fellows turned round to go back, and about we went. At this moment, however, seeing a lot of their cavalry coming on us, within fifteen yards, I holloaed to them (the remnants of the 4th and 11th, the only two regiments then in front) to 'front,' which they right gallantly did, when a cry arose, 'They are coming down on us in our rear, my lord;' and to our consternation we saw a regiment of Lancers (fresh disengaged ones) formed up in our rear, between us and our retreat. The case was now desperate. Of course, to retain the guns was out of the question. We went about again and had to cut away through this regiment, which had skilfully formed so as to attack us in flank (our then right flank).
>
> I holloaed 'Left shoulder forward!' but my voice was drowned, and I hesitate not to say that had that regiment behaved with common bravery not one of us would have returned. I am no swordsman, but was fortunate to disengage myself and get through them, and I had the worst of it, for in the mêlée I had got on the right flank (that exposed to them), and my horse was so dead-beat that I could not keep up, and saw the rest gradually leaving me at each step. Well, having got by them, we had to ride back a mile, through the murderous fire we had come through, of guns, shells, and Minié rifles from the hills of brushwood on each side; and all I can say is, that here I am, but how any of us got back I don't know ...

Our return was really a sort of triumph, the troops cheering us as we came up, and the fellows rushing forward to shake hands with us on our escape. As for myself, I take no credit — I could not help myself; I was ordered to go on, and go I must, but that in the whole of that devoted brigade there was not one man who hesitated was a noticeable fact now that one looks back at it.[2]

Private James Henry Herbert of the 4th Light Dragoons said that the horses were 'winded and terribly distressed' after their long galloping towards the Don Cossack battery, and when the remnants of the Light Brigade turned to retreat, the horses were too tired to move quickly:

As we came back I saw the officers commanding the Russians waving their swords as if they were trying to bring the flanks of the Lancers round, so as to hem us in; but they seemed to me either to be afraid to move, or not to know what their officers were driving at. It was, of course, a disgraceful thing that they allowed a single man of us to get back again down the valley. Strictly speaking, not a soul in the Light Brigade should have been permitted to return, in view of the superior numbers of the enemy, their freshness and our own exhausted state. We rushed in amongst them, and there was a renewal of the cutting, slashing, pointing and parrying of the earlier part of the fight. There was no fancy work, but just hard, useful business, and it fulfilled its object, for we cut our way through the opposing lancers.[3]

Another Private of the 4th Light Dragoons, John Whitehead, related his escape in more restrained tones than many of his comrades:

We advanced towards the enemy. The 17th Lancers leading men and horses falling wholesales. About three parts down the valley a shell landed just in front of my horse. When it exploded it caught her fair in the chest and brought her down. I shot over her head for a dozen yards but my poor mare didn't move, being instantly killed. The shots from the Russian guns were so thick that I had to lie down behind my horse for protection. When at last the firing ceased I retired on foot to where the Roll call of the Regiment was being called. I didn't do much in the actual Charge; but thank God, I have never had another such experience.[4]

In a letter, Private William Pennington of the 11th Hussars, writing from the General Hospital at Scutari to his father, and which appeared in the

Oldham Chronicle of 30 December, he related his escape after being wounded:

> As for myself, I never reached the guns in front, as a grapeshot went through my 'busby', about two inches above my head, knocking it on one side, another through the calf of my leg, and next through my horse's head (a fine black mare). Well, here I was at the mercy of their Lancers, whom I saw lancing our dismounted men. The demons give no quarter when you are down. At this moment the 8th Hussars came by with a horse without a rider. This I mounted, and formed in rear of the 8th as if it were my own regiment, and dashed on, but, worse again, we were obliged to wheel 'Right About', and to pass through a strong body of the enemy's cavalry which had gathered in our rear, cutting off our retreat.
>
> Of course with our handful it was life or death; so we rushed at them to break through them; but as soon as we got through one body there was another to engage. At any rate, with five or six of our fellows at my rear, I galloped on, parrying with the determination of one who would not lose his life, breaking the lances of the cowards who attacked us in the proportion of three or four to one, occasionally catching one a slap with the sword across the teeth, and giving another the point in his arm or breast. They still pressed on me till I got sight of our Heavies, when, thanks be to God, they stopped pursing me.

Some indication of just how desperate a struggle the remnants of the Light Brigade had in trying to return down the North Valley as the Russian horsemen surrounded them comes from Private John Firkins of the 13th Light Dragoons:

> By this time I could not see three men of our regiment. I of course thought I was lost but I turned my Mare's Head to try to get back if I could. I had only gone a few yards when I saw two Russian lancers coming towards me with clenched teeth and staring like savages. I prepared to meet them with as much coolness and determination as I could command. The first one made a thrust at me with his Lance. It is a heavy weapon and easily struck down which I did with my sword thrusting it at the same time through the fellow's neck. He fell from his horse with a groan. The shock [of the impact] nearly brought me from my saddle. The other fellow wheeled round his dying comrade and made a thrust at me. I had not the strength to strike down the blow for my sword fell from my grasp, but my time

was not yet come. One of our Lancers seeing the attack made on me came to my assistance and thrust his Lance clean through the fellow's body at the moment I lost my sword.[5]

Another trooper of the 13th Light Dragoons, Private George Badger, also lived to recount his experiences of that memorable day, which appeared in the *Shrewsbury Chronicle* of 15 January 1904:

> Three men on my right (next to me) and two on my left fell; I found my horse was wounded, but with a little reign and close leg, I managed to keep him up. Getting nearer the guns, I was struck with a piece of shell, which tore away part of my clothes and took a piece of my flesh away with it. Still we kept pushing on to the guns, and on reaching them I was attacked by a Russian gunner, who made a point at me, the steel entering my side before I could parry his thrust. Then fortunately, one of the 4th [Light] Dragoons came up and cut the man down.

As he tried to return back to the British lines, Badger's horse was hit a second time by a shell splinter, and fell down dead. One of the 8th Hussars happened to pass by Badger and he caught hold of the stirrup-iron of his saddle, but he was unable to hold on. The rest of George Badger's story was related in the *Midland Evening News*:

> Private Badger, wounded, and knocked silly when his horse had been brought down, recovered consciousness to see Captain Oldham lying nearby. The Captain had been thrown from his horse after it had been struck by a shell. Although unhurt, he was bowled over almost immediately by a musket ball. He called Badger across and asked him to take his personal treasures, but as Badger moved towards him another ball struck him and he fell back dead, still clutching the watch and purse he was holding out.

Badger saw that a number of Cossacks were galloping up, and he knew that he could never outrun them. Luckily, the Russians stopped to loot the dead British officer and Badger was able to make his escape.

Looting might also be the reason why Cornet Denzyl Chamberlain, also of the 13th Light Dragoons, managed to escape. As we have read, his charger Pimento was killed, being struck three times before it fell. Lieutenant Percy Smith was returning back down the valley when he saw Chamberlain, and he advised him to remove the saddle and bridle from Pimento as 'another horse you can get, but you will not get a saddle or bridle so easily', so the gallant rider was seen standing within range of the Russian batteries, the ground all around being ploughed up by shot and shell, coolly taking off the saddle and holsters, and with them on his arm he walked quietly up to the rising ground where what still remained of the gallant '600' had formed. It was there that he was received with a burst of cheering.

It has been said that he threaded his way through the Cossacks who were killing and pillaging the wounded British cavalrymen, the Russians most likely thought he was one of their own who had stolen the saddle from one of the Light Brigade. He returned to the British lines unchallenged.[6]

Corporal Nunnerley of the 17th Lancers also managed to escape, thanks in part, he claims, because of his physique:

> When I was within a few yards of the guns my horse was shot under me and fell on his head. I endeavoured to pull it up to dash at the gunners but found it was unable to move, its foreleg having been blown off. I left it and forced my way on foot when I was attacked by Russian cavalry through whom I cut my way, my more than ordinary height combined with a powerful frame proving most advantageous to me. I had no sooner got clear than I was knocked down and ridden over by riderless horses together with a few Hussars.[7]

Albert Mitchell's horse had been killed just as the 13th Light Dragoons reached the Don Cossack battery, with his left leg tramped underneath the animal. He was unable to move as the second line galloped towards, and over him.

Luckily he was not trampled by the onrushing cavalry, and he managed to extricate his leg and stand up. 'I still had my sword in my hand, and soon found there were numberless bullets flying around me which came from the infantry on the flank of their battery, who fired at us who were dismounted.' After trying to help a fellow light dragoon who was too severely wounded to be moved, Mitchel encountered his commanding officer:

> Just then Lord Cardigan came galloping up from the direction of the guns, passing me at a short distance, when he turned about again, and meeting me pulled up, and said: 'Where is your horse?' I answered: 'Killed, my Lord.' He then said in his usually stern, hoarse voice: 'You had better make the best of your way back as fast as you can go, or you will be taken prisoner.' I needed no telling, for

I was doing so as fast as I was able. He then rode a little farther down, and in a few moments returned past me at a gallop.[8]

Corporal John Buckton of the 11th Hussars was lucky to have escaped injury throughout the charge and the engagement with the Russian gunners. He heard the order to retire and turned back down the valley:

We saw, as we thought, the 17th Lancers, and we were going to retire under them, but we found that they were Polish Lancers, who had been stationed to cut our retreat off. On our way down the valley they had been behind a hill on our left, and now they emerged, and formed a line right in our front. How we got through them I don't exactly know … Our poor fellows – the mere handful that were left of them – hurrahed and halloed as loudly as they could, and they apparently had an effect upon the Polish horsemen, for it was evident their horses had not, like ours, been trained to withstand the noise and din of battle, and when they heard the British 'hurrahs' and saw our brave fellows rushing towards them at such a mad pace, they became restless and turned round and about and before they could form again in any kind of way, our men had bobbed through their ranks and were scampering up the hill before them.[9]

In the excitement of the battle, Private James Mustard of the 17th Lancers had not realised how close he had been to serious injury. As he was returning down the valley, Private John Ettridge of the 13th Light Dragoons rode up to Mustard and asked if he could lend him his sword as Ettridge had lost his in the fighting. 'I still had my lance,' Mustard later recounted,

though the shaft had been chipped by a bullet. I turned to draw my sword to hand it to Hetridge [sic], when, to my amazement, I had neither sword, scabbard, nor belt. A canister-shot had caught me on the left hip, and cut away sword, belt, overalls, and pants, and laid bare a great patch of bleeding flesh. Another inch would have smashed my hip and killed me.[10]

The account of the charge which appeared in the *Chester Chronicle* of Saturday 18 November 1854, included some details of the retreat:

Mr Cook of the 11th, also had a regular run for his life of a mile and a half, pursued by the Russian cavalry, to avoid them he ran under range of the guns of their batteries, and finally escaped. Major

Clarke, of the Greys, in addition to a bad cut in the neck, had his horses' tail almost cut off by a sabre cut.

Sergeant-Major Henry Franks learned of Lieutenant George Wombell's remarkable escape after his horse had been shot and,

> he found himself on foot amidst the crowd of dead and wounded men and horses. He was seized by two of the enemy, and perceiving that he was an Officer, they thought they had got a prize … One on each side, they were escorting him along, when a horse belonging to the Russians without a rider, came upon the scene. The Officer saw his chance, and embraced it quick as lightning. He threw his two Russian friends to each side, and with the agility of a circus rider he caught and mounted the Russian horse, and bending his body well over the horse's neck, he left the two astonished Russians spellbound; and the noble little trooper brought him safely into camp, where the few that escaped from slaughter were coming back.[11]

For Sergeant John Fitzgerald of the 13th Light Dragoons it was a case of every man for himself as he escaped from the avenging Russian cavalry:

> I had one horse shot under me at the very commencement and of course was running back to our own army the same as dozens of others when I saw a trumpeter of the 11th Hussars shot dead. He fell off his horse, poor fellow so I 'borrowed' his mount and jumped on … There was another Sergeant of the 11th Hussars running for this horse the same as I was, but I got there first and hopped into the saddle. I knew him well, poor fellow, and I can remember him saying, 'Fitz, that horse belongs to us', but I paid no attention to him. I was sorry to hear they killed him, but everything is fair in war time.[12]

By contrast, Private Morris White, also of the 13th Light Dragoons, went back to the British lines to get another horse for another man:

> On going into the Charge at Balaklava the horse of his Captain was shot and he, turning to White, said, 'Ride back and bring my second charger.' White rode back and brought his officer another horse, and he and his captain rode into, and out of, that 'valley of death'.[13]

Ryzhov watched the retreating British cavalry and spotted Cardigan trotting down the valley, though he mistakenly believed it was Lucan that he saw:

The only thing I regret is that Lord Lucan did not fall into our hands. For saving his life he is obliged to his magnificent and most swift horse. I saw with my own eyes how he went along, dodging and slipping away from his pursuers and swinging his sabre in the air right and left as if in a state of drunkenness.

Private Thomas Dudley of the 17th Lancers sent a letter to his parents on 18 December from the hospital at Scutari. He was hit during the advance down the valley but continued on into the Russian positions. After describing the charge, he wrote about the retreat:

Well, I got out of the melée, but, in returning, my poor horse was shot down, and me under him. Poor beast! I believe he struggled to release me. You will hardly think I took time to give the noble beast a last look, but I did though; he was a fine creature. Well I got to my legs, and was fortunate enough to catch an officer's charger, got up as well as I could, and so got to camp, and next day packed off to this place, and many times have I thought it a very lucky hit for me in two respects: first, if it had been an inch further to my neck, it would have been all up with me; next it sent me here to be laid up in lavender – at least, compared with what the poor fellows are undergoing at camp.[14]

Lieutenant Edward Phillips, of the 8th Hussars, was one of those that had a fortunate escape as he tried to return down the valley:

I had not gone far when I found my mare begin to flag and presently I think she must have been hit in the leg by a round shot, as she suddenly dropped behind and fell over on her side. I extricated myself as quickly as possible and ran for my life, the firing being as hard as ever. After going some distance I found myself cut off by some Lancers who had got in my front … I was sure my time was come; I drew my revolver but seeing they kept their distance, until an officer came up and ordered them back, as they were too far in advance, so I escaped this danger. Some little distance on I reached one of our poor fellows lying on the ground, dead or dying, his horse standing beside him; the saddle had turned round with what excitement and running for one's life I was so done that I had not the strength to right it, therefore undid the girths and by standing on the saddle managed to climb on his bare back. Never was I so happy as when I felt a horse under me again.[15]

Private Naylor's horse was another that lost its life:

> I was bleeding from two wounds myself … when my horse fell down dead giving me a nice toss over his head; how I got from the guns it must have been a miracle, as the Cossacks were lancing our poor fellows all round. The agony of my wounds by this time began to tell on me, my lower jaw shattered and wounded in my left shoulder.[16]

The *Daily News* of 24 November printed the following account from an un-named Trumpeter of the 8th Hussars:

> As we were coming back, our regiment and the 17th Lancers were attacked by another lot of Russian cavalry, so we had to make the best of our way through them. Their artillery and infantry were firing on us all the time. Our regiment lost 38 men and two officers killed, seventeen men and two officers wounded. Capt. Lockwood is missing, we suppose him to be killed. It was an awful sight to see our men falling on every side of me, but, thank God, I was spared. I had my horse shot under me, but I was no sooner down than I mounted a Russian's horse. I had not, however, the pleasure of riding it more than half an hour when one of the Russian lancers ran his lance through the horse's body. Then I was left without any, so I had to run for my life, which I did for three miles until I came to the French cavalry, where I remained until our regiment came back. You may guess I had a very narrow escape.

Another member of the 8th Hussars, Private Richard Owen Glendur, was taken prisoner but still escaped:

> At this time, my horse being wounded, and surrounded by Polish Lancers, I was taken prisoner, and being wounded myself in my sword arm, I was left by the Russians on the ground, while they followed the 8th Hussars out.
>
> At this time, with great exertion, I got a horse of the 4th Light Dragoons, which was coming out, which I mounted, and seeing the Busby Bags flying at the bottom of the valley, wheeled my horse and joined the 4th Light Dragoons and 11th Hussars as they were wheeling round at the right flank of the Battery, and retreating at a rapid gallop.[17]

Butcher Vahey of the 17th Lancers, having found himself surrounded by the Cossacks beyond the Don battery, was still 'thrashing about me like a windmill' when he heard a trumpet somewhere far in his rear sounding out 'Threes about'. At this, he disengaged and made his way back through the battery, 'knocking over an artilleryman or two' as he passed, meeting up with a little group that had formed around Colonel Shewell:

> I was as sober as a bishop by this time, take my word for it, and I joined them right cheerfully; but the chances of getting back again to our own side of the valley looked very blue. The Russian cavalry were hard on our heels and we suffered sorely from the devilish battery in our rear, which kept pelting into the thick of us, without much discrimination between friend and foe ... Soon what little formation we had got was knocked to pieces, and then the word was 'Every man for himself and God help the hindmost.'

According to Joseph Pardoe of the 1st Dragoons, Vahey went missing after the charge and it was thought that he had been killed. He then turned up three days later. It seems that he had made himself scare as he thought he would be disciplined for leaving his prison-tent. When he learned 'by some means' that he would be pardoned for breaking his arrest, he reappeared.[18]

Colonel Shewell certainly appears to have been the man who, in the apparent absence of Lord Cardigan, maintained a degree of control and rallied many of the men, enabling them to fight their way through the Russians who tried to cut off the Light Brigade's avenue of retreat. Sergeant James Donoghue of the 8th Hussars was one of those who was grateful that Shewell had kept his head in the mêlée:

> The 8th Hussars continued to advance, and when we had got considerably beyond the Russian battery which had been in our front, we were halted for a few seconds. Some Russian cavalry then formed in our rear to cut off our retreat. Colonel Shewell gave the word to wheel; we wheeled round, and under the orders of Colonel Shewell we cut our way through the Russian cavalry.
>
> After this my horse was shot. After I had recovered from the stunning effects of the fall, I stripped my horse of my kit, and placing it on my arm, I made the best of my way back to the regiment.[19]

What is even more remarkable about Shewell's efforts that day was that he had been lying ill in Balaklava when he heard the opening shots of the battle. Realising that at such an early hour Lord Cardigan would still be on his yacht, the forty-five-year-old had got up from his sick bed and hurried to his regiment, arriving just in time to take part in the charge. Henry Clifford, George Brown's aide-de-camp, was watching the disaster unfold from, it is presumed, the Sapoune Heights:

> Some time passed, I can't say how much, but it was *very* long, waiting to see if any would return. Horses without riders, galloped back in numbers, and men wounded on foot and men not hurt, but their horses killed, returned on foot, and then saw a horse or a man fall, who wounded, had come as far as he could and then fell and died.
>
> At length about 30 horsemen dashed through a line of Cossacks, who had reformed to interrupt their retreat, and then another larger body came in sight from the middle of the smoke and dust. Two hundred men! They were all that returned of 600-odd that charged. I don't know the names of the Officers who fell or were taken prisoner, but very few returned.[20]

Cornet John Yates, Adjutant of the 11th Hussars, was with Cardigan as he reached the cavalry camp:

> His horse seemed to have had enough of it, and his lordship appeared to have been knocked about, but was cool and collected. He returned his sword, undid a little of the front of his dress, and pulled down his under-clothing under his waist-belt ... He then in a quiet way, as if talking to himself, said, 'I tell you what it is – those instruments of theirs', alluding to the Russian weapons, 'are deuced blunt; they tickle up one's ribs!' [referring to the slight wound given him by the Cossacks] ... After this, he asked, 'Has any one seen my regiment?'[21]

The return of the brigade was fearful, wrote Baron de Bazancourt:

> Horses without riders, or dragging after them their riders mortally wounded, galloped and bounded wildly across a plain strewn with the dead and the dying; others, with torn and bleeding flanks, terrified by all this noise, this fearful tumult, this waste of blood, and with difficulty supporting themselves upon their trembling limbs, came, like frightened herds, to mingle with the heavy horse, and seek protection there. It was, indeed, a sad and heart-rending spectacle to see that splendid brigade, which its valiant General brought sorrowfully back to the English lines, battered by shot, and reduced by more than half its number.[22]

Private Edward Woodham was one of those survivors. He confessed in a surprisingly frank interview for the *Illustrated London News* on the first Balaklava Banquet in October 1875, that at one point he thought 'it was all up with me' – but help was at hand:

> Near to the end of the valley my horse was shot under me, and it fell with my left leg under it, so that I could not move; but happily I was afterwards released ... A corporal of the 13th Light Dragoons rode up and commenced pulling at my horse's head, thinking it was not dead. And so it proved, for the animal gave a bit of a struggle, which I took advantage of, and regained my feet. All was then smoke and confusion, and all of our men that I could see were cutting right and left, and making their way back to camp ... I began running away as hard as I could, when a soldier belonging to the 8th Hussars, who was lying under his horse shouted to me 'For God's sake, man, don't leave me here.'
>
> At this time the firing from the guns was incessant – indeed it was murderous; still I returned and strove hard to release him, but without effect, the horse being dead. The enemy at this time were coming up the valley, killing the wounded on their march, so I said to the man, 'It's no use my stopping here; we shall both be killed' The poor fellow said something in reply, but I don't recollect it now. I then reluctantly left him to his fate, and joined three or four of my comrades who, like myself, had been unhorsed, and were trying to escape on foot.

Private John Berryman of the 17th Lancers also had his horse shot from under him as he reached the battery, one of her hind legs being broken. He quickly mounted another rider-less charger, only to find himself on the ground again, a bullet or canister ball having struck the horse's brass breastplate which was driven into its chest. Now stranded on foot, he was about to make his way back down the valley when he saw Captain John Webb had halted his horse. The captain was badly wounded and could not continue. In an account printed in the *Morning Post* of 1 February 1855, Berryman explained how he ran over to the wounded officer:

> I found that his wound was so painful that he could not ride any further. Lieutenant George Smith, of my regiment, coming by, I got him to stand at the horse's head whilst I lifted the Captain off. Having accomplished this, I assisted Smith to mount Webb's horse and to ride for a stretcher, taking notice where we were. By this time

the Russians had got back to their guns and re-opened fire. I saw six men from my own regiment get together and recount to each other their escapes. Seeing their danger, I called to them to separate, but too late, for a shell dropped amongst them, and I don't think anyone of them escaped alive. Hearing me call to these men, Captain Webb asked what I thought the Russians would do? 'They are sure to pursue, Sir, unless the Heavy Brigade comes down.' He replied, 'Then you had better consult to your own safety and leave me.'
'Oh no, Sir, I shall not leave you now'
'Perhaps they will only take me prisoner.'
'If they do, we will go together.'
'Don't mind me, look to yourself.'
'Alright, Sir, only we will go together, whatever happens.'
Just at that time I saw Sergeant Farrell coming by. I called to him. He asked, 'Who is it?' When I told him, he came over.
I said, 'We must get Captain Webb out of this for we shall be pursued.' He, agreeing, we made a chair out of our hands and lifted the Captain up, and found that we could carry him with comparative ease.
We got about 200 yards in this manner, when the Captain complained that his leg was very painful. A Private [was] near[by called] Malone. I asked him would he be good enough to support Captain Webb's legs until we could procure a stretcher. He did so and several of the officers passed us'.

Unfortunately, Captain Webb later died of his wounds. All three men, Berryman, Dublin born John Farrell and Sergeant Joseph Malone from Eccles, were eventually awarded the Victoria Cross.

Also making his way back on foot was Private Samuel Parkes, Lord Paget's six-foot-two-inch orderly, who had been wounded and his horse shot from under him. As he was walking back down the valley he saw the horse of the 4th Light Dragoons' Trumpeter Hugh Crawford go down. Crawford was thrown to the ground and two Cossacks, seeing the trumpet-major prostrate and helpless, bore down upon him. Private James Henry Herbert saw what happened:

Many of our men were fighting dismounted, their horses having been killed by fire or steel. Some of them performed prodigies of valour, amongst them being Sam Parkes, a private of my own regiment. When we were mixed up with the guns Parkes was on foot, his horse having been killed. He was surrounded by Russians and fought like a demon.[23]

Parkes' fighting retreat was also seen by James Wightman:

> I then rode towards Private Samuel Parkes, of the 4th Light
> Dragoons, who, supporting with one arm the wounded Trumpet-
> Major (Crawford) of his regiment, was with the other cutting and
> slashing at the enemies surrounding them. I struck in to aid the
> gallant fellow, who was not overpowered until his sword was shot
> away, when he and the trumpet-major were taken prisoners, and it
> was with difficulty I was able to cut my way out.

Parkes and Crawford spent two years in captivity. Upon his return
Parkes told Lord Paget that as he and Crawford were trying to make
their way back down the valley before they were captured they spotted
Major John Halkett of their regiment with what Parkes described as a
bad body wound. 'In accordance with his cries, Crawford lifted him on
to Parkes' back, and he carried him a short distance, when, to save
himself from attacks from the Cossacks, knots of whom were hovering
around, he was forced to let him down and leave.' When they returned
over the same ground as prisoners, they saw Halkett dead and stripped
of everything save his blue dragoon jacket.[24] Like Berryman, Farrell and
Malone, Parkes was later awarded the Victoria Cross.

Captain William Morris, in command of the 17th Lancers, also missed the
Russian guns and galloped on into the Russian cavalry. With around
twenty of his men, Morris came upon a squadron of Russian Hussars.
Ordering his men to keep together, he rode straight at the Russian leader,
running him through with his sword with such force that the Russian
toppled him over the side of his horse, and Morris, unable to disengage his
hand from his sword, fell with him. Now on the ground, the Russians
closed in on Morris, and slashed at him with their sabres. He received a
sabre cut on the left side of his head which carried away a large piece of
bone and penetrating both plates of his skull. He was knocked unconscious
but recovered and was seen by Troop Sergeant Major Abraham Ranson:

> Then I saw an act of heroism; Morris was on foot, his head streaming
> with blood, engaging five or six Cossacks. I made the remark to
> Corporal Taylor near me that poor Captain Morris, I was afraid, was
> taken prisoner, there was so much odds against him.[25]

Kinglake, who had earlier described Captain Morris as a man 'richly
gifted with the natural qualities which tend to make a leader of cavalry',
continues the story:

Morris sought to defend himself by the almost ceaseless 'moulinet' or circling whirl of his sword and from time to time he found means to deliver some sabre cuts upon the thighs of his Cossack assailants. Soon, however, he was pierced in the temple by a lance-point, which splintered up a piece of bone and forced it under the scalp. This wound gave him great pain and ... he believed that his life must be nearly at its end.[26]

Incredibly, Morris managed to stagger back down the valley and was spotted by Sergeant Major George Loy Smith of the 11th Hussars:

After a time I saw one of the 17th Lancers in front of me. I sped on and when I got near I found that he was an officer and wore his forage cap, much to my surprise. When within a few yards of him, I said, 'This is warm work, sir.' He looked over his right shoulder at me but made no reply – his face was covered in blood and he had a very wild appearance. This officer was Captain Morris who led the 17th Lancers and behaved so gallantly. I now inclined to my right towards the centre of the valley and in another minute, lost sight of him.

Some time passed, I can't say how much, but it was *very* long, waiting to see if any would return. Horses without riders, galloped back in numbers, and men wounded on foot and men not hurt, but their horses killed, returned on foot, and then we saw a horse or a man fall, who wounded, had come as far home as he could and then fell and died.

At length about 30 horsemen dashed through a line of Cossacks, who had reformed to interrupt their retreat, and then another larger body came in sight from the middle of the smoke and dust. Two hundred men! They were all that remained of 600 odd that charged.[27]

Morris was taken prisoner but in the confusion of the fighting, managed to slip away, capture a horse and make a dash for freedom, only to fall from his horse due to his wounds. Pursued by the Russians through the thick smoke of the battlefield, he caught another horse, but fell again when the horse was shot. This time the horse fell on him, trapping his leg. When he regained consciousness, despite being in agony from a broken right arm, broken ribs and three deep head wounds, he managed to free his leg and stagger towards the British lines. By a strange coincidence he came across the body of his good friend Captain Nolan and lay down beside it.

Once again Morris lapsed into unconsciousness but he was spotted by one of Raglan's aides-de-camp, Captain Ewart, who was near No.4 Redoubt as the Light Brigade limped back towards camp. Ewart dismounted and spoke to him but Morris was almost insensible. As he could not lift Morris or the others by himself, Ewart rode back towards No.4 Redoubt. Ewart sought help in recovering the bodies and he got together a number of the Turks who, presumably, had previously been in the redoubt.

The recovery party reached the ground where Nolan and Morris lay. As the Turks were moving off with Nolan's body some Russian guns opened fire on them, probably from the Fedioukine Heights. The Turks dropped Nolan and ran away.

Ewart called to the nearest British cavalryman to get a stretcher. This, it seems, was Private George Smith of the 5th Dragoon Guards. According to Assistant-Surgeon William Cattell:

> Pte Geo. Smith informed Sgt. O'Hara of the spot where Morris lay and [General] Scarlett sent the staff surgeon with Tr. Sergt. Major Wooden to bring him in. They found a trooper trying to arrest the bleeding from the scalp. Presently some Cossacks attacked the party and the doctor, Mouat, said he had to draw his sword, which he described as 'a novel experience'

After dressing Morris' wounds, they succeeded in returning to their lines. For saving the life of Morris, who went on to become a Lieutenant Colonel, Surgeon Mouat, of the 6th Dragoons, was recommended for the Victoria Cross – however, German-born Wooden, who it is said was not a popular character, was not put forward for the award.

After the announcement of Mouat's VC, Wooden wrote to him saying that if the doctor was to receive a Victoria Cross then so should he as he had been at Mouat's side during the rescue of Morris. Luckily for Wooden, Dr. Mouat agreed and wrote to the Horse Guards supporting Wooden's claim. The reply to his letter reads:

> His Royal Highness [the Duke of Cambridge] feels very unwilling to bring any further claim for the Victoria Cross for an act performed at so distant a period but as the decoration has been conferred on Dr James Mouat for the part he took in the rescue of Lt. Col. Morris and Sergeant-Major Wooden appears to have acted in a manner very honourable to him on the occasion and, by his gallantry, been equally instrumental in saving the life of this officer, His Royal Highness is induced to submit the case.[28]

Wooden's Victoria Cross was gazetted on 26 October 1858, the very last of the Crimean War.

Having cut his way through the Russian lancers, Wightman, who it might be recalled was with privates Mustard and Fletcher, forced his way through 'ring after ring of enemies', meeting up with Private Peter Marsh, also of the 17th Lancers:

> And rode rearward, breaking through party after party of Cossacks, until we heard the familiar voice of Corporal [Thomas] Morley, of our regiment, a great, rough, bellowing Nottingham man. He had lost his lance hat, and his long hair was flying out in the wind as he roared 'Coom ere! Coom ere! Fall in, lads, fall in!' Well, with his shouts and oaths he had collected some twenty troopers of various regiments. We fell in with the handful this man of the hour had rallied to him, and there joined us also under his leadership [Troop] Sergeant Major [Abraham] Ranson and Private John Penn of the 17th. Penn, a tough old warrior who had served with the 3rd Light in the Sikh war, had killed a Russian officer, dismounted, and with great deliberation accoutred himself with the belt and the sword of the defunct, in which he made a great show.

Lieutenant Alexander Dunn, in charge of 'F' Troop, 11th Hussars, was also making his way back along the valley when he saw Sergeant William Bentley from his troop who was wrestling with his horse, which had been severely wounded. The Russians had also seen Bentley's difficulties and had singled him out as an easy target. Three of them concentrated their efforts to knock him out of his saddle and were preparing to finish him off. Seeing Bentley's predicament, Dunn wheeled around and galloped through a maze of dead and dying as well as rider-less horses charging about in all directions to rescue him. At six-foot-three and high in the saddle, Dunn, who was born in Toronto in Canada, had Wilkinson's Swords fashion a four-foot-long sabre for him, four-and-a-half inches longer than the 1853 Pattern Light Cavalry sabre:

> Prancing, side-wheeling, rearing his thoroughbred, he parried, thrusted and slashed at the assailants, felling them all in a matter of minutes. But Bentley was still in dire straights, desperately hanging on to his horse by one of the stirrups so Dunn dismounted, lifted Bentley back into his own saddle, then belted the horse on the rump to send it galloping towards the British lines. On foot Dunn suddenly caught sight of Private Robert Levett from his troop who had lost his mount and was in danger of being cut down by a

Russian hussar. Dunn rushed to his aid and skewered the enemy to death with his giant-sized sabre.

Bentley himself described the incident, which took place after Lieutenant Colonel John Douglas of the 11th Hussars had told his men to retire and re-form upon the lancers in the rear:

> I drew his [Douglas'] attention to the circumstance of their being Russians, and not our lancers, when we got his order 'Fight for your lives,' thereupon all retired. On passing them [the Russian lancers] I was attacked by an officer and several men, and received a slight wound from a lance. I was pursued by them, and cut the officer across the face. Lieutenant Dunn came to my assistance. I saw him cleave one almost to the saddle and can bear witness to his admirable and gallant fortitude.[29]

Unfortunately, Levette was killed. Bentley survived thanks to Alexander Dunn who, consequently, was awarded the Victoria Cross.

Despite meeting up with others, James Wightman and the men he was with, were chased by the Russian cavalry and very few of the group with Corporal Morley got through. Wightman was not among those that escaped, yet he survived to tell his astonishing story:

> As we rode up the valley, pursued by some Hussars and Cossacks, my horse was wounded by a bullet in the shoulder, and I had hard work to put the poor beast along. Presently we were abreast of the Infantry who had blazed into our right as we went down; and we had to take their fire again, this time on our left. Their fire was very impartial; their own Hussars and Cossacks following close on us suffered from it as well as we did … My horse was shot dead, riddled with bullets. One bullet struck me on the forehead, another passed through the top of my shoulder; while struggling out from under my horse a Cossack standing over me stabbed me with his lance once in the neck near the jugular, again above the collar-bone, several times in the back and once under the short rib; and when, having regained my feet, I was trying to draw my sword, he sent his lance through the palm of my hand. I believe he would have succeeded in killing me, clumsy as he was, if I had not blinded him for a moment with a handful of sand.

At the same time as Wightman was fighting for his life, Private Fletcher's horse was also wounded. The two men were taken prisoner by the Cossacks and dragged along by the tails of their coatees. When they got to their feet they were taken back up the valley, pushed forwards with lance-butts in their backs. Both men, though, were in very poor condition. 'With my shattered knee and the other bullet wound on the shin of the same leg, I could barely limp,' continued Wightman:

> Good old Fletcher said 'Get on my back, chum!' I did so, and then found that he had been shot through the back of the head. When I told him of this, his only answer was, 'Oh, never mind that, it's not much, I don't think'.

The heroic Fletcher's wound was far more serious than he made out, and a few days later it proved fatal. 'He was a doomed man himself, making light of a mortal wound, and carrying a chance comrade of another regiment on his back.' Wightman wrote that he, someone who had been wounded at least nine times in the leg, back, shoulder and hand, felt like a 'woman' having taken a ride on the back of a dying man. Though it is a great story, Wightman was mistaken. Though the date of his death is not known, Thomas survived, and lived until at least 1875.[30]

Private William Pearson of the 17th Lancers owed his escape to his horse, which he had taught to perform certain 'circus tricks'. This was revealed in his obituary which appeared in the *Yorkshire Evening Post* of Monday, 14 June 1909:

> Of the Balaklava Charge, Mr. Pearson often related a thrilling story ... Three Cossacks tried to cut young Pearson off, and he gave rein to his charger, which required no urging and would have cleared them, having beaten off all three with his lance, but a fourth appeared, wheeling right across his path.
>
> It was a moment in which the scales of life and death are balanced. There was no time for thought. More by inspiration than anything else, Pearson pressed his knees ... In response, the faithful animal reared itself and seemed as though it were to come down on the Cossack with its forefeet.
>
> The Cossack swerved, upset at this new mode of attack, and in a flash Pearson got through, not before, however, one of the three had jabbed him in the side with his lance. At the time he hardly felt the wound, although it had penetrated the left lung, and he reached the British lines in safety.

Pearson collapsed almost as soon as he reached the British positions, air having been sucked into his lungs through his wound. He survived to live to the age of eighty-four.

There were similar stories of survival amongst the *Chasseurs d'Afrique*, such as that described in the *Illustrated London News* of Saturday, 25 November 1854:

> With fearful impetuosity, they dashed upon a battery on the left of our army, which had been telling severely upon our men, and cutting down the gunners …Of course there were some very narrow escapes. One of my friends in the squadron had his horse killed in the very [infantry] square – in the midst of the enemy; but was fortunate enough to catch an artillery horse, which he mounted, and got off safely with his companions.

Another who was fortunate to survive the charge was Private John Doyle of the 8th Hussars:

> My horse got a bullet through his nose, above the noseband, which caused him to lose a great deal of blood, and every time he gave his head a chuck the blood spurted over me. That night when I opened my cloak, I found 23 bullets in it. There were five buttons blown off my dress jacket, the sling of my sabretache were cut off … I also had the right heel and spur blown off my boot.[31]

Private Thomas Perry of the 8th Hussars was amongst those of the Light Brigade who had been captured and taken prisoner. A letter that he sent to his parents from hospital in Simferopol was published in the *Huddersfield Chronicle* of 24 February 1855:

> I myself was shot through both thighs, and through the right shoulder, at the top part of the arm, two sword cuts in the head, and two lance wounds, one in the hand and one in the thigh; so I leave you to think I was in a bad state. I was taken up almost dead by the Russians; but after I got a doctor's attendance I began to do well.

Fanny Duberly had watched the return of the Light Brigade, feeling 'sick at heart':

> Colonel Shewell came up to me, looking flushed, and conscious of having fought like a brave and gallant soldier, and having earned his

laurels well. Many had a sad tale to tell. All had been struck with the exception of colonel Shewell, either themselves or their horses. Poor Lord Fitzgibbon was dead. Of Captain Lockwood no tidings had been heard; none had seen him fall, and none had seen him since the action. Mr Clutterbuck was wounded in the foot; Mr Seager in the hand. Captain Thompson's horse had been shot under him; Major De Salis's horse wounded. Mr Mussenden showed me a grape-shot which had 'killed my poor mare.' Mr Clowes was a prisoner. Poor Captain Goad, of the 13th is dead. Ah, what a catalogue!'[32]

Lieutenant Colonel George Bell of the Royals also described the fearful scene after the battle:

The dead are lying thick beside their horses, many of which are badly wounded; some unable to rise are biting at the short grass within their reach. Poor things, they must die of their wounds and starvation at last; 381 of ours lie dead. See the effect of our broadswords, such ghastly dead, such terrible wounds. That stout fellow how quiet he lies upon his back with his eyes open; an English sabre let out his life-blood under the left arm; his long grey-coat does not look very 'militaire' just now, it is drenched in gore–a shocking spectacle! That next body is more hideous to look on, his head nearly cleft in twain as if by an axe, his long beard matted with blood. He sleeps soundly. This fellow wears an embroidered hussar jacket. His bridal arm is cut in two, but it was that deep thrust between the ribs which sent his soul away … That one is very young, fair-headed, youthful soldier. His light-blue eyes are open wide, his two hands are clenched tight, as if grasped at something in agony before his soul took flight; he lies in a bloody bath. This one here was of another regiment. A sky-blue cloth shako, high and broad in the crown, lies beside him uninjured; it fell from his head, no doubt, in his fruitless combat … Many tears of sorrow may be shed for this poor youth, but who will ever know his fate?[33]

Though there was much sorrow at the terrible loss of life, there was also much relief; the survivors scarcely believing their luck. Amongst these was Lieutenant Edward Seager of the 8th Hussars:

Those that were left collected, shook hands and congratulated each other on escaping. We, about 5, sat down on the grass, and fared sumptuously on salt pork and biscuits, washed down by rations of rum, all brought on the ground by our quartermaster.[34]

Despite having taken part in the most famous cavalry action in history, and seemingly untroubled by the terrible losses his regiments had suffered, Lord Cardigan, upon his return to the British lines was more concerned with military protocol than reporting to his divisional commander:

> I rode slowly up the hill, and met General Scarlett. I said to him, 'What do you think, General, of the aide-de-camp [Nolan], after such an order being brought to us which has destroyed the Light Brigade, riding to the rear and screaming like a woman? Sir J. Scarlett replied, 'Do not say any more, for I have ridden over his body.'[35]

Private Daniel Deering of the 4th Light Dragoons had escaped back to the safety of the British end of the valley:

> When we got back to where we started from, I saw Lord Cardigan in front of us; he rode up and said, 'This has been a great blunder, but don't blame me for it.'

To this some of the men replied, 'Never mind, my lord! We are ready to go again,' Cardigan answering: 'No, no men! You have done enough'.

After a roll-call revealed only 195 mounted men present under arms, Cardigan trotted up to Raglan, who had descended into the valley with his staff, to make his report. 'What did you mean, sir,' asked the Commander-in-Chief, 'by attacking a battery in front, contrary to all the usages of warfare, and the customs of the service?'

'My Lord', replied Cardigan, 'I hope you will not blame me, for I received the order to attack from my superior officer in front of the troops.'[36]

Equally, Raglan and Lucan were already setting out their positons. In a confidential letter to the Duke of Newcastle, penned on the 25th, Raglan wrote that 'Lord Lucan had made a fatal mistake ... The written order sent to him by the Quarter-master General did not exact that he should attack at all hazards, and contained no expression which could bear that construction.'

As for Lucan, he was certain of his ground: 'I do not intend to bear the smallest particle of responsibility. I gave the order to charge under what I considered a most imperious necessity, and I will not bear one particle of the blame.'[37]

Who then was to blame?

Chapter 11

'Someone Had Blundered'

Though the Charge of the Light Brigade became one of the most celebrated actions of the Crimean War, in practical terms it had little bearing on the Battle of Balaklava. By the time Cardigan led his men down the North Valley the Russians had given up their attack upon the British-held port following the repulse of their cavalry by Scarlet and Campbell, and the British infantry had finally arrived to help Balaklava's defenders. Even the battle as a whole was of far less significance than the impression its famous incidents have had upon British perceptions. At the Alma, for instance, total Allied casualties amounted to more than 3,000 men; and by its conclusion, the Siege of Sevastopol would result in the death of 128,387 Allied troops, and a not hugely dissimilar number of Russians. The 271 casualties suffered by the Light Brigade on 25 October, whilst not trivial, were of no great consequence, other than the loss of a large proportion of the available British cavalry. In fact, the loss of 170 of the 500 Turks in No.1 Redoubt was proportionately little different from that suffered by the Light Brigade yet this is hardly ever reflected upon, and despite the heroics of the British and French infantry and cavalry, Russian casualties incurred during the battle amounted to only 238 killed and 312 wounded.[1] Balaklava was, in reality, little more than a minor clash amid a protracted and hugely costly war.

Though the loss of the Causeway Heights caused major logistical problems for the British over the subsequent winter, the months following the battle would see little opportunity for cavalry action in the static warfare of the siege, so even the loss of such a high percentage of men and horses from the Light Brigade had no material effect on the operations of the Allied army. As one British surgeon observed, three times the number of men lost in the charge would die of disease in a week and those in authority would 'think nothing of it'.[2] Temple

178

Godman of the 5th Dragoon Guards, for example, wrote to his brother Frederick about the charge eight days after the battle:

> Later in the day the Light Brigade charged down a valley, they had no business to have gone there, they lost about 300, but can't get the numbers exactly, they took twenty-five guns [sic] and killed an immense number, but were totally annihilated by batteries on each side of the valley. The weather is fearfully cold ... [3]

This was a single sentence in a long letter, placing the charge in its true context as one incident in a prolonged siege involving tens of thousands of troops on both sides. Godman had written to his father in more detail on the day after about the charge, but that was in the past, and in war, events move on rapidly. Similarly, Private Henry William Parker of the 11th Hussars, when writing to his father, regarded the fighting on the 25th, as nothing more than a 'skirmish'.[4]

The overriding sentiment in the British press, as we have seen, was largely positive. A mistake had been made, but mistakes happen in the heat of battle and the charge was seen as being so glorious no-one was going to delve too deeply into its causes – there was nothing to be gained in that.

Indeed, the causes of the mistaken charge might have been pushed aside had it not been for Lucan's objection to Raglan's official despatch on the battle, which was published in *The Times* on 13 November.

> As the enemy withdrew from the ground which they had momentarily occupied, I directed the cavalry, supported by the Fourth Division under Lieutenant-General Sir George Cathcart, to move forward, and take advantage of any opportunity to regain the heights; and, not having been able to accomplish this immediately, and it appearing that an attempt was making to remove the captured guns, the Earl of Lucan was desired to advance rapidly, follow the enemy in their retreat, and try to prevent them from effecting their objects.
>
> In the meanwhile the Russians had time to re-form on their own ground, with artillery in front and upon their flanks.
>
> From some misconception of the instruction to advance, the Lieutenant-General considered that he was bound to attack at all hazards, and he accordingly ordered Major-General the Earl of Cardigan to move forward with the Light Brigade.
>
> This order was obeyed in the most spirited and gallant manner. Lord Cardigan charged with the utmost vigour, attacked a battery

which was firing upon the advancing squadrons, and, having passed beyond it, engaged the Russian cavalry in its rear; but there his troops were assailed by artillery and infantry as well as cavalry, and necessarily retired, after having committed much havoc upon the enemy.

They effected this movement without haste or confusion; but the loss they have sustained has, I deeply lament, been very severe in officers, men, and horses, only counterbalanced by the brilliancy of the attack and the gallantry, order, and discipline which distinguished it, forming a striking contrast to the conduct of the enemy's cavalry which had previously been engaged with the heavy brigade.

Not only did Raglan appear to praise Lucan's hated brother-in-law for his 'gallant manner' but the despatch also stated, for all the world to see, that Lucan had misconceived the Commander-in-Chief's instructions. In other words, Lucan was responsible for the loss of the Light Brigade.

A furious Lucan immediately defended himself in a long letter to Raglan, asking the Commander-in-Chief to pass on the letter to the Duke of Newcastle. A row was brewing and very rapidly the mistaken charge became the subject of great interest both in the British camp and back in the UK after the publication of Russell's report in *The Times*. People wanted answers. How could such an inconceivable action have happened?

One of those who was intrigued by the growing dispute was Lieutenant Colonel George Dallas of the 46th Foot, who, like so many then and since, pondered on the question of who was to blame, or who would be blamed, for the loss of the Light Brigade:

> Who will answer for it, I don't know. Ld. Lucan *I am told* lays the blame on the A.D.C. who brought him the order, poor fellow! I knew him well, a most promising Officer, Captain Nolan, 15th Hussars.[5]

It was true that initially many men thought that Nolan was the one who had caused the light cavalry to charge the Don Battery, including Captain Robert Portal of the 4th Light Dragoons:

> Captain Nolan was shot dead the first shot, and we think it was a judgement on him for having been the cause of us getting into such a mess. Lord Lucan is dreadfully cut up about it, but says he 'can show the order in writing, which is his only comfort'.[6]

Kinglake was a nephew of Raglan and, understandably, saw nothing wrong with the orders the Commander-in-Chief sent to Lord Lucan:

> Whether taken alone, or as a command reinforcing the one before sent, this order has really no word in it which is either obscure or misleading. By assigning 'the guns' as the object, Lord Raglan most pointedly fixed the line of the Turkish redoubts as the direction in which to advance; and it must not be said that the expression left room in the mind of Lord Lucan for a doubt as to what guns were meant. He well knew that the guns indicated by the 'fourth order' were the English guns taken in the forts—in the forts crowning those very 'heights' which, more than half an hour before, he had been ordered to retake if he could.[7]

Kinglake goes on to say that Lucan, more than anyone, knew which guns Raglan was referring to as he had received the earlier order to try and recover the Causeway Heights:

> If collated with the third order, the written words brought down by Nolan seem to come with accumulated weight and decisiveness. By the third order, the commander of our cavalry had been directed to advance, and take any opportunity of recovering the heights—those heights, be it remembered, where the enemy was posted with the seven English guns he had captured; and now, by this fourth order, Lord Lucan—being requested to advance rapidly to the front, and try to prevent the enemy from carrying away the guns—was, for the second time, told that he must operate against the Russians on the Causeway Heights, and was furnished with a new and special motive for energy and despatch.
>
> Construed singly, the fourth order looks clear as day; read along with the former direction it looks equally clear, but even more cogent; for, when so considered, it appears to visit Lord Lucan with something like an expression of impatience and displeasure for having allowed more than half an hour to pass after the receipt of the third order without trying to recover the 'heights'.

Was Kinglake correct in stating that there was no ambiguity in the orders which were all on the same subject and Lucan could not possibly have misconstrued the last of them? Well, before Raglan's official despatch had been published, Lucan had already submitted his report on the Cavalry Division at the battle. What is most revealing in this report is that Lucan was indeed aware that he had been instructed to 'make a rapid advance to our front, to prevent the enemy carrying the guns lost by the Turkish troops in the morning.' This is exactly what Raglan had wished. So Lucan appears, as Kinglake stated, to have understood exactly what was required of him:

My Lord,— I have the honor to report that the cavalry division under my command was seriously engaged with the enemy on the 25th inst., during the greater part of which day it was under a heavy fire; that it made a most triumphant charge against a very superior number of the enemy's cavalry, and an attack upon batteries which, for daring and gallantry, could not be exceeded. The loss, however, in officers, men, and horses, has been most severe.

From half-past 6 in the morning, when the Horse Artillery first opened fire, till the enemy had possessed itself of all the different forts, the cavalry, constantly changing their positions, continued giving all the support they could to the Turkish troops, though much exposed to the fire of heavy guns and riflemen, when they took post on the left of the second line of redoubts by an order from your Lordship.

The Heavy Brigade had soon to return to the support of the troops defending Balaklava, was fortunate enough in being at hand when a large force of Russian cavalry was descending the hill. I immediately ordered Brigadier-General Scarlett to attack with the Scots Grays [sic] and Enniskillen Dragoons, and had his attack supported in second line by the 5th Dragoon Guards, and by a flank attack of the 4th Dragoon Guards.

Under every disadvantage of ground, these eight small squadrons succeeded in defeating and dispersed a body of cavalry estimated at three times their number and more.

The Heavy Brigade now having joined the Light Brigade, the division took up a position with a view of supporting an attack upon the heights, when, being instructed to make a rapid advance to our front, to prevent the enemy carrying the guns lost by the Turkish troops in the morning, I ordered the Light Brigade to advance in two lines, and supported them with the Heavy Brigade. This attack of the Light Cavalry was very brilliant and daring; exposed to a fire from heavy batteries on their front and two flanks, they advanced unchecked until they reached the batteries of the enemy, and cleared them of their gunners, and only retired when they found themselves engaged with a very superior force of cavalry in the rear. Major-General the Earl of Cardigan led this attack in the most gallant and intrepid manner; and his Lordship has expressed himself to me as admiring in the highest degree the courage and zeal of every officer, non-commissioned officer, and man who assisted.

The Heavy Brigade advanced to the support of the attack under a very galling fire from the batteries and infantry in a redoubt, and acted with most perfect steadiness, and in a manner to deserve all praise.

The losses, my Lord, it grieves me to state, have been very great indeed, and, I fear, will be much felt by you Lordship.

I cannot too strongly recommend to your Lordship the two General officers commanding the brigades, all the officers in command of regiments, as also the divisional and brigade staffs; indeed, the conduct of every individual, of every rank, I feel to be deserving of my entire praise, and, I hope, of your Lordship's approbation.

The conduct of the Royal Horse Artillery troop, first under the command of Captain Maude, and, after that officer was severely wounded, of Captain Shakespear, was most meritorious and praiseworthy. I received from these those two officers every possible assistance during the time they respectively commanded.

This is perhaps the most revealing document relating to the entire controversy surrounding the charge of the Light Brigade. In it, Lucan admits that he knew perfectly well that the objective was not to attack the Don Cossack battery at the head of the valley but to prevent the guns being removed from the redoubts. Raglan has been severely criticized by historians for his failure to adequately convey his instructions and this led to the confusion which resulted in the wrong guns being attacked. Whilst it will be seen that Raglan was indeed the perpetrator of the ill-judged charge, it was not due to a misunderstanding on Lucan's part. This complaint therefore can no longer be upheld. Lucan knew full well what Raglan intended, admitting this in his own words.

When Lucan wrote the above report it was immediately after the battle and he had no inkling of how celebrated the charge would become, or that he would be held responsible for the loss of the Light Brigade. As we shall see, as the disagreement escalated, Lucan would change his version of events.

Very shortly after the battle the subject of why the light cavalry charged the Russian guns was being discussed in the British camp. Henry Clifford, who as the aide-de-camp to George Brown of the Light

Division had no particular axe to grind, made the following observations on 27 October in a letter home. It is evident that it was widely seen that the feud between Lucan and Cardigan was, at least in part, responsible for the disaster:

> I must tell you that but little confidence has been placed in the commanding powers of Lord Lucan commanding the Cavalry and long and loud have been the feuds on public grounds, between his Lordship and Lord Cardigan (than whom, a braver soldier never held a sword) who commands the Light Brigade; and it was thought if a verbal order was sent to Lord L. it might be misunderstood, or not carried out. A written order was, therefore, sent from Lord Raglan by Captain Nolan, General Airey's A.D.C. ... desiring his Lordship to 'charge.' 'To charge what?' said Lord Lucan very naturally. 'Here are your orders,' said poor Nolan, pointing to the paper, *and there,* pointing to the Russian army, 'is the enemy,' and shouting 'Come on' to the Light Brigade of Cavalry, he dashed forward. He was wrong, poor fellow in doing so, he forgot his position, and his conduct was most insulting to Lord Lucan and Lord Cardigan, who at the head of his Brigade, pale with indignation, shouted to him to stop, that he would answer for his words and actions before Lord Raglan, but he was called to a higher tribunal, a shell struck him in the chest, and in a few minutes he was a mangled corpse.[8]

Two days later, Clifford wrote again about the charge after he had had a conversation with Cardigan. It shows, without any ambiguity whatsoever, that Cardigan knew exactly which guns Raglan was referring to:

> He gave me full particulars of it, which corresponds exactly with what I have written to you about it, except that the written order brought to Lord Lucan by poor Nolan was worded as follows: 'Lord L. will attack with Cavalry, and prevent the English guns in the redoubts being taken away by the enemy.' This order was written at some distance from Lord Lucan, and still greater from the guns and redoubts in question, which were in the hands of the Russians, and no attempt being made to carry them off, Lord Cardigan pointed out to Lord L the position the enemy held, the fact of no attempt being made to carry off the guns, and the distance at which the order had been written, all of which justified his demanding further explanations from Lord Raglan of the vague order sent by Captain

Nolan, for it was evident to every Officer and man in the Cavalry force, that it was sending men to certain destruction, to order some 600 to charge an army in position of 20,000!

Lord Cardigan says he would not have obeyed the order till it was made more clear to him what he was to charge, and if Lord Raglan intended the lives of so many brave soldiers to be thrown away for nothing, as nothing could be gained by it.

Lord Lucan then asked poor Nolan 'What he was to charge?' Nolan pointed to the paper and said 'There are your orders – and there is your enemy.'[9]

So, we now have both Lucan and Cardigan stating in the aftermath of the battle that they understood the objective of the Light Brigade was to prevent the guns in the redoubts being taken away. Poor though Raglan's orders were, in this regard they were understood. This, therefore, implies that Nolan not only knew which guns the order referred to but that he also communicated those orders accurately. Though we do not have Nolan's words to confirm this, a fellow officer wrote to the *Daily News* shortly after the battle:

> I cannot help remembering that Captain Nolan was one of our most distinguished cavalry officers – a man who ... had acquired a thorough knowledge of his arm, and who, more than any one else, was able to make a fair estimate of its capabilities ... he had also been a deep thinker on his profession, and was the author of one of the best books on cavalry service. To lead cavalry, unsupported by foot, through a cross-fire of two batteries, in order to cut down the support and gunners of the third, is so adventurous and unmilitary a proceeding that Captain Nolan is the last man whom I can believe of so much thoughtfulness and folly.[10]

Other members of the Light Brigade also seemed to believe they were aiming to prevent the guns in the redoubts being removed. Private Anthony Sheridan was with the 8th Hussars:

> Lord Raglan and his staff were on the hills above us, surveying the Russians with their field glasses, when they saw, as I supposed, the cowardly Turks leave their guns in the redoubt, and run for their lives. There were five guns left, and each one was loaded and not spiked when the Russians got up to them. Presently Captain Nolan, riding a horse of the 13th Light Dragoons, came up with a paper from Lord Raglan, and we imagined at once that we were to move.

> The order was ... to charge on the guns left by the Turks, in order, as I suppose, that we might recover them from the enemy.[11]

Private Charles Howell of the 1st Dragoons likewise was under no illusions as to the purpose of the charge:

> Now in front of the cavelery [sic] encamped there were 4 redoubts or batterys [sic] with 3 ships guns in each manned by, I was going to say Turkish soldier's but they hardly deserve the name. They fled from the guns and left them in the before the enemy got near them ... And it was to retake them that the fatal charge was made.[12]

Similarly, Robert Farquharson, understood the Light Brigade's objective:

> An aide-de-camp from Lord Raglan came up with an order that the Light Brigade of cavalry was to attack the enemy, and recapture, if possible, some guns they were carrying off from the Turkish redoubts.[13]

As we have seen Corporal Robert Grant of the 4th Light Dragoons, told the *Illustrated London News* that 'We then disabled as many gunners and drivers as we could, to prevent them taking away the guns, feeling they were ours'.[14] This is exactly the point. Liprandi's men occupied the valley and the adjoining heights contiguously and it was hard to differentiate between any of the guns held by the enemy. It must be remembered that many of the troopers and officers said they could see little amidst the gunsmoke which filled the valley.

Nolan, condemned by historians as being the perpetrator of the disaster that befell the Light Brigade, can now be cleared of all blame. He had faithfully communicated Raglan's instructions. Lucan, consequently, remained adamant that he had done no more than pass on Raglan's instructions to Cardigan, and he told William Russell that he was,

> quite content with *his* charge – he had ordered the Heavy Brigade to charge the Russian horse, and he had nothing to do with Lord Raglan's charge, except to pass on the orders he had received, that the Light Brigade was to charge – that he had not lost them, he had obeyed orders.

Lucan refused to accept any personal responsibility, and he insisted that his letter justifying his actions was passed onto Newcastle. Raglan asked

Airey to try and placate Lucan, advising him that 'it would not lead to his advantage in the slightest degree'. But Lucan was not to be dissuaded. He believed, and with some justification, that Raglan had persistently favoured Cardigan and this latest event, in which Cardigan had been praised and he himself, as he saw it, condemned, was the final straw. He demanded that his letter was sent to London.

Raglan duly despatched the lieutenant general's letter, but, naturally appended his own covering letter justifying his own actions:

> Lieutenant-General the Earl of Lucan complains that, in my despatch to your Grace of the 28th of October I stated that, 'from some misconception of the instruction to advance', the Lieutenant General considered that he was 'bound to attack at all hazards.' His lordship conceives this statement to be a grave charge, and an imputation reflecting seriously on his professional character, and he deems it incumbent upon him to state those facts which he cannot doubt must clear him from what he respectfully submits as altogether unmerited.
>
> I have referred to my despatch, and, far from being willing to recall one word of it, I am prepared to declare, that not only did the Lieutenant General misconceive the written instruction that was sent him, but that there was nothing in that instruction which called upon him to attack at all hazards, or to undertake the operation which led to such a brilliant display of gallantry on the part of the Light Brigade, and unhappily, at the same time, occasioned such lamentable casualties in every regiment composing it.
>
> In his lordship's letter, he is wholly silent with respect to a previous order which had been sent him. He merely says that the cavalry was formed to support an intended movement of the infantry.
>
> This previous order was in the following words:— 'The cavalry to advance and take advantage of any opportunity to recover the heights. They will he supported by infantry, which has been ordered to advance on two fronts.'
>
> This order did not seem to me to have been attended to, and therefore it was that the instruction by Captain Nolan was forwarded to him. Lord Lucan must have read the first order with very little attention, for he now states that the cavalry was formed to support the infantry, whereas he was told by Brigadier-General Airey, 'that the cavalry was to advance, and take advantage of any opportunity to recover the heights, and that they would be supported by infantry,' not that they were to support the infantry;

and so little had he sought to do as he had been directed, that he had no men in advance of his main body, made no attempt to regain the heights, and was so little informed of the position of the enemy that he asked Captain Nolan, 'Where and what he was to attack,' as neither enemy nor guns were in sight.

This, your Grace will observe, is the Lieutenant General's own admission. The result of his inattention to the first order was, that it never occurred to him that the second was connected with, and a repetition of, the first. He viewed it only as a positive order to attack at all hazards (the word 'attack,' be it observed, was not made use of in General Airey's note) an unseen enemy, whose position, numbers, and composition, he was wholly unacquainted with, and whom, in consequence of a previous order, he had taken no step whatever to watch.

I undoubtedly had no intention that he should make such an attack—there was nothing in the instruction to require it; and therefore I conceive I was fully justified in stating to your Grace, what was the exact truth, that the charge arose from the misconception of an order for the advance, which Lord Lucan considered obliged him to attack at all hazards. I wish I could say with his lordship that, having decided against his conviction to make the movement, he did all he could to render it as little perilous as possible. This, indeed, is far from being the case, in my judgment.

He was told that the horse-artillery might accompany the cavalry. He did not bring it up. He was informed that the French cavalry was on his left. He did not invite their co-operation. He had the whole of the heavy cavalry at his disposal. He mentions having brought up only two regiments in support, and he omits all other precautions, either from want of due consideration, or from the supposition that the unseen enemy was not in such great force as he apprehended, notwithstanding that he was warned of it by Lord Cardigan, after the latter had received the order to attack.

Whilst Raglan's imprecisely-worded orders, compounded by his shouted instruction to Nolan to tell Lucan to attack immediately, were undoubtedly the catalyst that set the whole unfortunate affair in motion, the Commander-in-Chief had made some valid points, none of which reflected well on Lucan. In particular, was the fact that Lucan had not kept up with the unfolding events of the battle and was unaware of the positions of the enemy, (unlike Captain Shakespear of 'I' Troop who, it may be recalled, had undertaken a personal reconnaissance). This was noted by Sergeant-Major Franks, who wrote that, 'neither the General in command of the Cavalry or anyone else of the two Brigades could see from where we were stationed what was going on on the other side of the ridge where the earthworks were thrown up, or in the valley beyond.'[15]

The other point was that Lucan had attacked without the horse artillery which was attached to, and was an integral part of, the Cavalry Division, and left the Light Brigade unsupported. These failings were remarked on by others, including Loy Smith:

> The same man that ordered Lord Cardigan with 670 men had to charge an army in position and them left them to their fate when he had at his command eight squadrons of Heavy Cavalry and two troops of Horse Artillery ... True, that he advanced two regiments of this brigade a short distance down the valley; but why did he not follow on? What did this avail us, for as soon as he came under fire, he began to retire.[16]

Airey was correct in warning Lucan that he would achieve nothing by involving the Government. The earl should simply have let the matter go, as he would emerge with little credit if his actions on the 25th were the subject of close scrutiny.

Lucan, as a matter of fact, would have been even more incensed had he seen the private letter sent by Raglan to Newcastle with his official despatch in which the Commander-in-Chief throws all responsibility for the charge upon Lucan. To add to his utter incapacity to command an army in the field, must be that of duplicity, sending disparaging reports to the Government behind the backs of his senior officers.

After complaining about the conduct of the Turks, Raglan wrote:

> But you will be much more shocked to see the loss sustained by our Light Cavalry. This, indeed is a heavy misfortune notwithstanding the brilliancy of their conduct and I feel it most deeply.
>
> The written order sent to him by the quarter master general did not exact that Lord Lucan should attack at all hazards and contained no expression which could bear that construction but he so considered it, taunted I believe by the Officer who carried it and who appears to have conducted himself with great impropriety and assumed an authority which was wholly *deplacé* and for which he ought to have been reproved instead of being listened to.
>
> This officer was General Airey's Aide de Camp Captain Nolan ...He was killed by the splinter of a shell which burst between the poor fellow and Cardigan.

> This latter who is as brave as a lion absolutely thought it his duty to point out to Lord Lucan the artillery that he was about to attack and that which would oppose him on the flanks but the latter retained the idea that he had imbibed and fancied that he had no discretion to exercise. Fatal Mistake! My only consolation is the admirable conduct of the Troops which was beyond all praise.[17]

The open dispute between the Commander-in-Chief and his cavalry commander soon became the talk of the British encampment. Everyone wanted to see how it would play out, and, of course, each person formed his own opinion on what had happened and who was to blame.

As has been mentioned, Temple Godman of the 5th Dragoon Guards wrote about the charge of the Light Brigade to his father the following day, the 26th. It is interesting to note that before describing what he saw, Godman said that the charge was the result of 'a mistake in an order which Captain Nolan brought from Lord Raglan'.[18] At this early stage it was believed that it was the order that was at fault, or the manner in which its contents had been relayed by Nolan, not Lucan or Cardigan's interpretation of the order.

In his journal, Paget had wisely observed that the charge would 'be the cause of much ill-blood and accusation', and, as we have seen, he was correct. He points the finger squarely at Nolan:

> There is, or rather was, an officer named Captain Nolan, who writes books, and was a great man in his own estimation, and who had already been talking very loud against the cavalry, his own branch of the service, and especially Lucan. Well, he rides up to Lucan with a written order signed 'R. Airey,' saying the cavalry were to recapture the guns taken in the morning. Lord Lucan says, 'But what guns?' on which he insultingly replied: 'There is your enemy, my lord.' Cardigan most gallantly led us on, arriving himself first at the guns. Nolan — the principal cause of this disaster — was the first man killed …
>
> Lucan is much cut up; and with tears in his eyes this morning he said how infamous it was to lay the blame on him, and told me what had passed between him and Lord Raglan. The fact is, we can fight better than any other nation, but we have no organisation.[19]

Paget was only too accurate with his prediction that the disastrous charge would be blamed upon Lucan. In fact, Lucan was recalled to the UK to explain how the Light Division had been lost. This was because the MP for Bristol, Henry Berkeley, asked for an inquiry, into the destruction of a particular portion of our army, namely, of a body of 300 soldiers, as brave as ever drew sword or put foot in stirrup, who, it was admitted, had been uselessly and wantonly sacrificed in an attempt of which there was no possibility of success, and where defeat was certain.[20]

It was on 26 January 1855, that Lord Hardinge wrote from the Horse Guards to Newcastle demanding that Lucan should be removed from his command:

> I concur with Lord Raglan that the terms he used in his despatch were appropriate; and as a good understanding between the Field-Marshal commanding the forces in the field and the Lieutenant-General commanding the Cavalry Divisions are conditions especially necessary for advantageously carrying on the public service, I recommend that Lieutenant-General Lord Lucan should be recalled.[21]

Consequently, the following day, the Secretary of State for War wrote to Raglan, telling him to inform Lucan that he should resign his command of the Cavalry Division and return to England, pointing out that, 'apart from any considerations of the merits of the question raised by Lord Lucan, the position in which he has now placed himself towards your lordship renders his withdrawal from the army under your command in all respects advisable'. Instead of letting things fade quietly away, Lucan had raised a storm and as a result he was being ignominiously dismissed from his post.

When he stood, at his own insistence, before the House of Lords to explain what had occurred during the Battle of Balaklava, Lucan gave a fuller account. His words here are taken up after he had received order No.3. As can be seen, his defence here is that the order he received was punctuated differently than the one produced by Raglan. In other words, Raglan, or Estcourt, subsequently changed the order to suit their version of events. There was no doubt about this, as Lucan had wisely sent the original soon after the accusations began to fly around to the British ambassador for safekeeping:

> I wish your Lordships to observe that the heavy cavalry were at this moment standing on the ground occupied by the Russian cavalry in the plan [not appended]. No. 3 order was to this effect— Cavalry to advance and take advantage of any opportunity to recover the heights. They will be supported by the infantry, which have been ordered. Advance on two fronts.

It is necessary here to observe that the copy given in Lord Raglan's letter of the 6th of December is incorrect, and materially so. In the original, which I hold in my hand, and which your Lordships can see, there is a full stop after the word 'ordered,' and the word 'Advance' is written with a large A, therefore making two distinct sentences. In Lord Raglan's copy the two sentences are made one by the omission of the stop, and by a small a being substituted for a large one. Therefore, whilst in the original, the order was for the cavalry to advance, in the copy it applied to the infantry. I do not wish to impute anything to Lord Raglan on account of this difference, as it is possible that the error was in the copy with which I furnished his Lordship. The cavalry were in consequence immediately mounted, and moved to the positions in the centre valley and on the ridge, as shown in the plan. No infantry had at this time arrived from the heights of Sebastopol. I remained myself between my two brigades, anxiously waiting their arrival. When they did arrive, instead of being formed for an attack, or to support an attack, they were, the greater part of them, sitting or lying down with their arms piled.[22]

We have already seen one version of the order, that supplied by Raglan. The one presented to the House of Lords was, as he said, only slightly different yet this made a significant difference to its meaning:

Cavalry to advance and take advantage of any opportunity to recover the Heights. They will be supported by infantry which have been ordered. Advance on two fronts.

This order makes no sense. How was the cavalry to advance on two fronts? What two fronts? It is easy to see why Lucan was confused with the turn of events and the orders he received. Furthermore, he took Raglan's instructions to mean that he was to attack the Heights when the infantry arrived. The idea of the cavalry alone trying to regain the Heights taken by the enemy was so preposterous that Lucan could not imagine it was what Raglan intended. Yet, as we have seen from the letter Raglan sent to Newcastle, the Commander-in-Chief really did expect the cavalry to attack the Heights with the infantry following on in support. Never imagining this to be the case, Lucan waited for the infantry, as he told his Peers:

From thirty to forty minutes had elapsed and the whole of the infantry had not arrived, when Captain Nolan galloped up to me with No. 4 order, in my opinion a fresh order, quite independent of any previous order, and having no connection with No. 3 or any other order. Indeed, I do positively affirm, that neither by my Lord Raglan, or General Airey, or any other person whatsoever, did I ever hear or suppose that any connection whatever existed, or was intended to exist, between this new order No. 4 and No. 3 the preceding one, or that they had the slightest reference to each other. No. 4 order is as follows — Lord Raglan wishes the cavalry to advance rapidly to the front, follow the enemy, and try to prevent the enemy carrying away the guns. Troop of horse artillery may accompany. French cavalry is on your left. Immediate.

As can be seen, Lucan has changed his declared understanding of the order completely from his report in *The Times*. There, it will be recalled, he had said that he had been ordered 'to prevent the enemy carrying the guns lost by the Turkish troops in the morning'. The guns were those in the redoubts on the Causeway Heights. Lucan's original report was made immediately after the Battle of Balaklava had been won, unaware that his actions would come under such public scrutiny. Now, seeking to shift the blame back Raglan, he had changed his tune. Lucan's statement to the House of Lords continued, which included an extract from the letter he sent to Raglan referred to earlier:

Your Lordships should be told, that when Lord Raglan gave this order, he was upon very high ground, and a quarter of a mile to my rear, from whence he could well see the whole position of the enemy; and you should be again told, that his Lordship at this time fancied, and he was not the only man who laboured under the same false impression (for I could produce half a dozen persons to testify to it), that the enemy were carrying away our guns from numbers 1, 2, and 3 redoubts, and therefore sent this order. I had, perhaps, better read from my letter to Lord Raglan of the 30th November how I acted on the receipt of number 4 order.

The extract is as follows — After carefully reading this order, I hesitated and urged the uselessness of such an attack, and the dangers attending it. The aide-de-camp [Nolan], in a most authoritative tone, stated that they were Lord Raglan's orders that the cavalry should attack immediately. I asked, 'Where, and what to do?' neither enemy nor guns being in sight. He replied in a most disrespectful but significant manner, pointing to the further end of the valley, 'There, my Lord, is your enemy; there are your guns!' So distinct, in my opinion, was your written instruction, and so positive and urgent were the orders delivered by the aide-de-camp, that I felt it was imperative on me to obey, and I informed Lord Cardigan that he was to advance, and to the objections he made, and in which I entirely agreed, I replied that the order was from your Lordship. Having decided, against my conviction, to make the movement, I did all in my power to render it as little perilous as possible. I formed the brigade in two lines, and led to its support two regiments of heavy cavalry, the Scots Grey and Royals, and only halted them when they had reached the point from which they could protect the retreat of the light cavalry in the event of their being pursued by the enemy, and when, having already lost many officers and men by the fire from the batteries and fort, any further advance would have exposed them to destruction.

My Lords, this I think is the time to show your Lordships what an aide-de-camp is. In page 59 of the Queen's Regulations, which cannot be violated with impunity, under the head of aides-de-camp, it is ordered, 'all orders sent by aides-de-camp are to be delivered in the plainest terms, and are to be obeyed with the same readiness as if delivered personally by the general officers to whom such aides-de-camp are attached.' I ask any military man, I ask the noble Duke near me (the Duke of Richmond), who was aide-de-camp to that great man, the late Duke of Wellington, whether an aide-de-camp is not the organ of his general? And whether a general officer who took upon himself to disobey an order brought by an aide-de-camp, verbal or written, would not risk the loss of his commission? If this were not so, why could not an orderly dragoon convey orders as well as an aide-de-camp? An aide-de-camp is chosen because he is an officer of education and intelligence, he is, therefore, supposed to deliver an order more correctly, and is considered as being in the confidence of his general. Shall I be told that Captain Nolan was not in General Airey's confidence? Why, he told me himself that he had given to Captain Nolan his instructions verbally, and it was only when that officer was turning his horse away, that he detained him, and committed the instructions to writing. I would ask any reasonable man, after this, whether any mistake was or could be committed by Captain Nolan? And how could I, at the time, or can now, doubt but that Captain Nolan was instructed to deliver to me the positive order to attack which he did?

If this note to Raglan had been written immediately after the battle, it would have great credibility. But it was written on 30 November, more than a month after the charge, and his original report he made no mention of any concern with the orders he received or that he expressed these concerns to Nolan. What is also interesting here is that he was quite certain that Nolan delivered Raglan's instructions faithfully, as we have already determined must have been the case.

'My Lords,' Lucan continued,

> I must direct your attention to this. In the order it is stated, 'French cavalry is on your left,' evidently for the purpose of informing me where the French cavalry were, an admission that they were out of my sight if not out of my reach, and again informing me that it was a combined movement in which they were to join and assist me. I felt, ordered as I was to advance immediately without an opportunity of sending to ask for further instructions that I could not fail to perform my part of this combined movement, and so leave the brunt of the affair to be borne by the French cavalry alone.
>
> Under these circumstances my course was clear to me; and I considered it a positive duty to order Lord Cardigan to advance with the light cavalry brigade, and to lead the heavy cavalry brigade to its support.
>
> Your Lordships are so well acquainted with the details of this charge, and so fully appreciate the extraordinary valour and gallantry displayed by the light cavalry on that occasion, and also the steadiness and bravery of the heavy brigade, more particularly the Scots Grey and Royals, the two regiments most exposed, that I would only add, that the brilliancy of the charge and the gallantry displayed by the whole of the cavalry, were never surpassed at any former period.
>
> Your Lordships should be told that the infantry, which I was informed was coming to support me, was composed of two divisions, the 1st commanded by His Royal Highness the Duke of Cambridge, and the 4th by an officer whose death the army and the country so much deplore, both my seniors, and therefore both my commanding officers.
>
> In the evening of the action, I saw Lord Raglan; his first remark to me was, 'You have lost the light brigade.' I at once denied that I had lost the light brigade, as I had only carried out the orders conveyed to me, written and verbal, by Captain Nolan. He then said that I was a lieutenant general, and should, therefore, have exercised my discretion, and not approving of the charge, should not have made it.

This is an astonishing statement for Raglan to make. What he was saying, in effect, was that his instructions were wrong and that he did not expect them to be carried out! This must be a unique occurrence in military history – a commander condemning a subordinate officer for *obeying* orders. Yet this would, indeed, form the basis of Raglan's defence.

Lucan simply could not have disobeyed a direct order. He could, of course, question an order or ask for further clarification. Interestingly, this was the course of action that Cardigan privately advocated, telling his other brother-in-law, Earl Howe, on 27 October that in his opinion 'the Lieutenant General ought to have had the moral courage to disobey the order till further instructions were issued.'[23] Major Forrest of the 4th Dragoon Guards agreed:

> If a lieutenant general will not take responsibility upon himself, a lance corporal might fill his place, he [Lucan] should have waited until the infantry on their way up had arrived, or sent to inquire whether that was not Lord Raglan's intention.[24]

This, though, was impractical, and entirely missed the point. Sending for further clarification would have taken too long, with the cavalry commander having been told to attack 'immediately'. Lucan, therefore had no choice but to obey, as George Paget agreed:

> Surely, then, for all that Lord Lucan knew, this might have been an order of such a nature, coming as it did from afar off, in the midst of a battle, the operations of which extended over a larger area than is common, and coming from a chief who was known to have sent his order from a position the most commanding in point of general view, and therefore one from which he apparently could form the best judgment on the effect that would result from any orders sent by him.[25]

What all this clearly demonstrates is that Raglan's orders were not just confusing but were downright wrong, as the Commander-in-Chief later conceded.

But if Lucan had disobeyed the order, there would have been only one alternative, according to Paget, 'to blow out his brains the moment he got back'. This seems to have been generally accepted, even by the editor of the *Daily News*, a newspaper not particularly favourable to Lucan, that an 'injustice' had been done to the commander of the Cavalry Division:

> We look in vain for any explanation that is intelligible, save the one that has been long since suggested itself to the public mind, namely,

that to satisfy national discontent, and to elude participation in the burthen of general responsibility, he, like others, has been sacrificed. This is the shabby upshot of the matter.

Lord Hardinge, from the comfortable benches of the House of Lords, and who was determined to support the Expeditionary Force's commander, picked on a phrase from Lucan's letter to Raglan, in which, it may be recalled, the Earl had written 'direct disobedience of orders … must have exposed me and the cavalry to aspersions, against which it might have been difficult to have defended ourselves.' Surely, Harding commented,

> when the noble Earl talks of possible aspersions, it shows that his decision to attack was taken, not upon any impression which he had of Lord Raglan's order, but upon the fear which he entertained of aspersions from his officers and soldiers.[26]

What Hardinge was saying, quite outrageously, was that Lucan ordered the cavalry to charge the Russian positions because of peer pressure from the officers and men under his command! Lucan replied to Hardinge's claim, by saying that:

> It is generally admitted that, had I disobeyed this order, I should for ever have been held responsible for the loss of the guns, which it was erroneously imagined were being removed. That such would have been the censure thrown upon me, that I could not have shown myself to my division; that my existence would have become intolerable, and I must have destroyed myself.

As will surely have been noticed, there was no reference throughout these exchanges of the Light Brigade having charged the wrong guns. The debate centred solely upon whether or not Lucan should have obeyed Raglan's order. Remarkable though it may seem, whilst it was abundantly clear that Raglan had made a mistake, Lord Lucan was the one being blamed.

The *Yorkshire Gazette* had its own view on the subject, following Lucan's explanation in the Lords:

> It now appears that the unfortunate order, which annihilated the Light Cavalry Brigade, originated entirely in a misapprehension, not by Lord Lucan, but, by the authority under which it was indited [*sic*], as to the actual state of affairs existing at the time. Lord Raglan was

anxious to prevent the Russians from carrying off our guns from the redoubts abandoned by the Turkish troops at the commencement of the affair ... The main question at issue is, whether or not the order was peremptory or discretionary! We have already ventured an opinion that Lord Lucan was bound to deem it as a peremptory order, and either to obey it or subject himself by refusal to a direct charge of insubordination and cowardice, from which no pretext would have excused him.[27]

Here we see that the 'main question' was not whether or not Lucan made a mistake and sent the Light Brigade against the wrong guns, but whether or not the cavalry commander had the freedom to act on his own intiative or had no choice in the matter. The newspaper then went onto explain the reasons behind its conviction that Lucan was merely 'following orders':

Our readers will remember that among the slain at the battle of Inkerman was the brave Sir George Cathcart. On the corpse of that distinguished warrior was found an unfinished letter to his wife, begun two days before, and in which more than one striking allusion is made to the engagement of the 25th October. Tales would, he foresaw, be cast upon those in command; but he declares, in the most unqualified terms, that 'neither Lord Lucan nor Lord Cardigan was to blame, *but on the contrary*, for they obeyed orders'. Such a sentence, from such an authority, written under such circumstances, ought at once to be accepted as a perfect justification of Lord Lucan; and although the War Office authorities may refuse to do the noble lord justice, we feel certain that he will receive justice from the British people.[28]

On the other hand, Captain Beauchamp Walker of the 7th Dragoon Guards, who was one of Lucan's aides and who went on to became a full General, wrote that 'Lord Lucan, instead of taking the order, and exercising his own judgement as to how he carried out, asked Captain Nolan what he was to attack'.[29] This, to some degree, supports Raglan's view that Lucan should have used his discretion in carrying out the attack. This was certainly how the Commander-in-Chief saw the matter, which is why in his official despatch, written on the 28th, see he stated that, 'the Lieutenant-General considered that he was bound to attack at all hazards, and he accordingly ordered Major-General the Earl of Cardigan to move forward with the Light Brigade'.

The two points of interest here are that Raglan stated in his despatch that the cavalry was to 'follow the enemy in their retreat', and that the misconception of the instructions was not that it charged in the wrong direction or against the wrong guns, but that the attack was made 'at all hazards'. Here we have confirmation. There was only one direction in which the Russians could have been retreating from the redoubts, i.e. down into the valley away from the British. If the Light Brigade was to 'follow' the Russians, they could only have followed them either along the Causeway Heights or down the valley. The cavalry, therefore, was to try and intercept the Russians before they reached their own lines. But when it became evident that this was no longer possible, it was expected by Raglan, that the Light Brigade would not press home its attack. But, as we know, Lucan was instructed to attack 'immediately'. So the Light Brigade did exactly that. There was no mention in Raglan's orders about the degree of danger to which the cavalry might be exposed to or that Lucan was to use his discretion and only attack if he considered such a move practicable without serious loss. Furthermore, Nolan would not have raced down the Heights if the order to attack was not an immediate necessity.

It may be recalled that there was no mention in the fourth order of attempting to recover the heights, as there had been in the third order. All that was expected of the cavalry was to try and save the guns as they were being taken towards the Russian lines. Yet it had taken Nolan, galloping as fast and recklessly as he dared, around a quarter of an hour to reach the valley floor, and further discussions between Nolan, Lucan and Cardigan had consumed more vital minutes. The result was that by the time the Light Brigade moved off it was already too late. If this should be doubted we have the impartial view of William Russell, whose reference to this was published in *The Times* on 1 March 1855.

> Now, it may be observed that when this order was given the enemy had actually, or I am mistaken, accomplished a part of that operation which the cavalry were ordered to try and prevent, and that they were actually carrying away the guns at the time it was issued; *a fortiori* they would-have completed the whole or very nearly the whole of the operation before Captain Nolan could have reached Lord Lucan with the orders in question. But, from the position of the cavalry, it would have been impossible, I think, for Lord Lucan to see either that the enemy had carried away the guns or where they were carrying them to; nor could he have beheld the masses

and disposition of the Russian guns and infantry, inasmuch as a ridge of hills of gentle elevation ran right in front of him across the valley and plain, and shielded their position from view.

As it happens, we now know that the Russians were not taking the guns away from the redoubts at this stage of the battle, though they did so later. What Russell, and presumably Raglan, probably saw was simply the Odessa Regiment moving back along the Causeway Heights after having abandoned both No.4 Redoubt and then No.3 Redoubt.[30] From the distant Sapoune Heights it would have been difficult to tell amid the constant movement of the troops during the battle, whether the Russians had a few guns in tow or not. This, however, shows how confused the whole affair was.

We know that Cardigan was fully aware which guns he was supposed to prevent being taken away. But as he reached the point where he could see the redoubts more clearly the Russian guns on the Fedioukine Heights opened fire upon the Light Brigade. What was Cardigan to do?

He could not have turned back as he had already had his objections to the attack dismissed by his divisional commander. Cardigan consequently knew that his attack was going to have to be undertaken 'at all hazards' and had pointed this out to his superior officer. Once he was on his way there was no turning back, otherwise he would have been accused of cowardice. 'Probably no Cavalry officer was ever in a greater predicament than Cardigan was as he approached that Battery,' remarked Whinyates:

> To have halted anywhere within 300 yards of the Battery could have done him no good, for he would have received the salvo of grape all the same, and the Artillerymen would not then have desisted for a moment, whereas by charging home, he at least shut up that number of guns from firing on his supports.[31]

That it was fully understood the objective of the charge was to prevent the guns from the redoubts being taken down from the Causeway Heights to the Russian positions was confirmed by Robert Farquharson of the 4th Light Dragoons:

> Lord Lucan gave his orders to Lord Cardigan, who ordered the brigade to move off at a walk. This pace was kept up until we were fairly off the hill and into a heavy ploughed field below, where we

broke into a trot, which we continued until getting on to grass, when we got into a gallop, all the time being exposed to a galling fire in front from an eight-gun battery which the enemy had placed in the centre of the valley, up which we were advancing to reach the guns we wanted to recapture.[32]

From this quote we can see that it was thought the Russians had already taken the guns down from the Causeway Heights to the rear of the Don Cossack battery. We now know that the guns were not removed at this stage of the battle, but there was movement along the Heights which, no doubt led to this widely-held misinterpretation.

So we have seen that Nolan had communicated Airey's instructions in an understandable manner, and that both Lucan and Cardigan knew the intended purpose of those orders, and that they had to be carried out 'immediately'. Let us then place ourselves in Cardigan's boots and see if we can possibly understand what happened.

We know that Lucan had not sent any scouts out to observe the unfolding of the battle and had little idea of the enemy dispositions – and neither, it would seem, had Cardigan. According to Sergeant-Major Franks, it was only as the cavalry rounded No.1 Redoubt that, 'the General and the whole of the Brigade saw for the first time the position [of the enemy]'.[33] Likewise, it may also be recalled that Paget stated: 'This battery [the Don Cossack], owing to the dust and confusion that reigned, had not been perceived by us (by me at least) until we got close upon it.'

Now, though, Cardigan he saw exactly what he had to face. But his objections had been dismissed and there was no going back. This is certainly how it was perceived by Sergeant Thomas Johnson of the 13th Light Dragoons:

We had scarcely advanced a few yards before they opened on us with grape and shell. It was a prefect level, the ground only wide enough for the 17th and 19th [sic] to advance, the rest of the brigade to follow. To our astonishment they had batteries on each side of the hills, which commanded the whole valley; consequently a dreadful cross fire was opened up on us from both sides and if front, but it was too late to do anything but advance, which we did in a style truly wonderful.[34]

It was, indeed, too late to do anything but advance as the Light Brigade moved up the valley coming under increasingly heavy fire. This was how it was understood by Captain W.P. Richards, Royal Artillery, whose battery arrived on the scene with the 1st Division:

> Lord Raglan gave an order that the Cavalry should charge and retake the guns (by the way no one knew where they were then), the consequence was, the cavalry charged slap into the centre of the Russian Army.[35]

The Russians were in strength, in both infantry, artillery and cavalry on the Causeway Heights, the slopes of which whilst gentle and low are rough and broken. To have followed the retreating enemy along them would have been no easy matter. If, alternatively, Cardigan would have wheeled around to the right to mount the Causeway Heights to cut off the retreating Russians, the brigade would have lost momentum, which would have been exacerbated by having to mount the rough slopes. The rear of the brigade would have been exposed to the fire from the Fedioukine Heights and its flank to the Don Cossack battery down the valley, as well that from the Heights in its front. Cardigan, through no fault of his own, was in the midst of the enemy, being fired on from all sides. There was to be no good outcome, whatever course of action he took. We know he commented 'Here goes the last of the Brudenells' before launching the attack, knowing full well the consequences of 670 men galloping into the heart of the Russian positions of more than 20,000 soldiers, which was the only way by that time that he could have intercepted the 'retreating' enemy that had left the Causeway Heights.

The truth is that when Raglan issued his order, he did not take into account three factors. The first is described by George Paget:

> If it be correct that the object of Lord Raglan's last order was that the cavalry should, instead of going down the valley, have made an advance *along* the Causeway Heights, to recapture the guns on the redoubts, then the nature of the ground must be considered; and I think I am right in saying that such an advance would have been attended with much difficulty, the ground being broken and uneven, and of such configuration that cavalry would have acted on it at a great disadvantage.[36]

If indeed the Russians had been attempting to remove the guns, it could only have been from Nos. 1, 2 and 3 redoubts i.e. those farthest away from the British lines. This would have meant the cavalry having to attack along almost the full length of the heights. Due to the nature of the ground, the Light Brigade would have been in a disordered state, and hardly in a position to mount a charge.

As a consequence, Cardigan had little choice but to travel down the North Valley before he could attempt to move up onto the Causeway Heights. But in doing this, the second factor that Raglan failed to take into account, was that in moving down the valley the cavalry would come under fire from all directions and be enveloped in gun smoke.

The third factor Raglan did not take into consideration was time. The fourth order to the Cavalry Division was timed at 10.45 hours. Nolan reached the Cavalry Division a little after 11.00 hours, and the Light Brigade moved off around ten minutes later. Almost half-an-hour had elapsed from the moment Raglan had believed he saw the Russians starting to remove the guns from the redoubts. In that time the situation had changed. After having abandoned No.4 Redoubt, the Odessa Regiment then abandoned No.3 Redoubt, the Russian force on the Causeway Heights then concentrating around the two most distant redoubts. This included two batteries, one heavy and one light, with fourteen pieces between them.

Whether Cardigan charged onto the Heights or along the valley he would encounter an enemy in overwhelming numbers. Rather than disturb the formation of his brigade or disrupt its momentum by wheeling round and charging the Heights, Cardigan rode on. Either way the Light Brigade would be charging directly into at least one fully-formed Russian battery.

It is usually stated that it was not Lucan or Cardigan or Nolan who lost the Light Brigade. The disaster, it is said, lay squarely at the feet of Lord Hardinge and the Duke of Newcastle. Kinglake, who witnessed the tragedy of the charge and who was a known supporter of Raglan, made it clear who he considered was responsible:

> If a minister were unhappily forced to cast his eyes over a crowd of officers who had none of them rendered war service, and to try to draw out from among them the three or four gifted men who could best be entrusted to act in the field as generals of cavalry, it would be senseless to blame him for failing in so hard a task; but ... it so happened that, notwithstanding the long duration of the peace which had been existing between the great Powers of Europe, England had a superb list of cavalry officers in the early prime of life who had done brilliant service in the field ... Well, elimination proceeded—a choice was made ... Incredible as it may seem, it is nevertheless true that, in nominating general officers for cavalry commands in the East, the names of the men who had done service

in the field were all set aside, and that from the peace-service residue exclusively the appointments in question were made.[37]

Lord George Paget who, as second-in-command of the Light Brigade was able to witness all that transpired between the two earls, had no doubt about where the 'tragedy of errors', as he put it, had its origin:

> We must look farther back, and condemn Lord Hardinge and the Cabinet for placing Lords Lucan and Cardigan in the relative posts to which they were appointed, for the disadvantage to the service of this arrangement (however good an officer in himself each may have been) is apparent from the well-known relations in which they stood to each other, and should have been so apparent to the Commander-in-Chief and the Cabinet, as to need no further comment.[38]

William Russell agreed that the Government had made a terrible mistake in its choice of cavalry commanders:

> Lord Lucan was a hard man to get on with. But the moment the Government of the day made the monstrous choice of his brother-in-law, Lord Cardigan, as the Brigadier of the Light Brigade of the Cavalry Division, knowing well the relations between the two officers and the nature of the two men, they became responsible for the disaster; they were guilty of treason to the Army – neither more nor less.[39]

Yet we may recall that behind the Light Brigade came Lucan with the Royals and the Scots Greys. When he pulled up the heavies he apparently said, 'They have sacrificed the Light Brigade: they shall not the Heavy, if I can help it'. He did not say that Cardigan had committed an error, which he would have had no hesitation in doing if he thought he could condemn his brother-in-law. Indeed, until the publication of Raglan's despatch, Lucan did not think that either he or Cardigan had done anything wrong. The 'they' he referred to was Raglan and his staff.

The relationship between the cavalry commander and his brigadier was irrelevant. Lucan received a direct order and Cardigan questioned that order when it was passed onto him. It is hard to see how anything would have changed even if the two men had been on the best of terms. Lucan received a confusing order, which he clearly had difficulty with, asking Nolan, 'Where, and what to do?', receiving little clarification from the aide-de-camp.

This where the actions of Nolan are of interest. It is usually thought that immediately before he was killed, he made a move across the front of the 17th Lancers. This has led to the conclusion that he was either trying to advise Cardigan that he was heading in the wrong direction, or was trying to wheel the brigade around to the right to mount the Causeway Heights. This was certainly the opinion of Kinglake after interviewing members of the 17th Lancers:

> He rode crossing the front of the brigade, and bearing away to the right front of our advancing squadrons, as though he would go on to the spot on the Causeway Heights where the Odessa regiment stood posted. Regarded in connection with this significant fact, the anxious entreaties which he sought to express by voice and by signs would apparently mean something like this — 'You are going quite wrong! You are madly going down this North Valley between flanking fires, where you won't have an enemy in your front for the next mile. This—the way you see me going — this is the direction to take for doing what Lord Raglan has ordered. Bring up the left shoulder, and incline to your right as you see me doing. This, this is the way to get at the enemy.[40]

Yet, as we have seen, many of the accounts of Nolan's death make no mention of any move by him until he was struck by the Russian shell. We have, for instance, the words of Cardigan's aide who was riding close to the Earl. In a letter to *The Times* on 28 July 1868, Fitz Maxse wrote: 'I have no recollection of his [Nolan's] divergence in the manner described by Mr. Kinglake either by deed or gesture until after he was struck.'

It must also be borne in mind that the front ranks of the Light Brigade had only travelled about 200 yards before Nolan was killed. The direction of the charge could not have been ascertained at that point. We have seen from Paget's observations that travelling *along* the Causeway Height 'would have been attended with much difficulty', and Cardigan, therefore, would have had to move down the valley for some distance before attempting to mount the Causeway Heights in the region of No.3 Redoubt. As Mark Adkin has correctly noted, the Light Brigade would have had to ride for at least 1,000 metres before the order to wheel would be given. Any suggestion that Nolan was trying to change the course of the charge is therefore highly improbable. The most logical conclusion is that Nolan's sudden movement was because he was struck by a shell splinter, just as most of the eye-witness accounts indicate. There is no mystery here.

There is only one reason why the Light Brigade was lost. It was, as William Russell wrote, 'The result of the confusion caused by Lord Raglan's lack of precision … Lord Raglan is utterly incompetent to lead an army through any arduous task.'[41]

It would have made little difference whether the Light Brigade attacked up the Causeway Heights or down the North Valley, in either case it would have had to face a line of enemy guns, be it the fourteen guns of No. 1 heavy and No.2 light batteries on the Heights or the eight guns of Don Cossack No.3 Battery [and possibly the four guns of No.12 Light Battery] in the valley. Once the lancers, hussars and light dragoons had started off towards the Russian positions their destruction was inevitable, whichever direction they took.

This was understood by William Russell, who wrote:

> I do not understand how the Light Cavalry could have succeeded in doing that which, it is said, Lord Raglan intended they should accomplish. The guns were in Redoubts Nos. 1, 2 and 3. The first was plainly inaccessible to horsemen – to have charged 2 and 3 in the face of Infantry, Artillery and Cavalry the enemy had within supporting distance of it, would have been quixotic in the extreme.[42]

This was understood by many of the officers, including Captain Christopher Blackett of the 93rd Highlanders:

> Every one who saw it says it was neither more nor less than driving brave men on to certain death … Lord Raglan may say what he likes in dispatches, but you may depend on it I have told you the real feeling in the army out here.[43]

The great debate over who said what, and which guns the Light Brigade should have ridden towards, can now be closed. By their own admission, Lucan and Cardigan knew which guns Raglan wanted to rescue. They both realised that what this entailed was nothing short of suicidal, whether this was attempted by mounting the heights or along the valley, but each in turn followed their respective commander's orders.

Raglan, when he believed he was going to lose cannon to the enemy, responded without thinking the situation through, and he ordered the cavalry to advance into the heart of the Russian positions.

Lieutenant, later Major, Clement Walker Heneage VC of the 8th Hussars had no doubt that it was the Commander-in-Chief who was to blame for the disaster:

It is wonderful to observe the way that fool the 'British public' kicks a man directly he is down, as in the instance of unlucky Lucan. I always hated him, and so did all the Cavalry Division, but for heaven's sake let a man have fair play – here is this unfortunate man catching over the heads and ears, merely because he obeyed an order given by the thick-headed Raglan through his still more stupid Q.M. General Airey, who is about the worst of the whole headquarters staff.[44]

Historians have speculated endlessly on who was to blame for the charge, but there is nothing to speculate about. Maps and diagrams, beautifully drawn and clear, give the impression of an ordered and precise movement. But it was nothing like that once the Russian guns opened fire. We have learnt that so dense was the gun smoke swirling around the valley many of the light cavalrymen, and particularly the 11th Hussars, charged down as far as the Tchernaya without even seeing the Don Cossack battery. On all sides were ranged 20,000 or more Russians, not divided neatly into those occupying the heights and those standing in the valley, but arranged contiguously to be mutually supporting on the low slopes and the adjoining plain.

In respect of time, the Light Brigade was already too late, with the Russians appearing to be dragging away the guns from the redoubts, though we know this was merely them moving along the Heights. Possibly at this point Raglan hoped the Light Brigade would rein back and not continue 'at all hazards', but this would be difficult if not impossible to effect on the valley floor amid the exploding shells, the round shot smashing into men and horses, the smoke, the noise, the wildly rampaging rider-less horses, and the screams.

No, Lucan had passed on Raglan's orders (which one newspaper called imbecile)[45] and Cardigan executed them in gallant fashion. Field Marshal Evelyn Wood, agreed, stating that the destruction of the Light Brigade was because of 'Lord Raglan's primary error of launching cavalry unsupported by infantry to the attack of 20,000 men in position'.[46]

Lucan was never going to be able to recover the Heights with his division whilst occupied in strength by the enemy and Cardigan could not prevent the Russians removing the guns if they so desired. But, as Tennyson so poetically wrote, 'It was not theirs to reason why'. The Light Brigade had been sent into the Valley of Death and had been sent there by Lord Raglan, no-one else was to blame, as one newspaper had no hesitation in declaring:

The fatal but brilliant error of Balaklava – leading to the destruction of our light cavalry brigade – has yet to be explained, although it cannot now be remedied. The mistake is generally said to have originated by Lord Raglan, who either gave orders for the advance of the cavalry to almost certain annihilation, or conveyed his instructions in such a loose or vague language, as to render them incomprehensible.[47]

The headline under which this article was written, was 'Lord Raglan's Promotion – Dangerous favouritism at the Horse Guards', which probably sums up the whole sorry, if glorious, mess.

Chapter 12

'Honour the Light Brigade'

Though he usually slept on his yacht, on the night of the 25th, Cardigan slept on the ground with his men, wrapped in his blanket, rather than retire to the comfort of his yacht. The earl showed genuine concern for his surviving men, as Mrs Farrel, one of three soldier's wives of the 5th Dragoon Guards who were left, unofficially, at Scutari on 'nursing' duties, recorded:

> We had two visits from Colonel [sic] Cardigan, Scarlett and a host of foreign Officers the day after the Lancers and Hussars charged the Russian guns, and what a sight those wounds of some were, shot through the bowels, legs, and chests. The trumpeter that sounded the charge for Colonel Cardigan was a most pitiful case, he begged that his Bugle should not be taken out of his sight. Colonel Cardigan spent half an hour with him soothing him, he is lying on some plank beds and Blankets, he belongs to the 17th Lancers. His name is Brittain [sic]. The sergeant of the 17th calls him Billy and keeps telling him to pluck up and get out soon to sound another charge. But there never was any chance for him though his lordship sees he has everything he wants.[1]

Mrs Farrel was correct about Billy Britten's chances as he died on 14 February 1855 at Scutari.

As the battle of the 25th had shown that the redoubts on the Causeway Heights could not stop a determined assault, Raglan and Canrobert decided not to attempt to regain them. Consequently, the two Commanders-in-Chief decided, 'that the English, abandoning their exterior lines of defence, should concentrate their forces on the narrow chain which closes the entrance of the valley of Balaklava towards the harbour, and on the hills which command the city'.

William Russell put it a little more succinctly:

> We had already found out that our position was too large to be readily defended. We made up our minds, therefore, to let the Russians have the redoubts Nos. 1, 2, and 3, and even 4 if they liked, and to content ourselves with keeping Balaklava and the communication with it open by the westerly and southerly heights behind our camp.[2]

The irony of this was surely not lost on Lord Lucan. The heights that he had been urged to take by Raglan, and which, mistakenly or otherwise, prompted the most famous cavalry charge in history and led to the loss of the Light Brigade, were now considered strategically unimportant.

Nevertheless, the effects of the charge were immediately felt. Major Charles Pyndar Beauchamp Walker, one of Lucan's aides, believed that, 'the two charges of the 25th have convinced the Russians that we are devils, devils in red they call us and they have now found out that there are also devils in blue among us'.[3] S. Kozhukhov of the Russian 12 Artillery Brigade agreed:

> It is difficult, if not impossible, to do justice to the feat of these mad cavalry, for, having lost a quarter of their number and being apparently impervious to new dangers and further losses, they quickly reformed their squadrons to return over the same ground littered with their dead and dying. With such desperate courage these valiant lunatics set off again, and not one of the living – even the wounded – surrendered.[4]

Two days after the battle, Lord George Paget wrote that in the evening:

> I rode up to head-quarters today and dined with Lord Raglan. I was very kindly received by him, and he grasped my hand two or three times in his congratulations; indeed, it was the same with them all, and it was very gratifying to hear all they said of us, which I must not repeat. They all saw it from the heights, and Lord Raglan showed great emotion, I believe. But I cannot omit one little speech, for it was one to have lived for, coming from such a man, and so neat. When among other things, I said I had lost my trumpeter, he said 'Never mind, George, you will never want another;' and Airey told me that he had said that, deplorable as the affair was, it would not be without its results, and would make a great impression on the Russians.[5]

Though a comparatively minor affair, the Charge of the Light Brigade immediately captured the public imagination, fuelled by letters from the Crimea printed in the local and national press. 'Oh what a sight it was to see our cavalry charging at their cavalry, and coming into contact with each other, men were falling on both sides,' wrote an anonymous trumpeter of the 8th Hussars in a letter that appeared in the *Daily News* of 24 November.

In the *Leeds Mercury* of 30 December, Sergeant John Baker of the 4th Light Dragoons wrote of the charge 'under the Earl of Cardigan. I was with him on that ever-memorable day, and I shall never forget it, even to the last day of my life.'

An officer of the 17th Lancers declared in the *Wakefield Journal & Examiner* that he heard from a man who had dined at Headquarters, that the Commander-in-Chief said 'our attack was an unheard of feat of arms, and that Lord Raglan says that the moral effect has been wonderful. The Russian prisoners taken at Sevastopol say the Russians were petrified at the audacity of the attack and the energy that could, after such a fire, break through their lines.'

Fanny Duberly, who published her *Journal kept during the Russian War* in 1855, wrote about 'our glorious and fatal charge'. She declared that, 'It has become a matter of world history'.[6]

Likewise, such hardened veterans such as Colonel George Bell of the 1st Royals who had been fighting since the Storming of Badajoz in 1812, wrote that, 'The story of this day will be told by a thousand tongues and in many languages'.[7]

Even the Editor of *The Times*, John Delane, whose attacks on the government's mishandling of the war was a major factor in the collapse of Lord Aberdeen's administration, had nothing but praise for the Light Brigade:

> The blood that was shed has not flowed in vain. The brave soldiers we lost nobly sacrificed their lives in arresting the course of an operation, the success of which would have cut off our communication with our fleet, turned our position and compromised the safety of the whole army. Never was a more costly sacrifice made for a more worthy object.[8]

But what stirred the nation perhaps more than any letter or report was Tennyson's immortal poem which has become the most quoted, and mis-quoted, poem in the English language. School children could thrill at the rhythmic pace of the Light Brigade charging into the Valley of Death with guns to the right of them and guns to the left. Even the illiterate labourer or farm hand could understand that theirs was not to reason why, theirs was to do and die, for it reflected their own circumstances.

The charge quickly became synonymous with men being asked to carry out ill-considered, or reckless attacks. After the assault upon the Redan at Sevastopol in June 1855, Colonel Burton of the 7th Royal Fusiliers wrote: 'I had but time for one glance at the position, but that was quite sufficient to show me that it was a regular Balaklava Charge which was expected of us.'

Cardigan did not remain long in the Crimea after the Battle of Balaklava. His health deteriorated over the course of the winter, as his close friend Fanny Duberly noticed in the first week of December 1854:

> Lord Cardigan is invalided and goes home in a day or two. I was discoursing him yesterday and he said 'My health is broken down, I have no brigade, my brigade is gone, if I had a brigade I am not allowed to command it [referring, of course, to the interference from Lucan], my heart & health are broken I must go home.[9]

When Cardigan arrived back in the UK, the man who had led the now celebrated charge was given a hero's welcome. When his ship berthed at the port of Folkestone on 13 January 1855, the townsfolk went wild and in London he was mobbed by an enthusiastic crowd. On 16 January, just three days after his return, he was invited to Windsor Castle where he related details of the charge to Victoria and Albert, which the Queen recorded in her journal:

> After dinner talked for some time with Ld. Cardigan, who is grown thinner & older though he does not look ill otherwise ... He spoke of the unfortunate murderous Charge ... Ld. Cardigan said that not one of the officers who went into that action, he believed, ever thought they would return out of it alive![10]

A banquet was also held in his honour at the Mansion House on 5 February, and whilst the Queen had noted in her diary that Cardigan had described the famous charge 'modestly', he was less restrained in the speech to the Lord Mayor and the great and the good of London:

> We advanced down a gradual descent of more than three-quarters of a mile, with the batteries vomiting forth upon us shells and shot, round ad grape, with one battery on our right flank and another on the left, and all the intermediate ground covered with the Russian

riflemen; so that when we came to within a distance of fifty yards from the mouths of the artillery which had been hurling destruction upon us, we were in fact surrounded and encircled by a blaze of fire, in addition to the fire of the artillery poured upon our rear, so that we had thus a strong fire upon our front, our flank, and our rear. We entered the battery – we went through the battery – the two leading regiments cutting down a great number of the Russian gunners in their onset. In the two regiments which I had the honour to lead, every officer, with one exception, was either killed ot wounded, or had his horse shot under him or injured. Those regiments proceeded, followed by the second line, consisting of two more regiments of cavalry, which continued to perform the duty of cutting down the Russian gunners.

Then came the third line, formed of another regiment, which endeavoured to complete the duty assigned to our brigade. I believe this was achieved with great success, and the result was that this body, composed of only about 670 men, succeeded in passing through the mass of Russian cavalry of – we have since learned – 5,240 strong; and having broken through that mass, they went, according to our technical military expression, 'three about', and retired in the same manner, doing as much execution in their course as they possibly could upon the enemy's cavalry. Upon our returning up the hill which we had descended in the attack, we had to run the same gauntlet and incur the same risk from flank fire of the Tirailleurs as we had encountered before. Numbers of our men were shot down – men and horses were killed, and many of the soldiers who had lost their horses were also shot down while endeavouring to escape.[11]

Cardigan was not the only Light Brigade survivor to have an audience with the Queen, as an article in the *Newcastle Courant* of 22 June 1855, related:

There is at present sojourning in this town, a sergeant of the 11th Hussars (Prince Albert's Own), who took part in the sanguinary but gallant charge of the light cavalry at Balaklava, and, where, unfortunately, he lost his right arm. His name is John Lawson, and he belongs to Horsley in this county, where he was born … Not a man (he says) quailed for a moment at the order, although they saw nothing but inevitable destruction before them. It was in the course of his return that Sergeant Lawson was wounded in his right arm by a spent shot, and his horse shot under him, but he succeeded in reaching the camp on foot. His arm was amputated on the field, after which he was removed to Scutari Hospital, where he remained from the 5th November to the 20th December during which time he was personally attended by Miss Nightingale ... On arriving in England he was an invalid in Chatham Hospital and while there was visited by her most gracious Majesty the Queen, who, after putting several questions to him, presented him with a silk pocket handkerchief, hemmed by the Princess Royal.

The charge became so celebrated that a series of supposedly 'true' stories about the Crimean War appeared in a weekly magazine, the *Young Englishman's Journal,* called 'Captain Jack; or One of the Light Brigade', written by a George Emmett. *Captain Jack,* was also published in twenty-one weekly one-penny parts, one of the notable 'penny dreadfuls'of that era. The *Captain Jack* stores appear to have been taken seriously at the time though there is no evidence that the author was ever a member of the Light Brigade.[12]

Over time the Charge of the Light Brigade became to be seen as exemplifying everything that was wrong, and what was right, about Britain and its society. In particular, the actions of those who had rode into the Valley of Death determined to do or die without reasoning why, were lauded for what was perceived as their English values of unquestioning courage. For example, on Balaklava Day (25 October) 1899, the *Birkenhead and Cheshire Advertiser and Wallasey Guardian* wrote of 'that thrilling event in the Crimean campaign at which "all the world wondered" the Charge of the Light Brigade.' When any one of the 'Six Hundred' died, his obituary featured in the local press. Ordinary soldiers, who otherwise would have died without ceremony, had become national icons.

In the grim Dickensian world of Victorian Britain, the Charge was seen as a symbol of unity in a sharply-divided society, as Prime Minister Palmerston was proud to proclaim:

> Talk to me of the aristocracy of England! Why, look to that glorious charge of the cavalry at Balaklava – look to that charge, where the noblest and wealthiest in the land rode foremost, followed by the heroic men from the lowest classes of the community, each rivalling the other in bravery, neither the peer who led nor the trooper who followed being distinguished the one from the other. In that glorious band there were sons of the gentry of England, leading were the noblest in the land, and following were the representatives of the people of the country.[13]

The local newspapers, always eager for a story, abounded with reports of survivors of the Charge found in their communities. One such report was given in the *Portsmouth Evening News* of 25 October 1904:

> Today is the fiftieth anniversary of the Charge of the Light Brigade Balaklava. A correspondent writes: It might be of interest to you to know that probably the oldest survivor of the Balaklava charge is living in your town, viz, Sergt-Major John Lincoln [or Linkon], 13th Light Dragoons, of Telephone Road, Southsea.
>
> He entered the 13th on October 2nd, 1835, and left the regiment on pension in August, 1861, after serving 26 years. He was present at the siege of Sebastopol and took part in the famous charge, in which he had two horses shot under him, and was taken prisoner and marched a thousand miles into the interior of Russia ... On October 31st he will celebrate his 89th birthday. He is in very good health for his age.

Another case was recounted in the *Yorkshire Chronicle* of 7 March 1891, which carried the headline 'Death of a Balaklava Hero at York':

> One of the few remaining British heroes who came back from 'the jaws of death' after the famous charge of the Light Brigade, has been summoned by the grim sentinel, Death, to the fate he averted under Lord Cardigan. Troop Serjt. Major William Bentley, late of the 11th (Prince Albert's Own) Hussars, was born in Kilnwick-on-the-Wolds, Yorkshire, in 1816, and at the age of 19 years enlisted at Beverley, serving 25 years in the regiment ... In the Balaklava Charge he would most assuredly have lost his life if it had not been for the timely intervention of the brave Lieutenant Roberts Dunn, who cut down three Russians who were attacking the Sergeant from the rear. He did, however, receive a lance prod in the neck and a bullet graze in the calf of his leg. His gallant rescue was publicly decorated with the Victoria Cross.

When the decision was made to introduce the Victoria Cross for deeds of the utmost valour with the Royal Warrant of 29 January 1856, the question of which members of the Light Brigade should be rewarded was a vexed one. This issue was raised by Victoria's Consort, Prince Albert:

> How is a distinction to be made ... between the individual services of the 200 survivors of Ld Cardigan's Charge? If you reward them all

> it [the Victoria Cross] becomes merely a Medal for Balaklava, to
> which the Heavy Brigade and the 93rd have equal claims.[14]

Of course it was impossible, and would have been highly invidious, to distinguish between any of those that had charged into the guns, as all had acted with equal valour. When officers of the Light Brigade were asked to submit names for the award it was, initially, at the level of one per regiment. However, the 8th Hussars failed to provide a name. This, it is believed, is because Colonel Shewell died whilst at home on sick leave and the subject of the awarding of the VC was overlooked. In the end six men of the Light Brigade received the Victoria Cross, in each case, as we have seen, it was not for attacking the Don Battery but for helping to rescue wounded colleagues in the retreat.

The problem of limiting the number of VCs caused commanding officers considerable difficulty. How this was resolved in the 13th Light Dragoons was told to a journalist in 1908 by Private James Lamb who, like so many, had lost his horse and was making his way back down the valley on foot:

> As I went on I saw one of the captains – Captain Webb it was – lying on the ground, and there was two troopers trying to help him. And one of them called to me. 'Lamb,' he says, 'can't you give Captain Webb a drink of water?'
>
> Now, my water bottle was strapped to my saddle; we could carry our bottles that way if we wanted, or strapped to ourselves, and I always kept mine strapped to the saddle to keep my sword arm free.
>
> So I hadn't any water, and there was Captain Webb, wounded and suffering. And afterwards he died, sir.
>
> Well, I felt that of course I must get that water for the captain, so I went back, picking my way over horses and men, looking for an un-smashed bottle. I suppose it seemed queerlike, to see me just walking back again the wrong way, but I never took thought o' that. I just wanted to get some water for Captain Webb, for he was a fine officer, and he was suffering. I wouldn't think of calling it bravery. I just wanted to get some water, and pretty soon I found it, strapped to the saddle of a dead horse.
>
> I unfastened it, and all in a minute it came to me that I never was so thirsty in all my life. That thirst, it was something awful the way it came over me the minute I got the water bottle in my hand. Till then I never thought of such a thing – you don't while you are fighting, you know. Well, I had never known such a thirst, and there

was I with water in my hand, and so I took a pull at it before I started back for Captain Webb.

There was enough for us both ...

I got back to the captain. 'Men leave me and save yourselves,' he was saying; but he felt better with the drink of water, and then the two troopers helped him to get ahead.

'And now I saw a lancer close by, and I helped him on, and carried him on my back for a little.

Now I don't think it was bravery at all. When there's something to do like this you don't notice shells or such things; that's all ...

I almost got the V.C. for that little matter of the drink of water. For some of the men or the officers saw it, and so, when it was decided to pick a man from each of the five regiments for the V.C. – for they said that though every man deserved it, yet they couldn't give it to every one of us – well for the 13th, it was decided that it was between my comrade Malone and me, and we were told to draw lots for it. And Malone, he drew first, and so he got it ... Well he's dead this many a year. A fair man he was, and he got the V.C. fair, but he had the first draw.[15]

Such was the celebrity status of a Light Brigade survivor, William Bentley was accorded full military honours at his funeral, with the route lined with onlookers:

The coffin, of plain oak, rested on the gun-carriage drawn by powerful black steeds in funeral trappings. The Union Jack over spread the bier and a black velvet pall was laid on the colours. The band headed the funeral procession ... the coffin itself flanked by six corporals who acted as bearers. The relatives and friends came next, followed by fourteen sergeants and sergeant-majors who composed the mourning party and wore black sashes ... The streets en-route to the cemetery were lined with spectators, whilst a considerable number gathered at the graveside.

Even in the far reaches of the Empire, stories of the Light Brigade made good copy. For example, the New South Wales *Windsor and Richmond Gazette* of October 1888, printed the following under the headline, 'A Neglected Hero':

Few people living but are acquainted, more or less fully, with the facts of the splendid feat of arms, immortalised by Tennyson and which will be known in history, when every individual hero of it shall be laid to rest, as 'The Charge of the Light Brigade'. It is not generally known that we have in Cootamundra ... one of the gallant 600, who rode into the very jaws of death with 'cannons to the right of them, cannons to the left of them, cannons in front of them,' – in the person of H. Steele, a vendor of oranges! This may sound like a coming down from the sublime to the ridiculous, but so it is. Mr Steele generally has about him the proud mementoes of the glorious campaign in the Crimea, in the shape of two silver medals, one being presented by Queen Victoria in person, bearing the name of his regiment (8th K R Hussars) also, on four silver lines, the names of the four great features of that campaign, Sebastopol, Inkerman, Balaklava and Alma. The other medal was presented by the Sultan of Turkey, 'La Crimea, 1855; One of the 600'.

As well as six survivors of the Light Brigade receiving the Victoria Cross and the Turkish Medal, a number of the men were awarded the *Medal Militaire*. Though generally well considered, its distribution in the case of the 13th Light Dragoons, quite arbitrary, as Trumpeter Harry Powell complained:

> When I returned to the Regiment from Brighton I found that the Commanding Officer had made a kind of lottery of the decorations given to the regiment by the French. One of the Trumpeters, R. Davis, by name, was lucky enough to draw and win one. One or two of the other men who also had a decoration were not actually under arms that day, so could not have been in the Charge.[16]

Many years after the war, Queen Victoria was still meeting former members of the Light Brigade, including the last surviving horse! The following incident occurred in the summer of 1872 during the Queen's visit to Aldershot Barracks:

> On Friday week on the occasion of the visit of Her Majesty to this station His Royal Highness the Commander-in-Chief, the Duke of Cambridge, presented Private [James] Malanfy of 'A' Troop (Captain Starkey's) to Her Majesty ... He was wounded by a musket-ball in the Charge, and owing the preservation of his life to a six-penny piece which he had in one of his trouser pockets. This coin caused the bullet to pass in an oblique direction and in the course of which a wound was inflicted.
> The horse on which he rode at the time was also shown to Her Majesty. The noble animal, whose name was 'Butcher', joined the

regiment as a three-year-old in 1851 and was wounded in the Charge and has been recently presented to the regiment, never to be sold …

After being presented to Her Majesty he was ordered to follow in the rear of the Regiment in order that the Royal Family might recognise him as he passed by on the horse that had been for so many years his companion in both peace and war.[17]

On Monday, 25 October 1875, the Charge was celebrated in the form of the Balaklava Banquet which was held at Alexander Palace in London. A large crowd turned up for the event, including a host of dignitaries, which was reported in my international as well as all the national and local newspapers:

> The Balaklava commemoration at the Alexandra Palace on Monday attracted about 20,000 persons to the palace. There was an exhibition of relics of the Crimean campaign, and at one o'clock a Balaklava trophy was unveiled in the Great Hall. In the afternoon about 120 survivors of the Light Brigade were entertained at a banquet, which was presided over by Colonel White, of the 12th Lancers, who was supported by Sir George Wombwell, Lord Tredegar, Colonel Treyelyan, and a few other officers, and by the Baron de Grancey. Military Attaché to the French Embassy, who, in the uniform of a Chasseur d'Afrique, took his seat on the right of the chairman. On the other side of the Baron was the Commandant Canavro, Naval Attaché to the Italian Legation.
>
> After the banquet there was a military concert, and at night there was a display of fireworks in the grounds. Sir Edward Lee, one of the directors of the Alexandra Palace, proposed what was the toast of the evening: 'The Survivors of the Six Hundred.' Perhaps, according to stricter etiquette, the greater portion of the audience, ought to have remained silent whilst in eloquent language Sir Edward spoke their praises. But in plain truth they did quite otherwise, cheering madly, and accepting the compliments with clapping hands.[18]

After further details of the various speeches and comments a 'most striking' incident occurred:

> The trumpeter who stood behind the chairman suddenly sounded the charge. Up leaped the Light Brigade as one man, and with a wild cheer, and a waving of sabreless sword-arms looked for a moment as if they really were going to do it again. But there was no enemy in sight, and

after going through some vigorous passes with imperceptible swords, they slowly and sorrowfully resumed their seats.

Two years later, in 1877, a Balaclava Commemoration Society was formed, which in 1879 restricted its members to those who had taken part in the Light Brigade action. On 25 October 1890, Alexandra Palace was the venue of the first annual Balaklava reunion dinner. These dinners continued on the anniversary of the battle until 1913, by which time there were few survivors left.

Private James Olley, who was one of the few that survived into the twentieth century, had earlier fallen on hard times and an appeal was made on his behalf by Mr H. Robinson JP writing from North Walsham, Norfolk, to *The Times* of 3 January 1888:

> A Balaklava Hero ... May I ask for a small space in your valuable paper to set forth the claims of one of the ever-famous Light Brigade, by name, James Olley [4th Light Dragoons], now residing in this parish? He had one horse shot under him in the charge. He received four wounds, and had his left eye shot out. He has a wife and six children, four of whom are under the age of ten, and utterly dependent upon him ... I have just seen a doctor's certificate stating that he is incapable of continuing his employment, owing, I believe, to heart disease.

Such was the reverence with which the Light Brigade was still held in the public consciousness that enough contributions were made to enable James Olley to start a little business, and to 'live out his out his life in better circumstances'. He died on 4 September 1920.

There were many other instances of survivors of the charge falling on hard times after the war, and this was brought to the attention of the public in a poem by Rudyard Kipling published in the *St James's Gazette* in May 1890, the opening lines of which are:

> There were thirty million English who talked of England's might,
>   There were twenty broken troopers who lacked a bed for the night.
>   They had neither food nor money, they had neither service nor trade;
>   They were only shiftless soldiers, the last of the Light Brigade.

When it was realised that indeed there were many survivors of history's most famous cavalry action who had been abandoned to the 'the streets and the workhouse' there was widespread outrage. Despite complaints of what was called 'a national disgrace', the Secretary of State for War refused to offer any assistance. As a result, the 'Light Brigade Relief Fund' was set up and, following an appeal in *The Times* by the Marquis of Hartington, money poured into the Fund.

By March 1891, the Relief committee had raised enough money for grants to those most in need, with a surplus of £3,000 to create annuities for the future. Amongst the fund-raising appeals was one of particular note made by Florence Nightingale. This took the form of one of the earliest sound recordings ever made. On 3 July 1890, at her home at 10 South Street, Park Lane, London, under the supervision of a representative of the Edison company, she recorded the following on a wax disc:

> When I am no longer even a memory, just a name, I hope my voice may perpetuate the great work of my life. God bless my dear old comrades of Balaclava and bring them safe to shore. Florence Nightingale.[19]

Earlier that year an appeal had been made to celebrate the Balaklava veterans which was given further impetus with the writing of a Music Hall song, 'Put them in the Lord Mayor's Show'. This worked and eleven open-top carriages, with four veterans in each one, formed part of the procession which travelled through the streets of London at the Lord Mayor's Show on 9 November 1890. The carriages flew banners which read 'Survivors of the Charge at Balaklava' and 'battle of Balaklava Heroes', and at their head rode Trumpeters Martin Landfried of the 17th Lancers and William Perkins of the 11th Hussars.

Another glorious pageant which took place in London was Queen Victoria's Diamond Jubilee. This included a procession through the streets of the capital on 22 June 1897. For this event, a publisher, Thomas Harrison Roberts, invited seventy-three survivors of the Light Brigade to an all-expenses-paid visit to his offices at 158 Fleet Street to watch the procession. In the midst of the immense cheering crowds, the Queen stopped her carriage to acknowledge the heroes of Balaklava.

It might seem all of those that survived the charge would thereafter be glorified and revered. But this was the second half of the nineteenth century, and the British Army was a brutal and unforgiving organisation, as this account from Private James Herbert of the 4th Light Dragoons sadly shows:

> I can tell you of a case as amazing in its way and one which shows up the brutal discipline of the Crimean period. There was a man of

our Regiment named [Private Christopher] Fox. When the order to advance was given, he was on duty in the camp. He rushed to his horse, rode in the Charge and came safely back. And to what? The cat! He was Court-martialled for leaving his post without orders and sentenced to receive 50 lashes. The remnant of the 4th was paraded for the degrading and monstrous punishment and Fox was tied to the wheel of a forge-cart. One of the farriers took a cat-o'-nine-tales and gave him 25 strokes. At that time when flogging was in vogue in the Army, one man never gave more than 25 lashes, a new man with a fresh cat being obtained. When half the punishment had been given, the Colonel said, 'Hold! I will forgive the other twenty-five'. Fox, who was an Irishman, answered, 'Oh, don't. Please, Colonel, I don't want to be beholden to you for anything. I'll take the other twenty-five'. The Colonel said sternly, 'Silence, sir!', and had him marched off to the hospital marquee. The balance was never given. Fox was a desperate character, and a rough customer to deal with, it is true; but he was a fine soldier and considering what he had gone through, his punishment was out of all proportion to his crime.[20]

In August 1927, it was announced to the world that the last surviving member of the Light Brigade had died, being buried at Layton Cemetery in Blackpool. This was reported in the *Brisbane Daily Mail* of the 14th of that month, with some almost laughable errors:

> The immortal charge of Light Brigade at Balaklava on October 26, 1854, is recalled by the death of the last survivor, Troop Sergeant-Major Edwin Hughes, at the age of 97.
>
> It was in this battle that a blunder of someone brought out a display of valour such as the world has seldom seen. In the order issued to the Earl of Cardigan, a comma had been put in the wrong place, and this error caused him to charge a Russian battery with his Light Brigade ... It is interesting to record that as the old warrior was placed to his rest, Tennyson's poem, The Charge of the Light Brigade, was recited, and the Last Post was sounded by the trumpeters of the 13th Hussars – his old regiment.

With the death of 'Balaklava Ned' Hughes, the last link with history's most famous cavalry charge was severed. Fascination with it, though, knows no end.

Chapter 13

Tarnished Glory

The virtual destruction of the Light Brigade at Balaklava was a serious blow to the Allies, reducing their cavalry force to little more than 1,000 men. Yet, instead of it being seen as the reprehensible blunder it truly was, the charge quickly became the most celebrated event of the entire war and its survivors would, upon their return to Britain, be lauded for their unquestioning courage. Unfortunately for the man who led the charge, at first heralded as the 'hero' of Balaklava, it all turned rather sour.

On 13 December 1856, the Honourable Somerset Calthorpe's memoir of the war, *Letters from Headquarters; or, the Realities of the War in the Crimea; by an Officer on the Staff*, was published anonymously by John Murray of London, in which Cardigan's conduct during the campaign in the East was severely criticized. Amongst the accusations directed at Cardigan was that he had driven the men and horses too hard during the reconnaissance from Varna, and that he allowed Russian prisoners to be released in the truncated pursuit at the end of the Battle of the Alma. These, though, were minor complaints compared with one particular accusation which cast a dark shadow over the Earl's newly-won heroic status. When the Light Brigade reached the Russian guns, according to Calthorpe,

> This was the moment when a general was most required, but unfortunately Lord Cardigan was not then present. On coming up to the battery (as he afterwards himself described it) a gun was fired close to him, and for a moment he thought his leg was gone. Such was not the case, as he remained unhurt; however, his horse took fright—swerved round—and galloped off with him to the rear, passing on the way by the 4th Light Dragoons and 8th Hussars before those regiments got up to the battery. [1]

Calthorpe had declared, for all the world to see, that Cardigan had ridden back before the last of his regiments had reached the Russian guns. As Paget's line was following just a few yards behind the preceding ones, there can only have been moments between them. The Earl, therefore according to Calthorpe, retired as soon as, or before, he reached the guns. A little further on in the book Calthorpe resorted to mockery of the Earl's leadership in the famous charge:

> I also see that Lord Cardigan has been feted at the Mansion-house, and made a speech on that occasion which has afforded considerable amusement and merriment amongst the officers of the Light Cavalry here, who naturally know better than any one else the very prominent part which his lordship took at the celebrated charge of Balaklava. I never read a more egotistical speech in my life, to say nothing of the wonderful way in which Lord Cardigan indulges his imagination.[2]

This, of course, was too much, and on 26 December that year a furious Cardigan wrote to the Commander-in-Chief, the Duke of Cambridge, seeking permission to prefer charges before a General Court-Martial against Calthorpe. Such an inquiry was likely to be little more than an embarrassing slanging-match which would do little for the Army's reputation which had already suffered at the hands of the press for its failures in Crimea. After all, Cardigan had led his men down the North Valley whilst Calthorpe watched safely from the heights above. He was hardly in a position to cast aspersions on any member of the Light Brigade. The Duke, therefore, declined Cardigan's request, stating that 'he did not conceive that it was his province to take notice of anonymous military publications, because such a precedent once established would lead to inevitable confusion in the administration of the discipline of the army'.[3] Calthorpe, after all, had not committed a military offence. It was a private matter and if the Earl wanted to pursue the matter he would have to do so through the civil courts.

Calthorpe, for his part, was unmoved by Cardigan's complaints and was determined to stand by what he had written. Worse was to come as a second edition of the book was published which included a footnote that was even more damning:

> The Earl of Cardigan has stated, since the publication of the first edition of this book, that he considers the account given of the part taken by him in the light cavalry charge unworthy of any reply, as it is well known that he led the light brigade up to the Russian cavalry in rear of the battery, and that the 8th Hussars did not advance as far

as the battery, but became engaged with the Russian cavalry short of it. The author has relied on Statements furnished him by officers actually engaged in the charge; but as the excellence of Lord Cardigan's horsemanship is unquestionable, the idea that his horse ran away with him is no doubt erroneous! Several officers of the 4th Light Dragoons and 8th Hussars bear witness to the fact that his Lordship retired between those regiments as they were advancing, and it has been confidently asserted to the author, by the two senior officers of the 8th Hussars who were present, that their regiment was not halted until it had gone 300 yards beyond the Russian battery, when it was wheeled about for the purpose of attacking the enemy's cavalry, which had assembled in its rear.[4]

Calthorpe's words were unbecoming of a fellow officer, and possibly even slanderous, and finally Cardigan acted. Firstly, he tried a reasonable approach by asking, on 9 January 1857, if Calthorpe (through the intermediary of his friend the Earl of Westmorland, Colonel the Lord Burghersh, who was related to Calthorpe, and who had been on the Staff in the Crimea) if he would retract the statements in the book:

> I am in a great difficulty about the 'Staff Officer'. I cannot let his slanders pass unnoticed, and it has been a subject of much reflection with me how I can dispose of this case in a tolerable satisfactory manner … I have sent you a document by Colonel Cotton, and you will there see that I have shown that every one of the Staff Officer's statements with regard to myself are without any truth or foundation … I asked [if the statement would be shown to] Major Calthorpe, and ask him whether, upon seeing that that which he has published is void of all truth and foundation, he will withdraw his statements, upon the plea that the cases had been misrepresented to him, or on any other grounds.

Included in his letter to Lord Burghersh, Cardigan gave an answer to all of Calthorpe's accusations, and these were passed onto Calthorpe, who replied on 22 January:

> I have carefully looked over the paper by Lord Cardigan in contradiction to various statements in 'Letters from Head-Quarters,' which you put in my hands a few days ago. I am at a loss how to answer them in a manner that can be satisfactory to Lord Cardigan, but you will, I think, admit the difficulty of the case when I have given you my explanation.

Calthorpe then detailed how he had reached the conclusions he had in his book. With reference to the Charge of the Light Brigade, he wrote:

> I only speak from what I was told by many officers present, that Lord Cardigan retired between the 4th Light Dragoons and 8th Hussars before either of these regiments arrived sat the Russian battery: there are several officers who witnessed it in both the above-mentioned regiments.

Cardigan was furious with Calthorpe's response and he tried to have him dismissed from his post as aide-de-camp to the Earl of Carlise who was at that time Lord-Lieutenant of Ireland. When this was rejected, Cardigan resorted to an appeal to his peers, making a lengthy statement to the House of Lords, speaking in the third person:

> The facts were these. His character had been maligned, his military reputation had been defamed, in a most extraordinary and uncalled-for manner by an officer holding a commission in the service; and that officer, although he had published his statement—his unfounded statement—under the name of 'A Staff Officer,' was in reality Major the Hon. Somerset Calthorpe ... First of all, it might be necessary for him to say that, barring one statement relating to a circumstance touching a certain number of horses, there was not a single statement made respecting him which was not utterly devoid of the slightest truth ... Under different circumstances, considering the insignificance of this officer, and if it had been merely a question of the present moment, he might have allowed his accusations to pass unnoticed; but published in a book, they became, if uncontradicted, matter of history; and somebody taking up this work twenty-five years hence might be led to believe that it showed the real tenor of his conduct as a general officer while serving in the Crimea.[5]

Cardigan said that, if duelling had not been illegal, he would have 'called out' the Honourable Calthorpe and settled the matter that way.

However, such a course of action was unavailable to him (having been prosecuted in 1841 for a duel with one of his former officers, being acquitted on a legal technicality) he then tried again to have Calthorpe dismissed, asking 'Whether an officer who had disgraced himself by propagating and publishing statements which were devoid of every vestige of truth should continue to receive even half-pay from the public purse?'

A personal dispute of this nature was hardly a suitable subject for the Lords to be discussing and Lord Panmure advised Cardigan to simply ignore the words of 'one so inferior in rank', and 'strongly recommend the noble Earl to rest upon the high testimonials which he had in his possession to refute the injustice to which he had been subjected'.

If Cardigan had taken the Secretary at State for War's advice, the whole subject would, no doubt, have quickly been forgotten. The Earl, though, was not the kind of man to forget such an insult, and two years later, in the autumn of 1859, Cardigan was able to exact revenge. Calthorpe, then an unattached major, applied to exchange into the 5th Dragoon Guards. The move was accepted by the Commander-in-Chief and by the Secretary at State for War as well as receiving royal sanction from Queen Victoria. Unfortunately for Calthorpe, the Colonel of the regiment was none other than the Earl of Cardigan, who blocked the move.

Calthorpe now realised that making an enemy of such a powerful man might not have been the smartest of moves, and he wrote to Lieutenant General Sir Charles Yorke, the Military Secretary at the Horse Guards, on 17 November 1859:

> I am willing now to admit, that I may have been indiscreet in bringing before the public statements calling into question the acts of a superior officer. Should H.R.H. [Duke of Cambridge] be pleased to recommend her Majesty to allow of my exchange taking place, I may confidently state that by my future conduct towards the Earl of Cardigan, I will shew that I am actuated by no personal feelings against his Lordship.

This was enough to secure Calthorpe the position in the 5th Dragoon Guards. He was then urged to go a little further and make some form of statement that might 'soothe' Lord Cardigan. But, having got the job he wanted, nothing more was forthcoming from Calthorpe and so, in 1860, Cardigan instructed his solicitors, Ward and Mills of Gray's Inn Square, to look into the possibility of undertaking a libel action against the author of the book.

Though the Earl was initiating legal action, Calthorpe stood by his comments, refusing to change anything he had written, saying that 'it was impossible … I consider my statements true; and I had no intention of altering in them'. Nevertheless, Calthorpe did agree to the following:

> I will undertake to say that but few copies [of the book] shall be issued from my publishers [John Murray], but I cannot recall those

in circulation; if Lord Cardigan likes to pay for the few copies that may be in circulation, of course he can do so – it will make no difference to me whether he dos or not.

Calthorpe then contacted John Murray to inform him of this decision, and it was agreed that only those copies that had already been bound, of which there were only a few, would be sold, and the remainder which were unbound, would be 'cut up and wasted'. This was duly carried out in June 1861. As John Murray later testified, 'In consequence of a communication made to me by Lieutenant Colonel the Hon. Somerset John Gough Calthorpe …of a wish expressed by Colonel Calthorpe, I caused 1,000 copies of the said work to be wasted. Since 1861 no effort has been made to effect a sale of the said work, by advertisement or otherwise.' This, Calthorpe hoped would satisfy Cardigan and end the matter. He could not have been more wrong.

On 4 February 1863, Cardigan's solicitors wrote to Calthorpe demanding that the book, unsold copies of which were still available in bookshops, should be withdrawn, and that Calthorpe should make a public retraction of the defamatory passages. If he failed to comply with these demands, proceedings would be instituted. Calthorpe remained intransigent, and was prepared to defend himself in court. Cardigan was about to fight his last battle. But before his day in court, the Earl had another appointment to keep.[6]

As both protagonists began to locate individuals who were prepared to act as witnesses in support of their respective claims, one particular person who submitted a statement for Calthorpe stood out above all others – Cardigan's brother-in-law. His statement included the following:

> Remaining in advance to watch the movements of the enemy and to be prepared to support the Light Brigade should they be pursued in their retreat, I saw Lord Cardigan gallop up from the direction of the enemy. When within a short distance of my front he brought his horse to a walk, and passed me going up the valley towards Sebastopol. He was at a distance of about 200 yards from me. When I first observed him, I called Lord William Paulet's attention to him. At this time no part of the Light Brigade was in my sight.
>
> Subsequently to this, Captain Lockwood, an aide-de-camp to Lord Cardigan, rode up to me, and said, 'My Lord, can you tell me where is Lord Cardigan? I replied that Lord Cardigan had passed me some time. Captain Lockwood then rode away, and was I believe killed.[7]

What Lucan implied with this statement, was that what Calthorpe had written was correct and Cardigan had abandoned his brigade and made his own way back, and indeed, was the first to make his escape, leaving his men to fend for themselves. As Cardigan blamed Lucan for the whole disastrous affair, he was enraged at what he saw as a betrayal. This time Cardigan did not hesitate, he immediately demanded 'satisfaction'. As duelling was illegal in Britain, the two Earls arranged to meet in France and settle their differences once and for all.

As with everything else that transpired between Lucan and Cardigan, they could not even arrange this matter properly. Lucan accepted Cardigan's challenge and went over to Paris. Cardigan, though, was delayed, and when he arrived at the appointed rendezvous, Lucan had set off back to England.

The case of Brudendell versus Calthorpe was brought before the Lord Chief Justice, Sir Alexander Cockburn, and three other judges, on 9 June 1863. Both Calthorpe and Cardigan were able to find a number of former, or serving, members of the Cavalry willing to provide statements. In Cardigan's case, there was considerable evidence that he charged into the guns and fought with the Russian cavalry, such as this letter from a member of the 8th Hussars:

> Lord Cardigan was entirely surrounded by Russian Hussars, and would have been killed but one of the 17th Lancers came up and ran one of them through the neck with his lance and beat the others off, so as to allow of his escaping.[8]

Private Patrick Rafferty of the 17th Lancers, who was on the front right of his regiment and, consequently, was in the centre of the brigade, did 'solemnly and sincerely declare' that on 25 October 1854:

> The Earl of Cardigan, who was in command, led the Brigade by the centre of the first line, just in front of me. That on nearing the Battery in our front my horse was killed, and about six other men and horses were at the same time disabled. That at about the same time I distinctly saw Lord Cardigan ride into and through the Battery, and that some short time after, when the remainder of the Brigade had passed us, and I had extricated myself, and was looking about to catch another horse, I noticed the General, Lord Cardigan, come away from where the guns were, and ride off at a hand canter up the Valley on the left-hand side going back – in which direction, having remounted myself, I also followed.[9]

An even more detailed letter was provided by William Barker, Troop Sergeant-Major, 17th Lancers:

> I remember seeing, after your Lordship had led the attack, the whole length of the valley under a tremendous fire from the whole of the enemy's guns; that your Lordship was the first to enter the battery, the officers and men following your Lordship, and taking possession of the battery by cutting down and spearing the artillery-men at their guns, amidst a deadly fire from the enemy's flank batteries, and from a large body of infantry formed in the left rear of the battery, causing death and destruction on all around. And, in consequence of the loss of officers as leaders and the ranks having to open out, so as to clear the guns, limber-carriages, etc., in the battery, the men became scattered, and all order lost, it being an impossibility to rally any number of men. I observed, after your Lordship had cleared the battery, and failed in restoring order, again dash forward, followed by about twenty or thirty men of both regiments mixed up together, and come in contact with a strong force of the enemy's cavalry advancing up the valley, at about two hundred yards in rear of the battery, when a hand-to-hand conflict ensued; but the men, seeing at once that there was no chance of success, turned their horses about and endeavoured to retire. I galloped away to the left, and came up to your Lordship as your Lordship, with sword in hand, was valorously resisting the attack, and putting to flight three or four of the enemy's Cossacks, a couple of squadrons of the enemy's cavalry advancing from their right flank across the valley at the same time, apparently with the intention of cutting off our retreat, your Lordship retiring at an easy canter up the valley under a fearful fire from all arms. I continued to ride near to your Lordship to the end of the valley, your Lordship halting frequently to make inquiries of the wounded ... I wish to add that I am prepared to swear that when your Lordship retired, and I followed you from the battery, that no part of the Light Brigade was advancing, but had already advanced and passed the flanks of the battery.[10]

The most senior officer to support Cardigan was General Scarlett, who stated:

> At the instant when the first line of the Light Brigade charged into the battery, it was almost impossible, from the dense smoke and confusion, to discover what took place; but a few minutes

afterwards I observed the remnants of the Light Brigade, as well as the remains of the second line, retreating towards the ground which they had occupied immediately before the charge; whilst dismounted men, and horses without riders, were scattered over the space which the brigade had just traversed. I recollect on this occasion pointing out to Lord Cardigan the broken remnants of his line as they were retreating up the hill. I firmly believe, from the information I received both at the time of the engagement and afterwards, that Lord Cardigan was the first to charge into the battery, and that he was amongst the last, if not the last, to return from behind the guns.

Calthorpe's version of the charge was also challenged by Private Richard Owen Glendur of the 8th Hussars:

> As the pace increased, the 4th Light Dragoons went right away to the left, the 8th Hussars advanced to the right of the guns, when the order was given 'left about wheel'. I was then on the left flank of the regiment, having had my horse shot at the 1st Battery, but got a remount of the 13th [Light Dragoons] which was riderless. As we retired out, the Russian cavalry formed partly across the valley, and the 8th cut their way out, and I distinctly remember seeing your Lordship returning to the position which we occupied in the morning, followed by some of the 13th Light Dragoons and 17th Lancers, *and at this moment no part of the Light Brigade was advancing.*
>
> At this time, my horse being wounded, and surrounded by Polish Lancers, I was taken prisoner, and being wounded myself in my sword arm, I was left by the Russians on the ground, while they followed the 8th Hussars out.
>
> At this time, with great exertion, I got a horse of the 4th Light Dragoons, which was coming out, which I mounted, and seeing the Busby Bags flying at the bottom of the valley, wheeled my horse and joined the 4th Light Dragoons and 11th Hussars as they were wheeling round at the right flank of the Battery, and retreating at a rapid gallop.[11]

After a preliminary hearing Calthope had been made aware of the various statements declaring that Cardigan had charged into the battery and before laying out his supporting evidence, he conceded that he was now able 'to cheerfully declare myself satisfied that the Earl of Cardigan entered the Russian battery,' but remained convinced that in every other respect the comments he made were true, particularly the one that 'This was the moment when a general was most required, but, unfortunately, Lord Cardigan was not then present'.

In support of his claims, Calthorpe was able to present a number of statements from members of the Light Brigade, but he explained that:

> In consequence of the lapse of time, I have found great difficulty in obtaining evidence. Some of my most important witnesses are dead, some are serving in India and in the colonies, and some object to give positive evidence on events which happened so long ago. A still more serious difficulty … is the reluctance of military men of all ranks to give voluntary evidence affecting the character of an officer in the high and influential position of the Earl of Cardigan.[12]

Nevertheless, he had found almost twenty men willing to condemn Cardigan. These included George Mayow, the Brigade Major, who, as we know, lost sight of Cardigan because of the dense smoke from the guns of the Don Cossack battery. He then explained in some detail that he never saw Cardigan again until after he had returned back to the British lines. As we have read earlier, after charging through the guns he made the decision to retreat with the men who were with him:

> I was induced to give these orders in consequence of not being able to see anything of Lord Cardigan on emerging from the smoke that hung over the Russian guns, and being the senior officer in his absence, until I joined Colonel Shewell, who assumed the command, led us to the charge. We broke through, and after we had broken through we repassed the Russian guns (which were all then unhorsed), and, galloping up the valley, reformed in rear of the Heavy Brigade. Whilst going up the valley I looked in every direction for Lord Cardigan (who would have been conspicuous for wearing the hussar dress of the 11th), and not being able to see him anywhere, I said to myself 'Lord Cardigan must be either killed or taken prisoner.' However, when I got in the rear of the Heavy Brigade, I found his Lordship there, and he spoke to me.[13]

Captain Daniel Clutterbuck, of the 8th Hussars, stated that:

> On our return to where the Heavy Brigade was drawn up I saw Lord Cardigan sitting quietly on his horse. I did not see Lord Cardigan at the lower end of the valley, nor did we receive any order from him while there.[14]

Major Edward Phillips, who had been a lieutenant in the 8th Hussars at the time of the Battle of Balaklava, said:

> The 8th Hussars and the 4th Light Dragoons, formed the second line, the 8th on the right. While the regiment was still advancing down the valley, I saw the Earl of Cardigan coming back. He passed the left flank of the regiment.

This was the most damning statement so far. It might be recalled that the second line was only 200 yards or so behind the first. If galloping as quickly as possible, the two lines could only be seconds apart. If Phillips was correct, it meant that Cardigan had turned back almost as soon as he reached the guns.

Phillip's account was backed up by James Donoghue, formerly a sergeant in the 8th Hussars. He was Field Trumpeter of the 8th and his position during the charge was in front of the centre of the regiment:

> As we were advancing, and after we had passed through the fire of the guns on the flanks, but before we had reached the guns in our front, I saw the Earl of Cardigan galloping passed us towards the rear, coming from the position of the Russian guns in front of us. I am sure it was Lord Cardigan: I saw him distinctly. He was mounted on a chestnut horse, and wore the uniform of the 11th Hussars. He passed to the left both of the 4th Light Dragoons and the 8th Hussars, and about 150 yards of the left flank of the 8th Hussars. I never felt more sure of anything in my life than I was at that moment, when Lord Cardigan passed us to the rear, that he was going to bring up the Heavy Brigade to our support.[15]

An intriguing, and what was in effect a third party testimony, came from Private Samuel Parkes VC of the 4th Light Dragoons whom, it may be recalled, had been taken prisoner by the Russians. Shortly after his capture he, along with other prisoners, was taken before General Liprandi. After asking if the Light Brigade had carried out their mad charge because the men were drunk,

> He further asked me if it was Lord Cardigan who went to the rear on a chestnut horse with white legs; we said 'Yes,' and he then said, 'If he had not had a good horse, he would never have got back.'[16]

The evidence submitted by Calthorpe certainly appeared to demonstrate that Cardigan had been the first man, or amongst the first men, to return from the charge. However, one man, Charles Whyte formerly a Private in the 8th Hussars, had sent the following letter to Lord Cardigan:

> On the 16th of May last, a person of the name of Bristol, a clerk to Mr Home, solicitor of Dublin, called on me, and said a criminal action was brought by Lord Cardigan against Colonel Calthorpe – something about the Light Cavalry Brigade charge of Balaklava – that his party acting for Colonel Calthorpe wanted to upset Lord Cardigan, and asked me if I could give him any information to help them, as, if so, it might be a few pounds in my pocket. I replied that I had no information to give him in the matter, but what was altogether favourable to Lord Cardigan, who not only in the action of Balaklava, but all through the campaign, behaved most nobly and bravely in every way as the General commanding the Brigade.
>
> That the same person called on me again on Friday, the 29th ultimo, and again urged me to give him some information, saying, that there were 'a lot of them going over to London together on the trial, and that as they had already beaten Lord Cardigan, I might as well go with them and have a jolly good spree,' and again said it would be a few pounds in my way.[17]

Nothing could have been worse for Calthorpe's defence. It was apparent that men were being bribed, or at least being offered money and a free day out, if they were prepared to condemn Lord Cardigan. This nullified all the statements made on Calthorpe's behalf, except those from senior officers for whom 'a few pounds' would have meant nothing.

The judges had little choice but to find in Cardigan's favour, except for one point, and this was the main basis of Calthorpe's team's defence – if, as he claimed, the publication of the book offended the Earl so much, why had he waited more than six years since the publication of the first edition of the book, when the initial claim that Cardigan had abandoned his men at the most crucial time, been made, and five years after the last edition, before taking legal action? If the Earl had lived with it for more than half a decade, the accusations cannot have troubled him that much.

The court was therefore unable to bring civil proceedings against Calthorpe and the case was dismissed. In his summation, nevertheless, Judge Cockburn had these words to say:

> There may be those who will say, Lord Cardigan, as a general, is open to criticism, but it should be a generous and liberal criticism, not one

that should seek to cast a stain upon his courage and personal honour as an officer. I cannot help, therefore, rejoicing, feeling as I said before, that the reputation and honour of every man who took part in that great scene should be dear to us all, and that this opportunity has been afforded of setting Lord Cardigan right in the estimation, not only of his own profession, but of the public generally.[18]

Neither Cardigan nor Calthorpe emerged from the affair with much credit. Certainly the Honourable Calthorpe had proven to be far from honourable, whilst on the other hand the statements made against the Earl hardly described the actions of the much-feted 'Hero of Balaklava'.

Consequently, Cardigan continued to press his case long after his appearance in the High Court, with the following being included in the sixth edition of Kinglake's history, published in 1877:

> The only point really to be considered is whether, after leading into the battery, and up to the Russian cavalry, and being wounded and nearly taken prisoner by the Cossacks, and having with difficulty got away from them—whether I was justified in returning slowly in rear of my own line, who were retreating up the hill.

In this Cardigan was effectively admitting that he had been amongst the first to retreat. He may have thought that this public appeal would help restore his reputation. Of course he was wrong. Even one of his friends, who wrote admiringly of Cardigan's equestrian skills under the pseudonym 'Thormanby' in a book entitle *The Kings of the Hunting-Field*, could offer no excuse for the earl's conduct during those crucial moments at Balaklava:

> He was the first to dash in at a gallop among the Russian guns, but, unfortunately for his reputation, he was not the last to come out. Beyond all question, he left the men, who he had so gallantly led to their goal, to find their way out of the tangle in which they were involved, as best they could. From the moment he got among the Russian cavalry he effaced himself as a leader ... Why he should so strangely have forgotten or ignored the duties of a leader is an enigma to which no one has offered a satisfactory solution.[19]

Thus it was that the Earl of Cardigan, who had paid a fortune for the honour to command a cavalry regiment, and bravely led his brigade in the greatest charge of all time, saw the glory he so fervently sought become forever tarnished.

References and Notes

Chapter 1: The Price of Glory

1. Hansard, HC Deb 29 March 1852 vol. 120 cc267-339.
2. Christopher Hibbert, *The Destruction of Lord Raglan, A Tragedy of the Crimean War 1854-55* (Penguin, London, 1985), pp.252-3.
3. Cecil Woodham-Smith, *The Reason Why* (Penguin, London, 1958), p.23.
4. *Report of the Commissioners appointed to inquire into the system of purchase and sale of commissions*, cited in Anthony Bruce, *The Purchase System in the British Army 1660-1871* (Royal Historical Society, London, 1980), p.45.
5. Hansard, HC Deb 04 March 1856 vol. 140 cc1791-850.
6. John Sweetman, *Raglan, From the Peninsula to the Crimea*, (Pen & Sword, Barnsley, 2010) p.189.
7. Quoted in Alister Massie, *The National Army Book of the Crimean War: The Untold Stories* (Pan Books, London, 2005), pp.24-5.
8. Kinglake, *The Invasion of the Crimea: Its Origin, and An Account of its Progress down to the Death of Lord Raglan* (William Blackwood, London, 1878), Vol.5, p.53.
9. Roy Dutton, *Forgotten Heroes, The Charge of the Light Brigade* (Infodial, Oxton, 2007), p.8.
10. Woodham-Smith, p.133.
11. John Sweetman, *Raglan*, p.172-3.
12. Robert Portal, *Letters from the Crimea: 1854-1855*, (Privately published, Winchester, 1900), p.71.
13. George Ryan, *Our Heroes of the Crimea: Being Biographical Sketches Of Our Military Officers, From The General Commanding-In-Chief To The Subaltern* (Routledge, London, 1855), p.47.

Chapter 2: Holy War

1. Reproduced in *The Times* 7 July 1853.
2. Reproduced in *The Times* 4 March 1854.
3. William Howard Russell, *The British Expedition to the Crimea* (Routledge, London, 1877), p.8.
4. Frederick Charles Arthur Stephenson, *At Home and on the Battlefield: Letters from the Crimea, China and Egypt, 1854-1888* (John Murray, London, 1915), p.69.
5. *The Times*, 3 July 1854.
6. Kinglake, vol. II, p.183.
7. Cambridge to Victoria, 13 May 1854 *The Letters of Queen Victoria, Volume III (of 3), 1854-1861, by Queen of Great Britain Victoria*, Edited by Arthur Christopher

Benson and Viscount Reginald Baliol Brett Esher, Project Gutenberg, 2009.
8. Albert Mitchell, *Recollections of One of the Light Brigade*, (R. Pelton, Tunbridge Wells, 1885), p.7.
9. General Sir Edward Hamley, *The Crimean War 1853-1856* (Parchment Publishing, 2012), pp.21-2.
10. Kinglake, vol.II, pp.114-5.
11. Baron Bazancourt, [translated by Robert Howe Gould] *The Crimean Expedition, to the Capture of Sevastopol, Chronicles of the War in the East, from Its Commencement to the Signing of the Treaty of Peace*, (Sampson Low, London, 1856) vol. I, pp.126-7.
12. *The Times*, 22 June 1854.
13. Henry Clifford, *His Letters & Sketches from the Crimea* (Michael Joseph, London, 1956), p. 36.
14. Clive Ponting, *The Crimean War, The Truth Behind the Myth* (Chatto & Windus, London, 2004), p70.
15. Julian Spillsbury, *The Thin Red Line, An eyewitness history of the Crimean War* (Weidenfeld & Nicolson, London), p.12.
16. ibid, p.14.
17. See Woodham-Smith, pp.153-4.
18. Kelly, Christine, *Mrs Duberley's War: Journal & Letters From the Crimea* (Oxford University Press, 2007), pp.33-4.
19. Quoted in Woodham-Smith, pp.163-4.

Chapter 3: Inaction at the Alma
1. 'The Army in the East', *Bristol Mercury*, 23 September 1854.
2. Hamley, p.39.
3. Quoted in Albert Seaton, *The Crimean War: A Russian Chronicle* (Batsford, London, 1977), pp.60-1.
4. The Honourable S.J.G. Calthorpe, *Letters from Headquarters; or, The Realities of the War in the Crimea, by an Officer on the Staff* (John Murray, London, 1858), p.55.
5. William Howard Russell, *Despatches from the Crimea* (Frontline Books, Barnsley, 2008), p.64.
6. Timothy Gowing, *A Soldier's Experience, or, A Voice from the Ranks* (Thos Forman & Sons Nottingham, 1903), 43-4.
7. C.S Paget, *The Light Cavalry Brigade in the Crimea. Extracts from the letters and journal of the late Gen. Lord G. Paget ... during the Crimean War* (John Murray, London, 1881), p.16.
8. Kelly, pp.63-4.
9. Mitchell, p.41
10. Kinglake vol.2, p.353.
11. Mitchell, p.42.
12. *Sheffield & Rotherham Independent*, 14 October 1854.
13. ibid.
14. Mitchell, pp.49-50.
15. Whinyates, Francis Arthur, *From Coruña to Sevastopol. The history of 'C' Battery, 'A' Brigade (late 'C' Troop), Royal Horse Artillery*, (W. H. Allen, London, 1884), pp.90-1.
16. Calthorpe, p.62.
17. Kinglake, vol.2, p.221.
18. Ian Fletcher and Ishenko Natalia, *The Battle of the Alma 1854, First Blood to the Allies in the Crimea* (Pen & Sword, Barnsley, 2004), p.91.
19. Reproduced from John Grehan and Martin Mace, *Despatches from the Front, British Battles of the Crimean War 1854-1856* (Pen & Sword, Barnsley, 2014), pp.54-5.

20. Edward Colebrooke, *Journal of Two Visits to the Crimea, in the Autumn of 1854 and 1855, with Remarks on the Campaign* (Privately printed by T. & W. Boone, London, 1856), pp.18-20.
21. Quoted in Seaton, p.92.
22. Gowing, p.47.
23. ibid, pp.47-8.
24. *Sheffield & Rotherham Independent*, 14 October 1854.
25. Quoted in Algernon Percy, *A Bearskin's Crimea, Colonel Henry Percy VC & His Brother Officers* (Pen & Sword, Barnsley, 2005), pp.20-30.
26. John Dugdale Astley, *Fifty Years of My Life* (Hurst and Blackett, London, 1894), Vol. I, pp.213-4.
27. Captain Alfred Tipping, 'Letters from the East during the Campaign if 1854', quoted in Michael Springman, *The Guards Brigade in the Crimea* (Pen & Sword, Barnsley, 2008), p.53.
28. *Hamley*, p.32.
29. Quoted in Ian Knight, *Marching to the Drums, Eyewitness Accounts of War from the Kabul Massacre to the Siege of Mafikeng* (Greenhill, London, 1999), pp.31-2.
30. Calthorpe, pp.71-2.
31. Quoted in Ponting, p.103.
32. *Sheffield & Rotherham Independent*, 14 October 1854. The only Russian gun taken was captured by Captain Edward Bell of the 23rd Royal Welch Fusiliers.
33. NAM, 1989-06-41, Journal of Captain Louis Nolan, 15th Hussars.
34. Calthorpe, p.73.
35. ibid, pp.73-4.
36. Bazoncourt, Baron de, [trans. By Robert Howe Goud], *The Crimean Expedition, to the Capture of Sebastopol, Chronicles of the War in the East*, Vol.1 (Smpson Lowe, London, 1856), p.263.

Chapter 4: The Flank March
1. *Sheffield & Rotherham Independent*, 7 October 1854.
2. George Shuldham Peard, *Narrative of a Campaign in the Crimea; including an account of the Battles of Alma, Balaklava, and Inkermann* (London, 1855), p.64.
3. Bazancourt, vol.19, p.270.
4. Hamley, pp.40-1.
5. William Howard Russell, *Despatches from the Crimea*, p.97.
6. Printed in the *Lancaster Gazette*, 4 November 1854.
7. Charles Alexandre Fay, *Souvenirs de la Guerre de Crimée, 1854-1856* (Paris, 1867), p. 63.
8. Grehan and Mace, p.61.
9. Mitchell, p.64.
10. Calthorpe, p.86.
11. 'Another letter from the Scots Greys', *Nottingham Guardian*, 26 October 1854.
12. Lieutenant Colonel Arthur Johnstone Lawrence, NAM. 1968-04-2.
13. Russell, *The British Expedition to the Crimea*, pp.166-7.
14. Journal of Captain Louis Nolan.

Chapter 5: Siege of Sevastopol
1. Robert Farquharson, *Reminiscences of Crimean Campaigning And Russian Imprisonment* (privately published, Glasgow, 1882), p.24.
2. Paget, p.45.
3. Quoted in Orlando Figes, *Crimea: The Last Crusade* (Penguin, London, 2010), p.235.
4. George Wrottesley, *Life and Correspondence of Field Marshal Sir John Burgoyne*, p.

(Richard Bentlet & Son, London, 1873), Vol.2, p.94.

5. Quoted in Sweetman, *Raglan*, p.234.
6. W. Edmund M. Reilly, *Account of the Military Operations Conducted by the Royal Artillery and Royal Naval Brigade Before Sevastopol in 1854 and 1855*, (War Office, London, 1859), p.1.
7. D. Bonner-Smith, and A.C. Dewar, *Russian War, 1854, Baltic and Black Sea Official Correspondence* (Navy Records Society, London, 1943), pp.323 & 325.
8. C.C.P. Fitzgerald, *Life of Vice Admiral Sir George Tyron, KCB* (Blackwood, London, 1897), p. 54.
9. Temple Godman explained what these referred to: 'An outlying piquet is a body of men, say perhaps thirty or forty … who go about five miles out in front or rear of the army to give an alarm of any approach of the enemy, and, if driven in, to keep them (the enemy) in check as long as possible, to give the main body time to get under arms. The inlying piquet is a body that remains within the encampment, ready under arms to turn at a moment's notice, see Philip Warner, *Letters Home from The Crimea, A young cavalryman's campaign from Balaklava and Sebastopol to victory* (Windrush, Moreton-in-Marsh, 1999), pp.67-8.
10. Farquharson, p.44.
11. Private letters from the Seat of War: Specially Communicated', *Nottinghamshire Guardian*, 18 November 1854).
12. Quoted in Alastair Massey, *A Most Desperate Undertaking* (National Army Museum, London, 2003), p.96.
13. Woodham-Smith, p.212.
14. Stuart, Brian [ed.], *Soldier's Glory, being 'Rough Notes of an Old Soldier by Major General Sir George Bell* (G. Bell & Sons, London, 1956), pp.230-1.
15. Michael Hargreave Mawson, *Eyewitness in the Crimea, The Crimean War Letters (1854-1856) of Lt. Col George Frederick Dallas* (Greenhill, London, 2001), p.35.
16. R.H. Vetch, *Life, Letters and Diaries of Lieut.-General Sir Gerald Graham* (Blackwood & Sons, London, 1901), p.37.
17. *Morning Chronicle*, 31 October 1854.
18. Wrottesley, p.106.
19. Quoted in David Buttery, *Messenger of Death, Captain Nolan & the Charge of the Light Brigade* (Pen & Sword, Barnsley, 2008), p.115.
20. Nolan's Journal.
21. Warner, pp.67-8.
22. The Siege of Sebastopol', *Supplement to the Illustrated London News* (11 November 1854), p. 496.
23. Russell, *Despatches*, pp.115-6.
24. Quoted in Anthony Dawson, *Voices from the Past, The Siege of Sevastopol* (Frontline Books, to be published 2017).
25. Edward Bruce Hamley, *The Story of the Campaign of Sebastopol, Written in the Camp* (Blackwood, London, 1855), p.71.
26. Portal, p.45.
27. Seaton, p.138.
28. 'Balaclava: Letter from an Officer of Royal Marines, Oct. 22', *Supplement to the Illustrated London News* (11 November 1854), p. 491.
29. See, Terry Brighton, *Hell Riders, The Truth About the Charge of the Light Brigade* (Penguin, London, 2005), pp.75-6, Hibbert, pp.130-1, and Woodham-Smith, p.216.

Chapter 6: The Brilliant Attack

1. H. C. Elphinstone and H.D. Jones, *Siege of Sebastopol 1854-5 - The Journal of the*

Operations Conducted by the Corps of Royal Engineers, (Eyre & Spottiswood, London, 1859), p.42.

2. Roy Dutton, *Forgotten Heroes, The Charge of the Heavy Brigade*, (InfoDial, Oxton, 2008), p.41

3. Kinglake, Vol.5, pp. 51-2.

4. 'Letter from a Soldier, a native of Aberford, near Leeds', *Leeds Intelligencer*, 14 April 1855.

5. Quoted, source incorrect, by Adkin, p.84.

6. Quoted from the *Royal Magazine* in Knight, p.35.

7. Paget, 161-2.

8. Seaton, 139-41.

9. Maude's diary, quoted in W.B. Pemberton, *Battles of the Crimean War* (Batsford, London, 1962), p.77.

10. Calthorpe, p.122.

11. Yevgenii Arbuzov, 'Reminiscences of the Campaign in the Crimean Peninsula in 1854 and 1855', *Voennyi Sbornik*, 1874, Vol. 96, No. 6, p. 396, quoted in http://marksrussianmilitaryhistory.info/Arbuzov.htm.

12. http://www.marksrussianmilitaryhistory.info/Liprandi.htm

13. Quoted in Kinglake, Vol.5, pp.68-9.

14. Quoted in Ponting, p.126.

15. William Howard Russell, *General Todleben's History of the Defence of Sebastopol, A Review* (D.Van Nostrand, New York, 1865), pp.134-5.

16. Quoted in Ian Fletcher and Ishenko Natalia, *The Crimean War, A Clash of Empires* (Spellmount, Staplehurst, 2004), pp.165-6.

17. Evelyn Wood, *The Crimea in 1854, and 1894* (Chapman & Hall, London, 1896).

18. Troop Sergeant-Major (later RSM and Riding Master) George Cruse, 1 Royal Dragoons, May 1854 to May 1855, NAM 1974-12-76.

19. *Bradford Observer*, 16 November 1854.

20. *Illustrated London News*, 30 October 1854.

21. George Loy Smith, *A Victorian RSM, From India to the Crimea* (D.J. Costello, Tunbridge Wells, 1987), p.126.

22. Woodham-Smith, pp.217-8.

23. Duberly, pp.92-3.

24. Loy Smith, p.127.

Chapter 7: That Thin Red Streak

1. http://www.marksrussianmilitaryhistory.info/Liprandi.htm

2. Calthorpe, p.125.

3. Russell, William Howard, *General Todleben's History of the Defence of Sebastopol, A Review* (D.Van Nostrand, New York, 1865), p.121.

4. Paget, pp.166-7.

5. Lieutenant Koribut-Kubitovich, *Recollections of the Balaklava Affair of 13 October, 1854,* translated by Mark Conrad,

6. On the Battle of Balaklava; Notes of Lieutenant General Iv. Iv. Ryzhov. .

7. *Birmingham Daily Post, 26 October 1889.*

8. Kinglake, vol.5. pp.78-9.

9. Quoted in Saul David, *Military Blunders* (Robinson, London, 1997), p.17.

10. Quoted in Spillsbury, p.145.

11. NAM 1968-07-270.

12. A private account held by Paul Patterson, and quoted in Roy Dutton, *Heavy Brigade*, p.52.

13. Cambridge University Library Special Collections, The Crimean War letters of Captain Blackett, Add.9587/16.

14. *The Times*, Monday, November 13, 1854.
15. Philip Warner, *A Cavalryman in the Crimea*, p.75.
16. 'Letters from a Dragoon and a Sailor to Leicester Friends, *Leicester Chronicle*, 3 January 1855.
17. Pemberton, pp.85-6.
18. NAM 1973-11-170.
19. *Reynold's Newspaper*, 26 November 1854.
20. Letters of Major W.C. Forrest, NAM 1963-09-5.
21. 'Extract from a letter of an officer in the heavy brigade', *Manchester Times*, 25 November 1854.
22. Henry Franks *Leaves from a Soldier's Notebook* (Mitre Pubns, June 1979), p.80.
23. Warner, *Temple Godman*, p.75.
24. http://www.marksrussianmilitaryhistory.info/Ryzhof.htm
25. Extracted from E. J. Boys website, Lives of the Light Brigade.
26. Lincolnshire Archives, DIXON 22/12/3/1, quoted in Dutton, *Heavy Brigade*, p.116.
27. Warner, *Temple Godman*, pp.78-9.
28. *The Times*, Tuesday, November 14, 1854.
29. 'Letters from a Dumfrieshire Dragoon', *The Morning Post*, 1 February 1855.
30. Donald Serrell Thomas, *Charge! Hurrah! Hurrah! Life of Cardigan of Balaclava*, (Routledge & Kegan Paul, 1974) p.237
31. James Wightman, 'One of the Six Hundred' *19th Century Magazine*, May 1892, quoted in M.J. Trow, *The Pocket Hercules, Captain Morris and the Charge of the Light Brigade* (Pen & Sword, Barnsely, 2006), p.91.
32. Kinglake, vol.5, pp.176-7.
33. ibid, pp.210-11.
34. Cardigan, James Thomas Brudenell, *Eight Months on Active Service* (William Clowes, London, 1855), p.89.
35. Whinyates, p.160.
36. Woodham-Smith, p.232.
37. ibid, pp.219-10.
38. Whinyates, p.137.

Chapter 8: Forward the Light Brigade
1. http://www.marksrussianmilitaryhistory.info/Liprandi.htm. Vladimir Shavshin, *The Valley of Death* [translated by Elena Kondrateva] (privately published, Sevastopol, 2005), states that the artillery on the Causeway Heights was the eight-gun Light Battery No.7, p.67.
2. ibid.
3. James Wightman, 'One of the "Six Hundred" in the Balaklava Charge', *The Nineteenth Century* magazine, May 1892.
4. Mitchell, p.83.
5. Kinglake, Vol.5, p.184.
6. Hibbert, pp.141-2.
7. General Fay, *Souvenirs de la Guerre de Crimée* (Berger-Levrault et Cie., Paris, 1889), 2e edition, p. 90, quoted in Anthony Dawson's forthcoming book, *Voices from the Past, The Siege of Sevastopol*, to be published by Frontline in 2017.
8. Calthorpe, p.128.
9. Bazancourt, vol.2, p.26.
10. Quoted in Anthony Dawson, *Letters from the Light Brigade* (Pen & Sword, Barnsley, 2014), p.127.
11. *Freeman's Journal*, 22 May 1888.
12. House of Lord Debates 02 March 1855, vol. 137 cc3-7.

13. Bazancourt, vol.2, p.31.
14. Kinglake, Vol.5, p.424.
15. NAM 1968-07-288.
16. Kinglake, Vol.5 p.404; H. Moyse-Bartlett, *Nolan of Balaklava, And his influence on the British Cavalry* (Leo Cooper, London, 1971), p.219.
17. *Morning Chronicle*, 17 November 1854.
18. *House of Lord Debates 02 March 1855, vol. 137 cc3-7.*
19. Paget, pp.170-1.
20. *Western Australia Times* 25 January 1876.
21. James Wightman, 'One of the Six Hundred' *19th Century Magazine*, May 1892.
22. Loy Smith, p.131.
23. Bazancourt, vol.2, p.32.

Chapter 9: Magnificent but not War
1. Wightman.
2. *Illustrated London News*, 30 October 1875.
3. E. Small, *Told From the Ranks, Recollections of service during the Queen's reign by privates and non-commissioned officers of the British Army* (A. Melrose, London, 1897), p.65.
4. Shavshin, p.67.
5. Kinglake, vol.5, p.405.
6. *Western Australia Times* 25 January 1876.
7. Kinglake, vol.5, pp. 220-1.
8. Calthorpe, p.130.
9. Quoted in Michael Barthorpe, *Heroes of the Crimea, The Battles of Balaklava and Inkerman*, (Blandford, London, 1991), p.50.
10. Quoted in Dutton, *Light Brigade*, pp.312-3.
11. *Daily Despatch*, 23 November 1905.
12. T. Morley, *The Cause of the Charge*, pp.9-10, quoted in Adkin, pp.159-60.
13. Yevgenii Arbuzov, quoted in http://marksrussianmilitaryhistory.info/Arbuzov.htm.
14. Shavshin, p.67.
15. http://www.marksrussianmilitaryhistory.info/ARTYOFF.html
16. *Vancouver News Advertiser* 16 September, 1892.
17. Franks, p.76.
18. *The Times* 3 April 1855.
19. Charles Pyndar Beauchamp Walker, *Days of a Soldier's Life, being letters written by the late General Sir C.P. Beauchamp Walker, K.C.B.*, (Chapman and Hall, London,1894), pp.135-6.
20. Archibald Forbes, 'Butcher Jack' in *Soldiering and Scribbling*, quoted in Dutton, *Light Brigade*, pp.337-9.
21. Quoted in Dutton, *Heavy Brigade*, p.67.
22. NAM 1983-11-9.
23. *The Morning Post*, 1 February 1855, p.5. Note that the James Melrose mentioned by Berryman was actually Private Frederick Melrose which itself was an assumed name. He had been a Shakespearean actor, as Berryman noted.
24. Bazancourt, vol.2, p.34.
25. Dutton, *Light Brigade*, p.133.
26. Paget, pp.71-2.
27. Calthorpe, p.130.
28. Clifford, pp.72-3.
29. 'Letters from the Crimea', *The Morning Post*, 1 February 1855.
30. Quoted, unsourced, in Brighton, p.135.

31. Mitchell, p.56.
32. Quoted in Fidges, p.249.
33. Paget, pp.180-1.
34. Calthorpe, p.130.
35. The *Dispatch*, 7 January 1855.
36. *The Times* on 14 November 1854.
37. Loy Smith, 131-2.
38. Cardigan, p.90.
39. Quoted in W.B. Pemberton, pp.85-6.
40. Loy Smith, 132-3.
41. Courtesy of .
42. E. Small, pp.65-6.
43. Paget, pp.182-3.
44. E. Small, p.66.
45. Vladimir Shavshin, p.67.
46. E. Small, pp.66-7.
47. Iz Krymskikh Vospominanii o Poslednei Voine', *Russkii Arkhiv*, 1869. Vol. 7, pp. 381-384, reproduced courtesy of .
48. Wood, p.120.
49. Bazancourt, vol.2, p.34.
50. *Western Australia Times* 25 January 1876.
51. See Dutton, *Light Brigade*, p.11.
52. Cardigan, p.90.
53. Kinglake, vol.5, p.108.
54. Cardigan v Calthorpe, *Affidavits filed by Lieut. Colonel The Hon. Somerset John Gough Calthorpe (5th Dragoon Guards) The Respondent* (London, John Murray, 1863), pp.26-7.
55. *Illustrated London News*, 30 October 1875.
56. Loy Smith, p.244.
57. Quoted in Seaton, p.150.
58. Cardigan v Calthorpe, pp.18-19.

Chapter 10: To Do or Die
1. All these Russians quotes, courtesy of http://www.marksrussian militaryhistory.info.
2. Paget, pp.69-70
3. *Illustrated London News*, 30 October 1875.
4. *Answers Magazine*, 26 October 1912.
5. NAM 1986-02-75.
6. Extracted from E. J. Boys website, Lives of the Light Brigade.
7. Quoted in Barthorpe, p.51.
8. Mitchell, p.85.
9. *Illustrated London News*, 30 October 1875.
10. Quoted in Lawrence Crider, *In Search of the Light Brigade* (Eurocommunica, 2004), p.494.
11. Franks, p.82.
12. Extracted from E. J. Boys website, Lives of the Light Brigade.
13. ibid.
14. Quoted in Dawson, *Letters*, pp.150-1.
15. Quoted in Pemberton, p.113.
16. *Western Australia Times* 25 January 1876.
17. *Not Published* (John Mitchell, London, 1864), NAM 1977-06-6-6, pp.16-17.
18. See Dutton, *Light Brigade*, p.67.

19. Cardigan v Calthorpe, pp.22-3.
20. Clifford, p.74.
21. Quoted in Anglesey, the Marquess of, *A History of the British Cavalry 1816 to 1919, Vol. II, 1851-1871* (Leo Cooper, Barnsley, 1975), p.101.
22. Bazancourt, pp.36-7.
23. Quoted in Spilsbury, p.169.
24. Paget, p.200.
25. Quoted in Trow, p.107.
26. Kinglake, vol.5, 255-6
27. Loy Smith, p.140.
28. TNA WO 32/7326. Crimean War: Recommendation concerning Sgt Major C Wooden, 17th Lancers for action at Balaclava, Crimea.
29. Loy Smith, pp. 237-8.
30. Dutton, *Light Brigade*, p.32.
31. John Doyle, *A Descriptive Account of the Famous Charge of the Light Brigade at Balaklava* (Privately published, Manchester, 1877).
32. Kelly, *Duberly*, p.95.
33. NAM 1983-11-9, Captain Edward Seager.
34. Stuart, *Soldier's Glory*, pp.239-40.
35. Kinglake, vol.5, p.405.
36. Anglesey, p.102.
37. Woodham-Smith, p.264.

Chapter 11: Someone had Blundered

1. Seaton, p.157.
2. Pemberton, p.115.
3. Warner, *Godman*, pp.77-80.
4. *Sheffield & Rotherham Independent*, 23 December 1854.
5. Dallas, p.40.
6. Portal, p.51.
7. Kinglake, vol.5, p.198.
8. Clifford, pp.72-3.
9. Clifford, pp.79-80.
10. *Daily News*, 18 November 1854.
11. *Illustrated London News*, 30 October 1875.
12. Quoted in Dutton, *Heavy Brigade*, p.52.
13. Farquharson, p.44.
14. *Illustrated London News*, 30 October 1875
15. Franks, p.73.
16. Russell, *The Great War with Russia* (London, 1895), p.160.
17. Quoted in Hugh Small, *The Crimean War, Queen Victoria's War with the Russian Tsars* (Tempus, Stroud, 2007), p.89.
18. Loy Smith, p.147.
19. Warner, *Godman*, 76-7.
20. Paget, pp.72-3 & p.219.
21. Hansard, HC Deb 29 March 1855 vol. 137 cc1310-54
22. Kinglake, vol.5, pp.428-9.
23. Hansard, HL Deb 06 March 1855 vol. 137 cc157-62.
24. Quoted in Buttery, *p.150.*
25. Joan Wake, *The Brundenells of Deene* (Cassel, London, 1959), p.408.
26. Hansard, HL Deb 19 March 1855 vol 137 cc730-73. Hugh Small, pp.77-8, has followed Hardinge's line of reasoning, claiming that 'the dissatisfaction and mutinous tendency in the Light Brigade's ranks', prompted Lucan 'to put

things right' by ordering them to charge the Russian guns. Small, (p.87) even goes as far as saying that 'The Charge was not a blunder; Lord Raglan's order was a blunder (we can all agree with that), but the Light Brigade were not told of and did not obey Raglan's order. The men substituted their own order, to charge the Russian cavalry and put them to flight.'

27. Paget, p.219.
28. Reproduced in the *Yorkshire Gazette*, 21 March 1855.
29. Beauchamp Walker, p.135.
30. Sweetman, *Balaklava*, p.79.
31. Whinyates, p.199.
32. Farquharson, p.45.
33. Franks, p.72.
34. Paget, p.205.
35. Letters from the Crimea of Captain William Powell Richards, transcribed at http://www.historyhome.co.uk/forpol/crimea/richards/biography.htm.
36. *Morning Post*, 20 November 1854.
37. Kinglake, Vol.5, pp.1-2.
38. Paget, p.204.
39. William Russell, *The Great War with Russia*, p.118.
40. Kinglake, vol.5, pp.218-9.
41. Nicholas Bentley [ed.], *Russell's Despatches from the Crimea* (Panther, London, 1970), p.125; Quoted in John Harris, *The Gallant Six Hundred* (Hutchinson, London, 1973), p.274.
42. Moyse-Bartlett, p.244.
43. Cambridge University Library Special Collections, The Crimean War letters of Captain Blackett.
44. Saul David, p.20.
45. *Kendal Mercury*, 18 November 1854.
46. Wood, p.123.
47. Reynold's Newspaper, 26 November 1854.

Chapter 12: Honour the Light Brigade

1. Quoted in Donald Thomas, *Cardigan, A Life of Lord Cardigan of Balaklava* (Cassell, London, 2002), pp.252-3.
2. Lambert & Badsey, p.116.
3. Beauchamp Walker, pp.137-8.
4. Quoted in Seaton, p.151.
5. Paget, pp.75-6.
6. Kelly, *Mrs Duberly's War*, p.94.
7. Stuart, p.238.
8. Tim Coates, *Delane's War, How front-line reports from the Crimean War brought down the British Government*, (Biteback, London, 2009), p.101.
9. Duberly, p.117.
10. Queen Victoria's Journal, entry for 16 January 1855, Royal Archives.
11. Quoted in Allan Mallinson, *The Making of the British Army, From the English Civil War to the War on Terror* (Bantam Press, London, 2009), pp.207-8.
12. Mike Huggins and J.A. Mangan, *Disreputable Pleasures, Less Virtuous Victorians at Play* (Frank Cass, London, 2004), p.115. See also http://john-adcock.blogspot.co.uk/2015/10/who-was-captain-jack.html.
13. For a detailed discussion of this subject, see John Grehan, *The First VCs, The Victoria Crosses in the Crimean War and the Definition of Courage* (Frontline, Barnsley, 2016).
14. Quoted in Nick Foulkes, *Dancing into Battle* (Phoenix, London, 2007), p.226.

15. *Harper's Monthly,* 1908, pp.305-6.
16. Harry Powell, *Recollections of a Young Soldier during the Crimean Campaign* (Privately published, Oxford, 1876), p.30.
17. Extracted from E. J. Boys website, Lives of the Light Brigade.
18. *Cardiff Times and South Wales Weekly News,* of 30 October 1875.
19. British Library Sound Archive, shelf mark 1CD0239287.
20. Dutton, *Light Brigade,* p.36.

Chapter 13: Tarnished Glory
1. Calthorpe, p.130.
2. ibid, p.250.
3. Hansard, HL Deb 05 February 1857 vol. 144 cc200-4.
4. Calthorpe, p.317.
5. Hansard, HL Deb 05 February 1857 vol. 144 cc200-4.
6. Donald Serrell Thomas, *Cardigan, A Life of Lord Cardigan of Balaklava,* (Cassell, London, 2002), p.295.
7. *Cardigan v Calthorpe,* pp.17-18.
8. Extracts from a letter from a private in the 8th Hussars', *Leeds Intelligencer,* 13 January 1855.
9. *Not Published,* printed by John Mitchell, London, 1864, p.17.
10. ibid, pp.14-15.
11. ibid, pp.16-17
12. *Cardigan v Calthorpe,* pp.16-17
13. ibid, pp.18-19.
14. *Not Published,* pp.10-12.
15. *Cardigan v Calthorpe,* pp.22-3.
16. This statement, regarding Liprandi asking if the Light Brigade were intoxicated, was repeated by other prisoners, see *Cardigan v Calthorpe,* p.28.
17. *Cardigan v Calthorpe,* pp.19-20.
18. Kinglake, vol.5, p.411.
19. 'Thormanby', *Kings of the hunting-field: memoirs and anecdotes of distinguished masters of hounds and other celebrities of the chase with histories of famous packs, and hunting traditions of great houses,* (Hutchinson, London, 1899), p.244, quoted in Saul David, *The Homicidal Earl,* p.494.

Bibliography and Sources

The Templer Centre, National Army Museum
Cardigan, Major General James Thomas Brudendell, Earl of, Memorandum on the Charge of the Light Brigade, NAM Acc. 1968-07-288.
Major Robert Nigel Fitzhardinge Kingscote, Scots Fusilier Guards, NAM 1963-11 70.
Cruise, George, Troop Sergeant-Major (later RSM and Riding Master), 1 Royal Dragoons, May 1854 to May 1855, NAM 1974-12-76.
Firkins, Private Edward John, 13th Regiment of (Light) Dragoons, NAM, 1986-02-75.
Forrest, Lieutenant Colonel Charles, 4th (Royal Irish) Regiment of Dragoon Guards, NAM 1963-09-5.
Lawrence, Lieutenant Colonel Arthur Johnstone, 2nd Battalion Rifle Brigade, NAM 1968-04-2.
Nolan, Journal of Captain Louis, 15th Hussars, NAM 1989-06-41.
Not Published (John Mitchell, London, 1864), NAM 1977-06-6.
Seager, Captain Edward, 8th (King's Royal Irish) Regiment of (Light) Dragoons (Hussars), NAM 1983-11-9.
Sterling, Lieutenant Colonel Anthony, Highland Brigade, NAM 1968-07-270.

The National Archives, Kew
TNA WO 32/7326, Crimean War: Recommendation concerning Sgt. Major C. Wooden, 17th Lancers for action at Balaclava, Crimea.

Cambridge University Library Special Collections
The Crimean War letters of Captain Blackett, Add.9587/16.
Published Books
Adkin, Mark, *The Charge, The Real Reason Why the Light Brigade Was Lost*, (Pen & Sword, Barnsley, 1996).
Anglesey, the Marquess of, *A History of the British Cavalry 1816 to 1919, Vol. II, 1851-1871* (Leo Cooper, Barnsley, 1975).
_____, *'Little Hodge', being extracts from the diaries and letters of Colonel Edward Cooper Hodge written during the Crimean War, 1854-1856* (Leo Cooper, London, 1971).
Astley, John Dugdale, *Fifty Years of My Life* (Hurst and Blackett, London, 1894.)
Bancroft, *Echelon, The Light Brigade Action at Balaklava, A New Perspective*

(Spellmount, Stroud, 2011).

Barnett, Correlli, *Britain and her Army* (Alan Lane, London, 1970).

Barthorpe, Michael, *Heroes of the Crimea, The Battles of Balaklava and Inkerman*, (Blandford, London, 1991).

Bazancourt, Baron, [translated by Robert Howe Gould] *The Crimean Expedition, to the Capture of Sevastopol, Chronicles of the War in the East, from Its Commencement to the Signing of the Treaty of Peace*, (Sampson Low, London, 1856).

Beauchamp Walker, Charles Pyndar, *Days of a Soldier's Life, being letters written by the late General Sir C.P. Beauchamp Walker, K.C.B.*, (Chapman and Hall, London,1894).

Bentley, Nicholas, [ed.], *Russell's Despatches from the Crimea* (Panther, London, 1970).

Bolithio, Hector, (ed.), *Letters of Queen Victoria From the Archives of Brandenburg-Prussia* (Yale University Press, New Haven, 1938).

Bonner-Smith, D., and Dewar, A.C., *Russian War, 1854, Baltic and Black Sea Official Correspondence* (Navy Records Society, London, 1943).

Brighton, Terry, *Hell Riders, The Truth About the Charge of the Light Brigade* (Penguin, London, 2005).

Buttery, David, *Messenger of Death, Captain Nolan and the Charge of the Light Brigade* (Pen & Sword, Barnsley, 2008).

Calthorpe, S.J.G., *Letters from Headquarters; or, The Realities of the War in the Crimea, by an Officer on the Staff* (John Murray, London, 1858).

Cardigan, James Thomas Brudenell, 7th Earl of, *Eight Months on Active Service* (William Clowes, London, 1855).

Cardigan v Calthorpe, *Affidavits filed by Lieut. Colonel The Hon. Somerset John Gough Calthorpe (5th Dragoon Guards) The Respondent* (London, John Murray, 1863).

Clifford, Henry VC, *His Letters & Sketches from the Crimea* (Michael Joseph, London, 1956).

Coates, Tim, *Delane's War, How front-line reports from the Crimean War brought down the British Government*, (Biteback, London, 2009).

Colebrooke, Edward, *Journal of Two Visits to the Crimea, in the Autumn of 1854 and 1855, with Remarks on the Campaign* (Privately printed by T. & W. Boone, London, 1856).

Crider, Lawrence, *In Search of the Light Brigade A Biographical Dictionary of the Members of the Five Original Regiments of the Light Brigade from Jan 1,1854 to Mar 31,1856* (Eurocommunica, 2004).

Dawson, Anthony, *Letters from the Light Brigade* (Pen & Sword, Barnsley, 2014).

_____, *Voices from the Past, The Siege of Sevastopol* (Frontline, Barnsley, 2017).

David, Saul, *Military Blunders, The how and why of military failure* (Robinson, London, 1997).

_____, *The Homicidal Earl, The Life of Lord Cardigan* (Abacus, London, 1998).

Doyle, John, *A Descriptive Account of the Famous Charge of the Light Brigade at Balaklava* (Privately published, Manchester, 1877).

Drummond, K., *Letters from the Crimea* (Norris & Son, London, 1855).

Duffy, Christopher, *Military Experience in the Age of Reason*, (Routledge and Kegan Paul, London, 1987).

Dutton, Roy, *Forgotten Heroes, The Charge of the Light Brigade* (InfoDial, Oxton, 2007).

_____, *Forgotten Heroes, The Charge of the Heavy Brigade*, (InfoDial, Oxton, 2008).

Edgerton, Robert B., *Death or Glory, The Legacy of the Crimean War* (Westview Press,

Oxford, 1999).
Elphinstone, Captain H.C. RE and. Jones, Maj.-Gen H.D., *Siege of Sebastopol 1854-5 - The Journal of the Operations Conducted by the Corps of Royal Engineers*, (Eyre & Spottiswood, London, 1859).
Farquharson, Robert, *Reminiscences of Crimean Campaigning And Russian Imprisonment* (privately published, Glasgow, 1882).
Fay, Charles Alexandre, *Souvenirs de la Guerre de Crimée, 1854-1856* (Paris, 1867).
Figes, Orlando, *Crimea: The Last Crusade* (Penguin, London, 2010).
Fitzgerald, C.C.P., *Life of Vice Admiral Sir George Tyron, KCB* (Blackwood, London, 1897),
ffrench Blake, R.L.V., *The Crimean War* (Pen & Sword, Barnsley, 2006).
Foulkes, Nick, *Dancing into Battle* (Phoenix, London, 2007).
Fortescue, Sir John, *A History of the British Army* (Macmillan, London, 1899-1930).
Fletcher, Ian, and Ishenko, Natalia, *The Battle of the Alma 1854, First Blood to the Allies in the Crimea* (Pen & Sword, Barnsley, 2004).
_____, *The Crimean War, A Clash of Empires* (Spellmount, Staplehurst, 2004).
Franks, Henry, *Leaves from a Soldier's Notebook* (Mitre Pubns, June 1979).
Goldfrank, David, *The Origins of the Crimean War* (Longman, London, 1994).
Gowing, Timothy, *A Soldier's Experience, or, A Voice from the Ranks* (Thos Forman & Sons Nottingham, 1903).
Grehan, John and Mace, Martin, *Despatches from the Front, British Battles of the Crimean War 1854-1856* (Pen & Sword, Barnsley, 2014).
_____, *The Crimean War: Images of War* (Pen & Sword, Barnsley, 2014).
Grehan, John, *The First VCs, The Stories Behind the First Victoria Crosses in the Crimean War and the Definition of Courage* (Frontline, Barnsley, 2016).
Hamley, General Sir Edward, *The Story of the Campaign of Sebastopol, Written in the Camp* (Blackwood, London, 1855).
_____, *The Crimean War 1853-1856* (Parchment Publishing, 2012).
Harris, John, *The Gallant Six Hundred* (Hutchinson, London, 1973).
Hibbert, Christopher, *The Destruction of Lord Raglan, A Tragedy of the Crimean War 1854-55* (Penguin, London, 1985).
Huggins, Mike and Mangan, J.A., *Disreputable Pleasures, Less Virtuous Victorians at Play* (Frank Cass, London, 2004).
Jocelyn, J.R.J., *The History of the Royal Artillery (Crimean Period)* (John Murray, London, 1911).
Kelly, Christine, *Mrs Duberley's War: Journal & Letters From the Crimea* (Oxford University Press, 2007).
Kinglake, A.W., *The Invasion of the Crimea: Its Origin, and An Account of its Progress down to the Death of Lord Raglan* (William Blackwood, London, 1878).
Knight, Ian, *Marching to the Drums, Eyewitness Accounts of War from the Kabul Massacre to the Siege of Mafikeng* (Greenhill, London, 1999).
Lambert, Andrew and Badsey, Stephen, *The War Correspondents, The Crimean War* (Bramley, Stroud, 1997).
Lummis, William M., and Wynn, Kenneth G., *Honour the Light Brigade* (Hayward, London, 1973).
Mallinson, Alan, *The Making of the British Army, From the English Civil War to the War on Terror* (Bantam Press, London, 2009).
Massie, Alastair, *A Most Desperate Undertaking, The British Army in the Crimea, 1854-56* (National Army Museum, London, 2003).
_____, *The National Army Museum Book of the Crimean War* (Pan, London, 2004).

Matineau, John, *The Life of Henry Pelham, Fifth Duke of Newcastle 1811-1864* (John Murray, London, 1908).

Mawson, Michael Hargreave, *The Crimean War Letters of Lieutenant Colonel George Frederick Dallas* (Greenhill, London, 2001).

Mercer, Patrick, *'Give Them a Volley and a Charge!' The Battle of Inkermannn 1854* (Spellmount, Stroud, 1998),

Mitchell, Albert, *Recollections of One of the Light Brigade*, (R. Pelton, Tunbridge Wells, 1885), republished by Lawrence W. Crider and Glenn Fisher for the Crimean War Research Society, 2009.

Mollo, John and Mollo, Boris, *Into the Valley of Death* (Windrow & Greene, London, 1991).

Morley, Thomas, *The Cause of the Charge of Balaclava* (Privately published, Nottingham, 1899).

Moyse-Bartlett, H., *Nolan of Balaklava, And his influence on the British Cavalry* (Leo Cooper, London, 1971).

Paget, C. S. (Ed.), *The Light Cavalry Brigade in the Crimea. Extracts from the letters and journal of the late Gen. Lord G. Paget … during the Crimean War. With a map*, (John Murray, London, 1881).

Parry, D.H., *Britain's Roll of Honour*, (Cassell, London, 1898).

Peard, George Shuldham, *Narrative of a Campaign in the Crimea; including an account of the Battles of Alma, Balaklava, and Inkermann* (London, 1855).

Pemberton, W. Baring, *Battles of the Crimean War* (Batsford, London, 1962).

Perrett, Bryan, *At All Costs! Stories of Impossible Victories* (Cassell, London, 1998).

Percy, Algernon, *A Bearskin's Crimea, Colonel Henry Percy VC & His Brother Officers* (Pen & Sword, Barnsley, 2005).

Ponting, Clive, *The Crimean War, The Truth Behind the Myth* (Chatto & Windus, London, 2004).

Portal, Robert, *Letters from the Crimea*, (Privately published, Winchester, 1900).

Powell, Harry, *Recollections of a Young Soldier during the Crimean Campaign* (Privately published, Oxford, 1876).

Reilly, W. Edmund M., *Account of the Military Operations Conducted by the Royal Artillery and Royal Naval Brigade Before Sevastopol in 1854 and 1855*, (War Office, London, 1859).

Russell, William Howard, *General Todleben's History of the Defence of Sebastopol, A Review* (D.Van Nostrand, New York, 1865).

_____, *The Great War with Russia, the invasion of the Crimea. A personal retrospect* (Routledge, London, 1895).

_____, *Despatches from the Crimea* (Frontline Books, Barnsley, 2008).

Ryan, George, *Our Heroes of the Crimea: Being Biographical Sketches Of Our Military Officers, From The General Commanding-In-Chief To The Subaltern* (Routledge, London, 1855),

Seaton, Albert, *The Crimean War, A Russian Chronicle* (Batsford, London, 1977).

Shavshin, Vladimir, *The Valley of Death* (Sevastopol, 2005).

Slade, Adolphus, *Turkey and the Crimean War* (Smith, Elder & Co., London, 1867).

Small, E., *Told From the Ranks, Recollections of service during the Queen's reign by privates and non-commissioned officers of the British Army* (A. Melrose, London, 1897).

Small, Hugh, *The Crimean War, Queen Victoria's War with the Russian Tsars* (Tempus, Stroud, 2007).

Smith, George Loy, *A Victorian RSM, From India to the Crimea* (D.J. Costello, Tunbridge Wells, 1987).

Spilsbury, Julian, *The Thin Red Line, An eyewitness history of the Crimean War*

(Weidenfeld & Nicolson, London).

Springman, Michael, *The Guards Brigade in the Crimea* (Pen & Sword, Barnsley, 2008).

Stephenson, Frederick Charles Arthur, *At Home and on the Battlefield: Letters from the Crimea, China and Egypt, 1854-1888* (John Murray, London, 1915).

Sterling, Anthony, *The Story of the Highland Brigade in the Crimea, Founded on Letters Written During the Years 1854, 1855, and 1856* (Absinthe Press, Minneapolis, 1995).

Stuart, Brian (Ed.), *Soldier's Glory, being 'Rough Notes of an Old Soldier by Major General Sir George Bell* (G. Bell & Sons, London, 1956).

Sweetman, John, *Balaklava 1854, The Charge of the Light Brigade* (Osprey, London, 1990).

_____, *Raglan, From the Peninsula to the Crimea* (Pen & Sword, Barnsley, 2010).

Thomas, Donald Serrell, *Charge! Hurrah! Hurrah! Life of Cardigan of Balaclava,* (Routledge & Kegan Paul, 1974).

_____, *Cardigan, A Life of Lord Cardigan of Balaklava* (Cassell, London, 2002).

'Thormanby', *Kings of the hunting-field: memoirs and anecdotes of distinguished masters of hounds and other celebrities of the chase with histories of famous packs, and hunting traditions of great houses,* (Hutchinson, London, 1899).

Trow, M.J., *The Pocket Hercules, Captain Morris and the Charge of the Light Brigade* (Pen & Sword, Barnsley, 2006).

Vetch, R.H., *Life, Letters and Diaries of Lieut.-General Sir Gerald Graham* (Blackwood & Sons, London, 1901).

Wake, Joan, *The Brundenells of Deene* (Cassel, London, 1959).

Wantage, Harriet S., *Lord Wantage, VC, KCB: A Memoir by His Wife* (Smith Elder, London, 1907).

Warner, Philip, *Letters Home from The Crimea, A young cavalryman's campaign from Balaklava and Sebastopol to victory* (Windrush, Moreton-in-Marsh, 1999).

_____*A Cavalryman in the Crimea: The Letters of Temple Godman, 5th Dragoon Guards* (Pen & Sword, Barnsley, 2009).

Whinyates, Francis Arthur, *From Coruña to Sevastopol. The history of 'C' Battery, 'A' Brigade (late 'C' Troop), Royal Horse Artillery,* (W.H. Allen, London, 1884).

Wood, Evelyn, *The Crimea in 1854, and 1894* (Chapman & Hall, London, 1896).

Woodham-Smith, Cecil, *The Reason Why* (Penguin, London, 1958).

Wolseley, Field Marshal Viscount, *The Story of a Soldier's Life* (Archibald Constable, Westminster, 1903).

Wrottesley, The Hon. George (Ed.), *Life and Correspondence of Field Marshal Sir John Burgoyne* (Richard Bentley, London, 1873)

Periodicals
Aberdeen Journal
Answers Magazine
Bath Chronicle and Weekly Gazette
Birkenhead and Cheshire Advertiser and Wallasey Guardian
Birmingham Daily Post
Bradford Observer
Brisbane Daily Mail
Bristol Mercury
Britain at War Magazine
Cambridge Chronicle
Cardiff Times and South Wales Weekly News

Carlisle Patriot
Chester Chronicle
Daily Mail
Daily News
Dispatch
Evening Post
Guardian
Harper's Monthly Magazine
Huddersfield Chronicle
Illustrated London News
Journal of the Victoria Cross Society
Journal of the Society for Army Historical Research
Kendal Mercury
Leamington Spa Courier
Leeds Intelligencer
Leeds Mercury
Leicester Chronicle
Manchester Courier
Manchester Times
Midland Evening News
Morning Post
Nottinghamshire Gazette
Nottinghamshire Guardian
Oldham Chronicle
Portsmouth Evening News
Reynold's Newspaper
St James's Gazette
Sheffield & Rotherham Independent
Shrewsbury Chronicle
Strand Magazine
The Chronicle
The London Gazette
The Times
Western Australia Times
Windsor and Richmond Gazette
York Herald
Yorkshire Gazette

On-line Resources
Hansard archived debates for the House of Commons and the House of Lords;
www.HYPERLINK "http://www.hansard-archive.parliament.uk/"hansardHYPERLINK "http://www.hansard-archive.parliament.uk/"-HYPERLINK
"http://www.hansard-archive.parliament.uk/"archiveHYPERLINK
"http://www.hansard-archive.parliament.uk/".HYPERLINK
"http://www.hansard-archive.parliament.uk/"parliamentHYPERLINK
"http://www.hansard-archive.parliament.uk/".uk
http://www.historyhome.co.uk
Lives of the Light Brigade, The E.J. Boys Archive
The Letters of Queen Victoria, Volume III (of 3), 1854-1861, by Queen of Great Britain Victoria, Edited by Arthur Christopher Benson and Viscount Reginald Baliol Brett Esher, Project Gutenberg, 2009.
http://www.marksrussianmilitaryhistory.info

Index

Wombell, Lieutenant George, 162
Wood, Field Marshal Sir Henry Evelyn VC, 83, 84, 148, 207
Wooden, Lieutenant Charles VC, 171-2,
Woodham, Private Edward, 85, 86, 138, 151, 152, 167
Woronzow (Woronzoff) road, 63, 129-30

Yates, Cornet John, 166
Yeropkin Colonel, 81, 127,
York, Duke of, 4, 6
Yorke, Lieutenant Colonel John, 131-2

Zhaboritski (Zhabokritsky), Major General O.P., 109, 122, 127, 149